Three Translations of The Bhagavad Gita

Three Translations of The Bhagavad Gita

Mohandas K. Gandhi
Sir Edwin Arnold
Swami Swarupananda

The Bhagavad Gita According to Gandhi

Mohandas K. Gandhi

Translated to English by Mahadev Desai

Table of Contents

Foreword

The following pages by Mahadev Desai are an ambitious project. It represents his unremitting labours during his prison life in 1933-'34. Every page is evidence of his scholarship and exhaustive study of all he could lay hands upon regarding the Bhagavad Gita, poetically called the Song Celestial by Sir Edwin Arnold. The immediate cause of this labour of love was my translation in Gujarati of the divine book as I understood it. In trying to give a translation of my meaning of the Gita, he found himself writing an original commentary on the Gita.

The book might have been published during his lifetime, if I could have made time to go through the manuscript. I read some portions with him, but exigencies of my work had to interrupt the reading. Then followed the imprisonments of August 1942, and his sudden death within six days of our imprisonment. All of his immediate friends decided to give his reverent study of the Gita to the public. He had copies typed for his English friends who were impatient to see the commentary in print. And Pyarelal, who was collaborator with Mahadev Desai for many years, went through the whole manuscript and undertook to perform the difficult task of proof reading. Hence this publication.

Frankly, I do not pretend to any scholarship. I have, therefore, contended myself with showing the genesis of Mahadev Desai's effort. In so far as the translation part of the volume is concerned, I can vouch for its accuracy. He carried out the meaning of the original translation. I may add too that Pyarelal has interfered with the original only and in rare cases where it was considered to be essential, an interference which Mahadev Desai would, in my opinion, have gladly accepted, had he been alive.

On the train to Madras

M. K. Gandhi

20th January, 1946

Introduction

It was at Kosani in Almora on 24th June, 1929, i.e., after two years' waiting, that I finished the introduction to my translation of the Gita. The whole was then published in due course. It has been translated in Hindi, Bengali and Marathi. There has been an insistent demand for an English translation. I finished the translation of the introduction at the Yeravda prison. Since my discharge it has lain with friends and now I give it to the reader. Those, who take no interest in the Book of Life, will forgive the trespass on these columns.[1] To those who are interested in the poem and treat it as their guide in life, my humble attempt might prove of some help. –M.K.G.

I

1. Just as, acted upon by the affection of co-workers like Swami Anand and others, I wrote My Experiments with Truth, so has it been regarding my rendering of the Gita. "We shall be able to appreciate your meaning of the message of the Gita, only when we are able to study a translation of the whole text by yourself, with the addition of such notes as you may deem necessary. I do not think it is just on your part to deduce ahimsa etc. from stray verses," thus spoke Swami Anand to me during the non-cooperation days. I felt the force of his remarks. I, therefore, told him that I would adopt his suggestion when I got the time. Shortly afterwards I was imprisoned. During my incarceration I was able to study the Gita more fully. I went reverently through the Gujarati translation of the Lokamanya's great work. He had kindly presented me with the Marathi original and the translations in Gujarati and Hindi, and had asked me, if I could not tackle the original, at least to go through the Gujarati translation. I had not been able to follow the advice outside the prison walls. But when I was imprisoned I read the Gujarati translation. This reading whetted my appetite for more and I glanced through several works on the Gita.

2. My first acquaintance with the Gita began in 1888-89 with the verse translation by Sir Edwin Arnold known as the Song Celestial. On reading it, I felt a keen desire to read a Gujarati translation. And I read as many translations as I could lay hold of. But all such reading can give me no passport for presenting my own translation. Then again my knowledge of Sanskrit is limited, my knowledge of Gujarati too is in no way scholarly. How could I then dare present the public with my translation?

3. It has been my endeavor, as also that of some companions, to reduce to practice the teaching of the Gita as I have understood it. The Gita has become for us a spiritual reference book. I am aware that we ever fail to act in perfect

accord with the teaching. The failure is not due to want of effort, but is in spite of it. Even though the failures we seem to see rays of hope. The accompanying rendering contains the meaning of the Gita message which this little band is trying to enforce in its daily conduct.

4. Again this rendering is designed for women, the commercial class, the so-called Shudras and the like who have little or no literary equipment, who have neither the time nor the desire to read the Gita in the original and yet who stand in need of its support. In spite of my Gujarati being unscholarly, I must own to having the desire to leave to the Gujaratis, through the mother tongue, whatever knowledge I may possess. I do indeed wish that at a time when literary output of a questionable character is pouring upon the Gujaratis, they should have before them a rendering the majority can understand of a book that is regarded as unrivalled for its spiritual merit and so withstand the overwhelming flood of unclean literature.

5. This desire does not mean any disrespect to the other renderings. They have their own place. But I am not aware of the claim made by the translators of enforcing their meaning of the Gita in their own lives. At the back of my reading there is the claim of an endeavour to enforce the meaning in my own conduct for an unbroken period of forty years. For this reason I do indeed harbour the wish that all Gujarati men or women wishing to shape their conduct according to their faith, should digest and derive strength from the translation here presented.

6. My co-workers, too, have worked at this translation. My knowledge of Sanskrit being very limited, I should not have full confidence in my literal translation. To that extent, therefore, the translation has passed before the eyes of Vinoba, Kaka Kalelkar, Mahadev Desai and Kishorlal Mashruwala.

II

7. Now about the message of the Gita.

8. Even in 1888-89, when I first became acquainted with the Gita, I felt that it was not a historical work, but that, under the guise of physical warfare, it described the duel that perpetually went on in the hearts mankind, and that physical warfare was brought in merely to make the description of the internal duel more alluring. This preliminary intuition became more confirmed on a closer study of religion and the Gita. A study of the Mahabharata gave it added confirmation. I do not regard the Mahabharata as a historical work in the accepted sense. The Adiparva contains powerful evidence in support of my opinion. By ascribing to the chief actors superhuman or subhuman origins, the great Vyasa made short work the history of kings and their peoples. The persons

therein described may be historical, but the author of the Mahabharata has used them merely to drive home his religious theme.

9. The author of the Mahabharata has not established the necessity of physical warfare; on the contrary he has proved its futility. He has made the victors shed tears of sorrow and repentance, and has left them nothing but a legacy of miseries.

10. In this great work the Gita is the crown. Its second chapter, instead of teaching the rules of physical warfare, tells us how a perfected man is to be known. In the characteristics of the perfected man of the Gita, I do not see any to correspond to physical warfare. Its whole design is inconsistent with the rules of conduct governing the relations between warring parties.

11. Krishna of the Gita is perfection and right knowledge personified; but the picture is imaginary. That does not mean that Krishna, the adored of his people, never lived. But perfection is imagined. The idea of a perfect incarnation is an after growth.

12. In Hinduism, incarnation is ascribed to one who has performed some extraordinary service of mankind. All embodied life is in reality an incarnation of God, but it is not usual to consider every living being an incarnation. Future generations pay this homage to one who, in his own generation, has been extraordinarily religious in his conduct. I can see nothing wrong in this procedure; it takes nothing from God's greatness, and there is no violence done to Truth. There is an Urdu saying which means, "Adam is not God but he is a spark of the Divine." And therefore he who is the most religiously behaved has most of the divine spark in him. It is in accordance with this train of thought that Krishna enjoys, in Hinduism, the status of the most perfect incarnation.

13. This belief in incarnation is a testimony of man's lofty spiritual ambition. Man is not at peace with himself till he has become like unto God. The endeavour to reach this state is the supreme, the only ambition worth having. And this is self-realization. This self-realization is the subject of the Gita, as it is of all scriptures. But its author surely did not write it to establish that doctrine. The object of the Gita appears to me to be that of showing the most excellent way to attain self-realization. That which is to be found, more or less clearly, spread out here and there in Hindu religious books, has been brought out in the clearest possible language in the Gita even at the risk of repetition.

14. That matchless remedy is renunciation of fruits of action.

15. This is the centre round which the Gita is woven. This renunciation is the central sun, round which devotion, knowledge and the rest revolve like planets. The body has been likened to a prison. There must be action where there is body. Not one embodied being is exempted from labour. And yet all religions

proclaim that it is possible for man, by treating the body as the temple of God, to attain freedom. Every action is tainted, be it ever so trivial. How can the body be made the temple of God? In other words how can one be free from action, i.e. from the taint of sin? The Gita has answered the question in decisive language: "By desireless action; by renouncing fruits of action; by dedicating all activities to God, i.e., by surrendering oneself to Him body and soul."

16. But desirelessness or renunciation does not come for the mere talking about it. It is not attained by intellectual feat. It is attainable only by a constant heart-churn. Right knowledge is necessary for attaining renunciation. Learned men possess a knowledge of a kind. They may recite the Vedas from memory, yet they may be steeped in self-indulgence. In order that knowledge may not run riot, the author of the Gita has insisted on devotion accompanying it and has given it the first place. Knowledge without devotion will be like a misfire. Therefore, says the Gita, "Have devotion, and knowledge will follow." This devotion is not mere lip worship, it is a wrestling with death. Hence, the Gita's assessment of the devotee's quality is similar to that of the sage.

17. Thus the devotion required by the Gita is no soft-hearted effusiveness. It certainly is not blind faith. The devotion of the Gita has the least to do with the externals. A devotee may use, if he likes, rosaries, forehead marks, make offerings, but these things are no test of his devotion. He is the devotee who is jealous of none, who is a fount of mercy, who is without egotism, who is selfless, who treats alike cold and heat, happiness and misery, who is ever forgiving, who is always contented, whose resolutions are firm, who has dedicated mind and soul to God, who causes no dread, who is not afraid of others, who is free from exultation, sorrow and fear, who is pure, who is versed in action and yet remains unaffected by it, who renounces all fruit, good or bad, who treats friend and foe alike, who is untouched by respect or disrespect, who is not puffed up by praise, who does not go under when people speak ill of him who loves silence and solitude, who has a disciplined reason. Such devotion is inconsistent with the existence at the same time of strong attachments.

18. We thus see that to be a real devotee is to realize oneself. Self-realization is not something apart. One rupee can purchase for us poison or nectar, but knowledge or devotion cannot buy us salvation or bondage. These are not media of exchange. They are themselves the thing we want. In other words, if the means and the end are not identical, they are almost so. The extreme of means is salvation. Salvation of the Gita is perfect peace.

19. But such knowledge and devotion, to be true, have to stand the test of renunciation of fruits of action. Mere knowledge of right and wrong will not make one fit for salvation. According to common notions, a mere learned man

will pass as a pandit. He need not perform any service. He will regard as bondage even to lift a little lota. Where one test of knowledge is non-liability for service, there is no room for such mundane work as the lifting of a lota.

20. Or take bhakti. The popular notion of bhakti is soft-heartedness, telling beads and the like, and disdaining to do even a loving service, least the telling of beads etc. might be interrupted. This bhakti, therefore, leaves the rosary only for eating, drinking and the like, never for grinding corn or nursing patients.

21. But the Gita says: No one has attained his goal without action. Even men like Janaka attained salvation through action. If even I were lazily to cease working, the world would not perish. How much more necessary then for the people at large to engage in action.

22. While on the one hand it is beyond dispute that all action binds, on the other hand it is equally true that all living beings have to do some work, whether they will or no. Here all activity, whether mental or physical is to be included in the term action. Then how is one to be free from the bondage of action, even though he may be acting? The manner in which the Gita has solved the problem is to my knowledge unique. The Gita says: 'Do your allotted work but renounce its fruit—be detached and work—have no desire for reward and work.'

This is the unmistakable teaching of the Gita. He who gives up action falls. He who gives up only the reward rises. But renunciation of fruit in no way means indifference to the result. In regard to every action one must know the result that is expected to follow, the means thereto, and the capacity for it. He, who, being thus equipped, is without desire for the result and is yet wholly engrossed in the due fulfillment of the task before him is said to have renounced the fruits of his action.

23. Again let no one consider renunciation to mean want of fruit for the renouncer. The Gita reading does not warrant such a meaning. Renunciation means absence of hankering after fruit. As a matter of fact, he who renounces reaps a thousandfold. The renunciation of the Gita is the acid test of faith. He who is ever brooding over result often loses nerve in the performance of his duty. He becomes impatient and then gives vent to anger and begins to do unworthy things; he jumps from action to action never remaining faithful to any. He who broods over results is like a man given to objects of senses; he is ever distracted, he says goodbye to all scruples, everything is right in his estimation and he therefore resorts to means fair and foul to attain his end.

24. From the bitter experiences of desire for fruit the author of the Gita discovered the path of renunciation of fruit and put it before the world in a most convincing manner. The common belief is that religion is always opposed to material good. "One cannot act religiously in mercantile and such other

matters. There is no place for religion in such pursuits; religion is only for attainment of salvation," we here many worldly-wise people say. In my opinion the author of the Gita has dispelled this delusion. He has drawn no line of demarcation between salvation and worldly pursuits. On the contrary he has shown that religion must rule even our worldly pursuits. I have felt that the Gita teaches us that what cannot be followed out in day-to-day practice cannot be called religion. Thus, according to the Gita, all acts that are incapable of being performed without attachment are taboo. This golden rule saves mankind from many a pitfall. According to this interpretation murder, lying, dissoluteness and the like must be regarded as sinful and therefore taboo. Man's life then becomes simple, and from that simpleness springs peace.

25. Thinking along these lines, I have felt that in trying to enforce in one's life the central teaching of the Gita, one is bound to follow Truth and ahimsa. When there is no desire for fruit, there is no temptation for untruth or himsa. Take any instance of untruth or violence, and it will be found that at its back was the desire to attain the cherished end. But it may be freely admitted that the Gita was not written to establish ahimsa. It was an accepted and primary duty even before the Gita age. The Gita had to deliver the message of renunciation of fruit. This is clearly brought out as early as the second chapter.

26. But if the Gita believed in ahimsa or it was included in desirelessness, why did the author take a warlike illustration? When the Gita was written, although people believed in ahimsa, wars were not only not taboo, but nobody observed the contradiction between them and ahimsa.

27. In assessing the implications of renunciation of fruit, we are not required to probe the mind of the author of the Gita as to his limitations of ahimsa and the like. Because a poet puts a particular truth before the world, it does not necessarily follow that he has known or worked out all its great consequences or that having done so, he is able always to express them fully. In this perhaps lies the greatness of the poem and the poet. A poet's meaning is limitless. Like man, the meaning of great writings suffers evolution. On examining the history of languages, we noticed that the meaning of important words has changed or expanded. This is true of the Gita. The author has himself extended the meanings of some of the current words. We are able to discover this even on superficial examination. It is possible that, in the age prior to that of the Gita, offering of animals as sacrifice was permissible. But there is not a trace of it in the sacrifice in the Gita sense. In the Gita continuous concentration on God is the king of sacrifices. The third chapter seems to show that sacrifice chiefly means body-labour for service. The third and fourth chapters read together will use other meanings for sacrifice, but never animal-sacrifice. Similarly has the

meaning of the word sannyasa undergone, in the Gita, a transformation. The sannyasa of the Gita will not tolerate complete cessation of all activity. The sannyasa of the Gita is all work and yet no work. Thus the author of the Gita, by extending meanings of words, has taught us to imitate him. Let it be granted, that according to the letter of the Gita it is possible to say that warfare is consistent with renunciation of fruit. But after forty years' unremitting endeavor fully to enforce the teaching of the Gita in my own life, I have in all humility felt that perfect renunciation is impossible without perfect observance of ahimsa in every shape and form.

28. The Gita is not an aphoristic work; it is a great religious poem. The deeper you dive into it, the richer the meanings you get. It being meant for the people at large, there is pleasing repetition. With every age the important words will carry new and expanding meanings. But its central teaching will never vary. The teacher is at liberty to extract from this treasure any meaning he likes so as to enable him to enforce in his life the central teaching.

29. Nor is the Gita a collection of do's and dont's. What is lawful for one may be unlawful for another. What may be permissible at one time, or in one place, may not be so at another time, and in another place. Desire for fruit is the only universal prohibition. Desirelessness is obligatory.

30. The Gita has sung the praises of Knowledge, but it is beyond the mere intellect; it is essentially addressed to the heart and capable of being understood by the heart. Therefore the Gita is not for those who have no faith. The author makes Krishna say: "Do not entrust this treasure to him who is without sacrifice, without devotion, without the desire for this teaching and who denies Me. On the other hand, those who will give this precious treasure to My devotees will, by the fact of this service, assuredly reach me. And those who, being free from malice, will with faith absorb this teaching, shall, having attained freedom, live where people of true merit go after death".

[1] This translation appeared in the columns of the Young India, 6-8-1931, from where it has been reproduced here.

Discourse I

No knowledge is to be found without seeking, no tranquility without travail, no happiness except through tribulation. Every seeker has, at one time or another, to pass through a conflict of duties, a heart-churning.

Dhritarashtra Said:

1. Tell me, O Sanjaya, what my sons and Pandu's assembled, on battle intent, did on the field of Kuru, the field of duty.

The human body is the battlefield where the eternal duel between right and wrong goes on. Therefore it is capable of being turned into a gateway to Freedom. It is born in sin and becomes the seed-bed of sin. Hence it is also called the field of Kuru. The Kuravas represent the forces of Evil, the Pandavas the forces of Good. Who is there that has not experienced the daily conflict within himself between the forces of Evil and the forces of Good?

Sanjaya Said:

2. On seeing the Pandava's army drawn up in battle array, King Duryodhana approached Drona, the preceptor, and addressed him thus:

3. Behold, O preceptor, this mighty army of the sons of Pandu, set in array by the son of Drupada, thy wise disciple.

4. Here are brave bowmen, peers of Bhima and Arjuna in fighting: Yuyudhana and Virata, and the 'Maharatha' Drupada.

5. Dhrishtaketu, Chekitana, valorous Kashiraja, Purujit the Kuntibhoja, and Shaibya, chief among men;

6. Valiant Yudhamanyu, valorous Uttamaujas, Subhadra's son, and the sons of Draupadi—each one of them a 'Maharatha'.

7. Acquaint thyself now, O best of Brahmanas, with the distinguished among us. I mention for thy information, the names of the captains of my army.

8. Thy noble self, Bhishma, Karna, and Kripa, victorious in battle, Ashvatthaman, Vikarna, also Somadatta's son;

9. There is many another hero, known for his skill in wielding diverse weapons, pledged to lay down his life for my sake, and all adepts in war.

10. This our force, commanded by Bhishma, is all too inadequate; while theirs, commanded by Bhima, is quite adequate.

11. Therefore, let each of you, holding your appointed places, at every entrance, guard only Bhishma.

12. At this, the heroic grandsire, the grand old man of the Kurus, gave a loud lion's roar and blew his conch to hearten Duryodhana.

13. Thereupon, conches, drums, cymbals and trumpets were sounded all at once. Terrific was the noise.

14. Then Madhava and Pandava, standing in their great chariot yoked with white steeds, blew their divine conches.

15. Hrishikesha blew the Panchajanya and Dhananjaya the Devadatta; while the wolf-bellied Bhima of dread deeds sounded his great conch Paundra.

16. King Yudhishthira, Kunti's son, blew the Anantavijaya, and Nakula nd Sahadeva their conches, Sughosha and Manipushpaka.

17. And Kashiraja, the great bowman, Shikhandi the 'Maharatha', Dhrishtadyumna, Virata and Satyaki, the unconquerable;

18. Drupada, Draupadi's sons, the strong-armed son of Subhadra, all these, O King, blew each his own conch.

19. That terrifying tumult, causing earth and heaven to resound, rent the hearts of Dhritarashtra's sons.

20-21. Then, O King, the ape-bannered Pandava, seeing Dhritarashtra's sons arrayed and flight of arrows about to begin, took up his bow, and spoke thus to Hrishikesha: "Set my chariot between the two armies, O Achyuta!"

22. That I may behold them drawn up, on battle intent, and know whom I have to engage in this fearful combat;

23. And that I may survey the fighters assembled here anxious to fulfil in battle perverse Duryodhana's desire.

Sanjaya Said:

24-25. Thus addressed by Gudakesha, O King, Hrishikesha set the unique chariot between the two armies in front of Bhishma, Drona and all the kings and said: Behold, O Partha, the Kurus assembled yonder.

26-28. Then did Partha see, standing there, sires, grandsires, preceptors, uncles, brothers, sons, grandsons, comrades, fathers-in-law and friends in both armies. Beholding all these kinsmen ranged before him, Kaunteya was overcome with great compassion and spake thus in anguish:

Arjuna Said:

28-29. As I look upon these kinsmen, O Krishna, assembled here eager to fight, my limbs fail, my mouth is parched, a tremor shakes my frame and my hair stands on end.

30. Gandiva slips from my hand, my skin is on fire, I cannot keep my feet, and my mind reels.

31. I have unhappy forebodings, O Keshava; and I see no good in slaying kinsmen in battle.

32. I seek not victory, nor sovereign power, nor earthly joys. What good are sovereign power, worldly pleasures and even life to us, O Govinda?

33. Those for whom we would desire sovereign power, earthly joys and delights are here arrayed in battle, having renounced life and wealth—

34. Preceptors, sires, grandsires, sons and even grandsons, uncles, fathers-in-law, brothers-in-law, and other kinsmen.

35. These I would not kill, O Madhusudana, even though they slay me, not even for kingship of the three worlds, much less for an earthly kingdom.

36. What pleasure can there be in slaying these sons of Dhritarashtra, O Janardana? Sin only can be our lot, if we slay these, usurpers though they be.

37. It does not therefore behove us to kill our kinsmen, these sons of Dhritarashtra. How may we be happy, O Madhava, in killing our own kins?

38. Even though these, their wits warped by greed, see not the guilt that lies in destroying the family, nor the sin of treachery to comrades;

39. How can we, O Janardana, help recoiling from this sin, seeing clearly as we do the guilt that lies in such destruction?

40. With the destruction of the family perish the eternal family virtues, and with the perishing of these virtues unrighteousness seizes the whole family.

41. When unrighteousness prevails, O Krishna, the women of the family become corrupt, and their corruption, O Varshneya, causes a confusion of varnas.

42. This confusion verily drags the family-slayer, as well as the family, to hell, and for want of obsequial offerings and rites their departed sires fall from blessedness.

43. By the sins of these family-slayers resulting in confusion of varnas, the eternal tribal and family virtues are brought to naught.

44. For we have had it handed down to us, O Janardana, that the men whose family virtues have been ruined are doomed to dwell in hell.

45. Alas! What a heinous sin we are about to commit, in that, from greed of the joy of sovereign power, we are prepared to slay our kith and kin!

46. Happier far would it be for me if Dhritarashtra's sons, weapons in hand, should strike me down on the battlefield, unresisting and unarmed.

Sanjaya Said:

47. Thus spake Arjuna on the field of battle, and dropping his bow and arrows sank down on his seat in the chariot, overwhelmed with anguish.

Thus ends the first discourse, entitled 'Arjuna Vishada Yoga' in the converse of Lord Krishna and Arjuna, on the science of Yoga as part of the knowledge of Brahman in the Upanishad called the Bhagawadgita.

Discourse II

By reason of delusion, man takes wrong to be right. By reason of delusion was Arjuna led to make a difference between kinsmen and non-kinsmen. To demonstrate that this is a vain distinction, Lord Krishna distinguishes between body (not-Self) and Atman (Self) and shows that whilst bodies are impermanent and several, Atman is permanent and one. Effort is within man's control, not the fruit thereof. All he has to do, therefore, is to decide his course of conduct or duty on each occasion and persevere in it, unconcerned about the result. Fulfillment of one's duty in the spirit of detachment or selflessness leads to Freedom.

Sanjaya Said:

1. To Arjuna, thus overcome with compassion, sorrowing, and his eyes obscured by flowing tears, Madhusudana spake these words:

The Lord Said:

2. How is it that at this perilous moment this delusion, unworthy of the noble, leading neither to heaven nor to glory, has overtaken thee?

3. Yield not to unmanliness, O Partha; it does not become thee. Shake off this miserable faint-heartedness and arise, O Parantapa!

Arjuna Said:

4. How shall I, with arrows, engage Bhishma and Drona in battle, O Madhusudana, they who are worthy of reverence, O Arisudana?

5. It were better far to live on alms of this world than to slay these venerable elders. Having slain them I should but have blood-stained enjoyments.

6. Nor do we know which is better for us, that we conquer them or that they conquer us, for here stand before us Dhritarashtra's sons having killed whom we should have no desire to live.

7. My being is paralysed by faint-heartedness; my mind discerns not duty; hence I ask thee; tell me, I pray thee, in no uncertain language, wherein lies my good. I am thy disciple; guide me; I see refuge in thee.

8. For I see nothing that can dispel the anguish that shrivels up my senses even if I should win on earth uncontested sovereignty over a thriving kingdom or lordship over the gods.

Sanjaya Said:

9. Thus spoke Gudakesha Parantapa to Hrishikesha Govinda, and with the words 'I will not fight' became speechless.

10. To him thus stricken with anguish, O Bharata! between the two armies, Hrishikesha, as though mocking, addressed these words:

The Lord Said:

11. Thou mournest for them whom thou shouldst not mourn and utterest vain words of wisdom. The wise mourn neither for the living nor for the dead.

12. For never was I not, nor thou, nor these kings; nor will any of us cease to be hereafter.

13. As the embodied one has, in the present body, infancy, youth and age, even so does he receive another body. The wise man is not deceived therein.

14. O Kaunteya! contacts of the senses with their objects bring cold and heat, pleasure and pain; they come and go and are transient. Endure them, O Bharata.

15. O noblest of men, the wise man who is not disturbed by these, who is unmoved by pleasure and pain, he is fitted for immortality.

16. What is non-Being is never known to have been, and what is Being is never known not to have been. Of both these the secret has been seen by the seers of the Truth.

17. Know that to be imperishable whereby all this is pervaded. No one can destroy that immutable being.

18. These bodies of the embodied one who is eternal, imperishable and immeasurable are finite. Fight, therefore, O Bharata.

19. He who thinks of This (Atman) as slayer and he who believes This to be slain, are both ignorant. This neither slays nor is ever slain.

20. This is never born nor ever dies, nor having been will ever not be any more; unborn, eternal, everlasting, ancient, This is not slain when the body is slain.

21. He who knows This, O Partha, to be imperishable, eternal, unborn, and immutable—whom and how can that man slay or cause to be slain?

22. As a man casts off worn-out garments and takes others that are new, even so the embodied one casts off worn-out bodies and passes on to others new.

23. This no weapons wound, This no fire burns, This no waters wet, This no wind doth dry.

24. Beyond all cutting, burning, wetting and drying is This-eternal, all-pervading, stable, immovable, everlasting.

25. Perceivable neither by the senses nor by the mind, This is called unchangeable; therefore knowing This as such thou shouldst not grieve.

26. And if thou deemest This to be always coming to birth and always dying, even then, O Mahabahu, thou shouldst not grieve.

27. For certain is the death of the born, and certain is the birth of the dead; therefore what is unavoidable thou shouldst not regret.

28. The state of all beings before birth is unmanifest; their middle state manifest; their state after death is again unmanifest. What occasion is there for lament, O Bharata?

29. One looks upon This as a marvel; another speaks of This as such; another hears thereof as a marvel; yet having heard This none truly knows This.

30. This embodied one in the body of every being is ever beyond all harm, O Bharata; thou shouldst not, therefore, grieve for any one.

Thus far Lord Krishna, by force of argument based on pure reason, has demonstrated that Atman is abiding while the physical body is fleeting, and has explained that if, under certain circumstances, the destruction of a physical body is deemed justifiable, it is delusion to imagine that the Kauravas should not be slain because they are kinsmen. Now he reminds Arjuna of the duty of a Kshatriya.

31. Again, seeing thine own duty thou shouldst not shrink from it; for there is no higher good for a Kshatriya than a righteous war.

32. Such a fight, coming unsought, as a gateway to heaven thrown open, falls only to the lot of happy Kshatriyas, O Partha.

33. But if thou wilt not fight this righteous fight, then failing in thy duty and losing thine honour thou wilt incur sin.

34. The world will for ever recount the story of thy disgrace; and for a man of honour disgrace is worse than death.

35. The Maharathas will think that fear made thee retire from battle; and thou wilt fall in the esteem of those very ones who have held thee high.

36. Thine enemies will deride thy prowess and speak many unspeakable words about thee. What can be more painful than that?

37. Slain, thou shalt gain heaven; victorious, thou shall inherit the earth: therefore arise, O Kaunteya, determined to fight.

Having declared the highest truth, viz. the immortality of the eternal Atman and the fleeting nature of the physical body (11-30), Krishna reminds Arjuna that a Kshatriya may not flinch from a fight which comes unsought (31-32). He then (33-37) shows how the highest truth and the performance of duty incidentally coincide with expediency. Next he proceeds to foreshadow the central teaching of the Gita in the following shloka.

38. Hold alike pleasure and pain, gain and loss, victory and defeat, and gird up thy loins for the fight; so doing thou shalt not incur sin.

39. Thus have I set before thee the attitude of Knowledge; hear now the attitude of Action; resorting to this attitude thou shalt cast off the bondage of action.

40. Here no effort undertaken is lost, no disaster befalls. Even a little of this righteous course delivers one from great fear.

41. The attitude, in this matter, springing, as it does, from fixed resolve is but one, O Kurunandana; but for those who have no fixed resolve the attitudes are many-branched and unending.

When the attitude ceases to be one and undivided and becomes many and divided, it ceases to be one settled will, and is broken up into various wills of desires between which man is tossed about.

42-44. The ignorant, revelling in the letter of the Vedas, declare that there is naught else; carnally-minded, holding heaven to be their goal, they utter swelling words which promise birth as the fruit of action and which dwell on the many and varied rites to be performed for the sake of pleasure and power; intent, as they are, on pleasure and power their swelling words rob them of their wits, and they have no settled attitude which can be centered on the supreme goal.

The Vedic ritual, as opposed to the doctrine of Yoga laid down in the Gita, is alluded to here. The Vedic ritual lays countless ceremonies and rites with a view to attaining merit and heaven. These, divorced as they are from the essence of the Vedas and short-lived in their result, are worthless.

45. The Vedas have as their domain the three gunas; eschew them, O Arjuna. Free thyself from the pairs of opposites, abide in eternal truth, scorn to gain or guard anything, remain the master of thy soul.

46. To the extent that a well is of use when there is a flood of water on all sides, to the same extent are all the Vedas of use to an enlightened Brahmana.

47. Action alone is thy province, never the fruits thereof; let not thy motive be the fruit of action, nor shouldst thou desire to avoid action.

48. Act thou, O Dhananjaya, without attachment, steadfast in Yoga, even-minded in success and failure. Even-mindedness is Yoga.

49. For action, O Dhananjaya, is far inferior to unattached action; seek refuge in the attitude of detached action. Pitiable are those who make fruit their motive.

50. Here in this world a man gifted with that attitude of detachment escapes the fruit of both good and evil deeds. Gird thyself up for Yoga, therefore. Yoga is skill in action.

51. For sages, gifted with the attitude of detachment, who renounce the fruit of action, are released from the bondage of birth and attain to the state which is free from all ills.

52. When thy understanding will have passed through the slough of delusion, then wilt thou be indifferent alike to what thou hast heard and wilt hear.

53. When thy understanding, distracted by much hearing, will rest steadfast and unmoved in concentration, then wilt thou attain Yoga.

Arjuna Said:

54. What, O Keshava, is the mark of the man whose understanding is secure, whose mind is fixed in concentration? How does he talk? How sit? How move.

The Lord Said:

55. When a man puts away, O partha, all the cravings that arise in the mind and finds comfort for himself only from Atman, then he is called the man of secure understanding.

To find comfort for oneself from Atman means to look to the spirit within for spiritual comfort, not to outside objects which in their very nature must give pleasure as well as pain. Spiritual comfort or bliss must be distinguished from pleasure or happiness. The pleasure I may derive from the possession of wealth, for instance, is delusive; real spiritual comfort or bliss can be attained only if I rise superior to every temptation even though troubled by the pangs of poverty and hunger.

56. Whose mind is untroubled in sorrows and longeth not for joys, who is free from passion, fear and wrath—he is called the ascetic of secure understanding.

57. Who owns attachment nowhere, who feels neither joy nor resentment whether good or bad comes his way—that man's understanding is secure.

58. And when, like the tortoise drawing in its limbs from every side, this man draws in his senses from their objects, his understanding is secure.

59. When a man starves his senses, the objects of those senses disappear from him, but not the yearning for them; the yearning too departs when he beholds the Supreme.

The shloka does not rule out fasting and other forms of self-restraint, but indicates their limitations, these restraints are needed for subduing the desire for sense-objects, which however is rooted out only when one has a vision of the Supreme. The higher yearning conquers all the lower yearnings.

60. For, in spite of the wise man's endeavour, O Kaunteya, the unruly senses distract his mind perforce.

61. Holding all these in check, the yogi should sit intent on Me; for he whose senses are under control is secure of understanding.

This means that without devotion and the consequent grace of God, man's endeavour is vain.

62. In a man brooding on objects of the senses, attachment to them springs up; attachment begets craving and craving begets wrath.

Craving cannot but lead to resentment, for it is unending and unsatisfied.

63. Wrath breeds stupefaction, stupefaction leads to loss of memory, loss of memory ruins the reason, and the ruin of reason spells utter destruction.

64. But the disciplined soul, moving among sense-objects with the senses weaned from likes and dislikes and brought under the control of Atman, attains peace of mind.

65. Peace of mind means the end to all ills, for the understanding of him whose mind is at peace stands secure.

66. The undisciplined man has neither understanding nor devotion; for him who has no devotion there is no peace, and for him who has no peace whence happiness?

67. For when his mind runs after any of the roaming senses, it sweeps away his understanding, as the wind a vessel upon the waters.

68. Therefore, O Mahabahu, he, whose senses are reined in on all sides from their objects, is the man of secure understanding.

69. When it is night for all other beings, the disciplined soul is awake; when all other beings are awake, it is night for the seeing ascetic.

This verse indicates the divergent paths of the discipline ascetic and sensual man. Whereas the ascetic is dead to the things of the world and lives in God, the sensual man is alive only to the things of the world and dead to the things of the spirit.

70. He in whom all longings subside, even as the waters subside in the ocean which, though ever being filled by them, never overflows—that man finds peace; not he who cherishes longing.

71. The man who sheds all longing and moves without concern, free from the sense of 'I' and 'Mine'—he attains peace.

72. This is the state, O partha, of the man who rests in Brahman; having attained to it, he is not deluded. He who abides in this state even at the hour of death passes into oneness with Brahman.

Thus ends the second discourse, entitled 'Sankhya Yoga' in the converse of Lord Krishna and Arjuna, on the science of Yoga as part of the knowledge of Brahman in the Upanishad called the Bhagawadgita.

Discourse III

This discourse may be said to be the key to the essence of the Gita. It makes absolutely clear the spirit and the nature of right action and shows how true knowledge must express itself in acts of selfless service.

Arjuna Said:

1. If, O Janardana, thou holdest that the attitude of detachment is superior to action, then why, O Keshava, dost thou urge me to dreadful action?

2. Thou dost seem to confuse my understanding with perplexing speech; tell me, therefore, in no uncertain voice, that alone whereby I may attain salvation.

Arjuna is sore perplexed, for whilst on the one hand he is rebuked for his faint-heartedness, on the other he seems to be advised to refrain from action (II.49-50). But this, in reality, is not the case as the following shlokas will show.

The Lord Said:

3. I have spoken, before, O sinless one, of two attitudes in this world—the Sankhayas', that of Jnana yoga and the Yogins', that of karma yoga.

4. Never does man enjoy freedom from action by not undertaking action, nor does he attain that freedom by mere renunciation of action.

'Freedom from action' is freedom from the bondage of action. This freedom is not to be gained by cessation of all activity, apart from the fact that this cessation is in the very nature of things impossible (see following shloka). How then may it be gained? The following shlokas will explain.

5. For none ever remains inactive even for a moment; for all are compelled to action by the gunas inherent in prakriti.

6. He who curbs the organs of action but allows the mind to dwell on the sense-objects,—such a one, wholly deluded, is called a hypocrite.

The man who curbs his tongue but mentally swears at another is a hypocrite. But that does not mean that free rein should be given to the organs of action so long as the mind cannot be brought under control. Self-imposed physical restraint is a condition precedent to mental restraint. Physical restraint should be entirely self-imposed and not super-imposed from outside, e.g. by fear. The hypocrite who is held up to contempt here is not the humble aspirant after self-restraint. The shloka has reference to the man who curbs the body because he cannot help it while indulging the mind, and who would indulge the body too if he possibly could. The next shloka puts the thing conversely.

7. But he, O Arjuna, who keeping all the senses under control of the mind, engages the organs in Karma yoga, without attachment—that man excels.

The mind and body should be made to accord well. Even with the mind kept in control, the body will be active in one way or another. But he whose mind is truly restrained will, for instance, close his ears to foul talk and open them only to listen to the praise of God or of good men. He will have no relish for sensual pleasures and will keep himself occupied with such activity as ennobles the soul. That is the path of action. Karma yoga is the yoga (means) which will deliver the self from the bondage of the body, and in it there is no room for self-indulgence.

8. Do thou thy allotted task; for action is superior to inaction; with inaction even life's normal course is not possible.

9. This world of men suffers bondage from all action save that which is done for the sake of sacrifice; to this end, O Kaunteya, perform action without attachment.

'Action for the sake of sacrifice' means acts of selfless service dedicated to God.

10. Together with sacrifice did the Lord of beings create, of old, mankind, declaring:

"By this shall ye increase; may this be to you the giver of all your desires.

11. "With this may you cherish the gods and may the gods cherish you; thus cherishing one another may you attain the highest good.

12. "Cherished with sacrifice, the gods will bestow on you the desired boons." He who enjoys their gifts without rendering aught unto them is verily a thief.

"Gods" in shlokas 11 and 12 must be taken to mean the whole creation of God. The service of all created beings is the service of the gods and the same is sacrifice.

13. The righteous men who eat the residue of the sacrifice are freed from all sin, but the wicked who cook for themselves eat sin.

14. From food springs all life, from rain is born food; from sacrifice comes rain and sacrifice is the result of action.

15. Know that action springs from Brahman and Brahman from the Imperishable; hence the all-pervading Brahman is ever firm-founded on sacrifice.

16. He who does not follow the wheel thus set in motion here below, he, living in sin, sating his senses, lives, O Partha, in vain.

17. But the man who revels in Atman, who is content in Atman and who is satisfied only with Atman, for him no action exists.

18. He has no interest whatever in anything done, nor in anything not done, nor has he need to rely on anything for personal ends.

19. Therefore, do thou ever perform without attachment the work that thou must do; for performing action without attachment man attains the Supreme.

20. For through action alone Janaka and others achieved perfection; even with a view to the guidance of mankind thou must act.

21. Whatever the best man does, is also done by other men, what example he sets, the world follows.

22. For me, O Partha, there is naught to do in the three worlds, nothing worth gaining that I have not gained; yet I am ever in action.

An objection is sometimes raised that God being impersonal is not likely to perform any physical activity, at best He may be supposed to act mentally. This is not correct. For the unceasing movement of the sun, the moon, the earth etc. signifies God in action. This is not mental but physical activity. Though God is without form and impersonal, He acts as though He had form and body. Hence though He is ever in action, He is free from action, unaffected by action. What must be borne in mind is that, just as all Nature's movements and processes are mechanical and yet guided by Divine Intelligence or Will, even so man must reduce his daily conduct to mechanical regularity and precision, but he must do so intelligently. Man's merit lies in observing divine guidance at the back of these processes and in an intelligent imitation of it rather than in emphasizing the mechanical nature thereof and reducing himself to an automation. One has but to withdraw the self, withdraw attachment to fruit from all action, and then not only mechanical precision but security from all wear and tear will be ensured. Acting thus man remains fresh until the end of his days. His body will perish in due course, but his soul will remain evergreen without a crease or a wrinkle.

23. Indeed, for were I not, unslumbering, ever to remain in action, O Partha, men would follow my example in every way.

24. If I were not to perform my task, these worlds would be ruined; I should be the same cause of chaos and of the end of all mankind.

25. Just as, with attachment, the unenlightened perform all actions, O Bharata, even so, but unattached, should the enlightened man act, with a desire for the welfare of humanity.

26. The enlightened may not confuse the mind of the unenlightened, who are attached to action; rather must he perform all actions unattached, and thus encourage them to do likewise.

27. All action is entirely done by the gunas of prakriti. Man, deluded by the sense of 'I', thinks, 'I am the doer'.

28. But he, O Mahabahu, who understands the truth of the various gunas and their various activities, knows that it is the gunas that operate on the gunas; he does not claim to be the doer.

As breathing, winking and similar processes are automatic and man claims no agency for them, he being conscious of the processes only when disease or similar cause arrests them, in a similar manner all his acclivities should be automatic, without his arrogating to himself the agency or responsibility thereof. A man of charity does not even know that he is doing charitable acts, it is his nature to do so, he cannot help it. This detachment can only come from tireless endeavour and God's grace.

29. Deluded by the gunas of prakriti men become attached to the activities of the gunas; he who knows the truth of things should not unhinge the slow-witted who have not the knowledge.

30. Cast all thy acts on Me, with thy mind fixed on the indwelling Atman, and without any thought of fruit, or sense of 'mine' shake off thy fever and fight!

He who knows the Atman inhabiting the body and realizes Him to be a part of the supreme Atman will dedicate everything to Him, even as a faithful servant acts as a mere shadow of his master and dedicates to him all that he does. For the master is the real doer, the servant but the instrument.

31. Those who always act according to the rule I have here laid down, in faith and without cavilling—they too are released from the bondage of their actions.

32. But those who cavil at the rule and refuse to conform to it are fools, dead to all knowledge; know that they are lost.

33. Even a man of knowledge acts according to his nature; all creatures follow their nature; what then will constraint avail?

This does not run counter to the teaching in II. 61 and II. 68. Self-restraint is the means of salvation (VI. 35; XIII. 7). Man's energies should be bent towards achieving complete self-restraint until the end of his days. But if he does not succeed, neither will constraint help him. The shloka does not rule out restraint but explains that nature prevails. He who justifies himself saying, 'I cannot do this, it is not in my nature,' misreads the shloka. True we do not know our nature, but habit is not nature. Progress, not decline, ascent, not descent, is the nature of the soul, and therefore every threatened decline or descent ought to be resisted. The next verse makes this abundantly clear.

34. Each sense has its settled likes and dislikes towards its objects; man should not come under the sway of these, for they are his besetters.

Hearing, for instance, is the object of the ears which may be inclined to hear something and disinclined to hear something else. Man may not allow himself to be swayed by these likes and dislikes, but must decide for himself what is conducive to his growth, his ultimate end being to reach the state beyond happiness and misery.

35. Better one's own duty, bereft of merit, than another's well-performed; better is death in the discharge of one's duty; another's duty is fraught with danger.

One man's duty may be to serve the community by working as a sweeper, another's may be to work as an accountant. An accountant's work may be more inviting, but that need not draw the sweeper away from his work. Should he allow himself to be drawn away he would himself be lost and put the community into danger. Before God the work of man will be judged by the spirit in which it is done, not by the nature of the work which makes no difference whatsoever. Whoever acts in a spirit of dedication fits himself for salvation.

Arjuna Said:

36. Then what impels man to sin, O Varshneya, even against his will, as though by force compelled?

The Lord Said:

37. It is Lust, it is Wrath, born of the guna—Rajas. It is the arch-devourer, the arch-sinner. Know this to be man's enemy here.

38. As fire is obscured by smoke, a mirror by dirt, and the embryo by the amnion, so is knowledge obscured by this.

39. Knowledge is obscured, O Kaunteya, by this eternal enemy of the wise man, in the form of Lust, the insatiable fire.

40. The senses, the mind and the reason are said to be its great seat; by means of these it obscures knowledge and stupefies man.

When Lust seizes the senses, the mind is corrupted, discrimination is obscured and reason ruined. See II. 62-64.

41. Therefore, O Bharatarshabha, bridle thou first the senses and then rid thyself of this sinner, the destroyer of knowledge and discrimination.

42. Subtle, they say, are the senses; subtler than the senses is the mind; subtler than the mind is the reason; but subtler even than the reason is He.

43. Thus realizing Him to be subtler than the reason, and controlling the self by the Self (Atman), destroy, O Mahabahu, this enemy—Lust, so hard to overcome.

When man realizes Him, his mind will be under his control, not swayed by the senses. And when the mind is conquered, what power has Lust? It is indeed a subtle enemy, but when once the senses, the mind and the reason are under the control of the subtlemost Self, Lust is extinguished.

Thus ends the third discourse entitled 'Karma Yoga' in the converse of Lord Krishna and Arjuna, on the science of Yoga, as part of the knowledge of Brahman in the Upanishad called the Bhagawadgita.

Discourse IV

This discourse further explains the subject-matter of the third and describes the various kinds of sacrifice.

The Lord Said:

1. I expounded this imperishable yoga to Vivasvat; Vivasvat communicated it to Manu, and Manu to Ikshvaku.

2. Thus handed down in succession, the royal sages learnt it; with long lapse of time it dwindled away in this world, O Parantapa.

3. The same ancient yoga have I expounded to thee today; for thou art My devotee and My friend, and this is the supreme mystery.

Arjuna Said:

4. Later was Thy birth, my Lord, earlier that of Vivasvat. How then am I to understand that Thou didst expound it in the beginning?

The Lord Said:

5. Many births have we passed through, O Arjuna, both thou and I; I know them all, thou knowest them not, O Parantapa.

Though unborn and inexhaustible in My essence, though Lord of all beings, yet assuming control over My Nature, I come into being by My mysterious power.

7. For whenever Right declines and Wrong prevails, then O Bharata, I come to birth.

8. To save the righteous, to destroy the wicked, and to re-establish Right I am born from age to age.

Here is comfort for the faithful and affirmation of the truth that Right ever prevails. An eternal conflict between Right and Wrong goes on. Sometimes the latter seems to get the upper hand, but it is Right which ultimately prevails. The good are never destroyed, for Right—which is Truth—cannot perish; the wicked are destroyed, because Wrong has no independent existence. Knowing this let man cease to arrogate to himself authorship and eschew untruth, violence and evil. Inscrutable Providence—the unique power of the Lord—is ever at work. This in fact is avatara, incarnation. Strictly speaking there can be no birth for God.

9. He who knows the secret of this My divine birth and action is not born again, after leaving the body; he comes to Me, O Arjuna.

For when a man is secure in the faith that Right always prevails, he never swerves therefrom, pursuing to the bitterest end and against serious odds, and as no part of the effort proceeds from his ego, but all is dedicated to Him, being ever one with Him, he is released from birth to death.

10. Freed from passion, fear and wrath, filled full with Me, relying on Me, and refined by the fiery ordeal of knowledge, many have become one with Me.

11. In whatever way men resort to Me, even so do I render to them. In every way, O Partha, the path men follow is Mine.

That is, the whole world is under His ordinance. No one may break God's law with impunity. As we sow, so shall we reap. This law operates inexorably without fear or favor.

12. Those who desire their actions to bear fruit worship the gods here; for in this world of men the fruit of action is quickly obtainable.

Gods, as indicated before, must not be taken to mean the heavenly beings of tradition, but whatever reflects the divine. In that sense man is also a god. Steam, electricity and the other great forces of Nature are all gods. Propitiation of these forces quickly bears fruit, as we well know, but it is short-lived. It fails to bring comfort to the soul and it certainly does not take one even a short step towards salvation.

13. The order of the four varnas was created by Me according to the different gunas and karma of each; yet know that though, therefore, author thereof, being changeless I am not the author.

14. Actions do not affect Me, nor am I concerned with the fruits thereof. He who recognizes Me as such is not bound by actions.

For man has thus before him the supreme example of one who though in action is not the doer thereof. And when we are but instruments in His hands, where then is the room for arrogating responsibility for action?

15. Knowing this did men of old, desirous of freedom, perform action; do thou, then, just as they did—the men of old in days gone by.

16. 'What is action? What is inaction?'—here even the wise are perplexed. I will then expound to thee that action knowing which thou shalt be saved from evil.

17. For it is meet to know the meaning of action, of forbidden action, as also inaction. Impenetrable is the secret of action.

18. Who sees action in action and action in inaction, he is enlightened among men, he is a yogi, he has done all he need do.

The 'action' of him who, though ever active, does not claim to be the doer, is inaction; and the 'inaction' of him who, though outwardly avoiding action, is always building castles in his own mind, is action. The enlightened man who has grasped the secret of action knows that no action proceeds from him, all proceeds from God and hence he selflessly remains absorbed in action. He is the true yogi. The man who acts self-fully misses the secret of action and cannot distinguish between Right and Wrong. The soul's natural progress is towards selflessness and purity and one might, therefore, say that the man who strays from the path of purity strays from selflessness. All actions of the selfless man are naturally pure.

19. He whose every undertaking is free from desire and selfish purpose, and he who has burnt all his actions in the fire of knowledge—such an one the wise call a pandita.

20. He who has renounced attachment to the fruit of action, who is ever content, and free from all dependence,—he, though immersed in action, yet acts not.

That is, his action does not bind him.

21. Expecting naught, holding his mind and body in check, putting away every possession, and going through action only in the body he incurs no stain.

The purest act, if tainted by 'self', binds. But when it is done in a spirit of dedication, it ceases to bind. When 'self' has completely subsided, it is only the body that works. For instance, in the case of a man who is asleep his body alone is working. A prisoner doing his prison tasks has surrendered his body to the prison authorities and only his body, therefore, works. Similarly, he who has voluntarily made himself God's prisoner, does nothing himself. His body mechanically acts, the doer is God, hot he. He has reduced himself to nothingness.

22. Content with whatever chance may bring, rid of the pairs of opposites, free from ill-will, even-minded in success and failure, he is not bound though he acts.

23. Of the free soul who has shred all attachment, whose mind is firmly grounded in knowledge, who acts only for sacrifice, all karma is extinguished.

24. The offering of sacrifice is Brahman; the oblation is Brahman; it is offered by Brahman in the fire that is Brahman; thus he whose mind is fixed on acts dedicated to Brahman must needs pass on to Brahman.

25. Some yogins perform sacrifice in the form of worship of the gods, others offer sacrifice of sacrifice itself in the fire that is Brahman.

26. Some offer as sacrifice the sense of hearing and the other senses in the fires of restraint; others sacrifice sound and the other objects of sense in the fires of the senses.

The restraint of the senses—hearing and others—is one thing; and directing them only to legitimate objects, e.g. listening to hymns in the praise of god, is another, although ultimately both amount to the same thing.

27. Others again sacrifice all the activities of the senses and of the vital energy in the yogic fire of self-control kindled by knowledge.

That is to say, they lose themselves in the contemplation of the Supreme.

28. Some sacrifice with material gifts; with austerities; with yoga; some with the acquiring and some with the imparting of knowledge. All these are sacrifices of stern vows and serious endeavour.

29. Others absorbed in the practices of the control of the vital energy sacrifice the outward in the inward and the inward in the outward, or check the flow of both the inward and the outward vital airs.

The reference here is to the three kinds of practices of the control of vital energy—puraka, rechaka, and kumbhaka.

30. Yet others, abstemious in food, sacrifice one form of vital energy in another. All these know what sacrifice is and purge themselves of all impurities by sacrifice.

31. Those who partake of the residue of sacrifice—called amrita (ambrosia)—attain to everlasting Brahman. Even this world is not for a non-sacrificer; how then the next, O Kurusattama?

32. Even so various sacrifices have been described in the Vedas; know them all to proceed from action; knowing this thou shalt be released.

Action here means mental, physical and spiritual action. No sacrifice is possible without this triple action and no salvation without sacrifice. To know this and to put the knowledge into practice is to know the secret of sacrifice. In fine, unless man uses all his physical, mental and spiritual gifts in the service of mankind, he is a thief unfit for Freedom. He who uses his intellect only and spares his body is not a full sacrificer. Unless the mind and the body and the soul are made to work in unison, they cannot be adequately used for the service of mankind. Physical, mental and spiritual purity is essential for the harmonious working. Therefore man should concentrate on developing, purifying, and turning to the best of all his faculties.

33. Knowledge-sacrifice is better, O-Parantapa, than material sacrifice, for all action which does not bind finds its consummation in Knowledge (jnana).

Who does not know that works of charity performed without knowledge often result in great harm? Unless every act, however nobel its motive, is informed with knowledge, it lacks perfection. Hence the complete fulfillment of all action is in knowledge.

34. The masters of knowledge who have seen the Truth will impart to thee this Knowledge; learn it through humble homage and service and by repeated questioning.

The three conditions of knowledge—homage, repeated questioning and service—deserve to be carefully borne in mind in this age. Homage or obeisance means humility and service is a necessary accompaniment; else it would be mock homage. Repeated questioning is equally essential, for without a keen spirit of inquiry, there is no knowledge. All this presupposes devotion to and faith in the person approached. There can be no humility, much less service, without faith.

35. When thou hast gained this knowledge, O Pandava, thou shalt not again fall into such error; by virtue of it thou shalt see all beings without exception in thyself and thus in Me.

The adage 'Yatha pinde tatha brahmande'—'as with the self so with the universe') means the same thing. He who has attained Self-realization sees no difference between himself and others.

36. Even though thou be the most sinful of sinners, thou shalt cross the ocean of sin by the boat of knowledge.

37. As a blazing fire turns its fuel to ashes, O Arjuna, even so the fire of Knowledge turns all actions to ashes.

38. There is nothing in this world so purifying as Knowledge. He who is perfected by yoga finds it in himself in the fullness of time.

39. It is the man of faith who gains knowledge—the man who is intent on it and who has mastery over his senses; having gained knowledge, he comes ere long to the supreme peace.

40. But the man of doubt, without knowledge and without faith, is lost; for him who is given to doubt there is neither this world nor that beyond, nor happiness.

41. He who has renounced all action by means of yoga, who has severed all doubt by means of knowledge—him self-possessed, no actions bind, O Dhananjaya!

42. Therefore, with the sword of Self-realization sever thou this doubt, bred of ignorance, which has crept into thy heart! Betake thyself to yoga and arise, O Bharata!

Thus ends the fourth discourse, entitled 'Jnana-Karma-Sannyasa-Yoga' in the converse of Lord Krishna and Arjuna, on the science of Yoga, as part of the knowledge of Brahman in the Upanishad called the Bhagawadgita.

Discourse V

This discourse is devoted to showing that renunciation of action as such is impossible without the discipline of selfless action and that both are ultimately one.

Arjuna Said:

1. Thou laudest renunciation of actions, O Krishna, whilst at the same time thou laudest performance of action; tell me for a certainty which is the better.

The Lord Said:

2. Renunciation and performance of action both lead to salvation; but of the two, karmayoga (performance) is better than sannyasa (renunciation).

3. Him one should know as ever renouncing who has no dislikes and likes; for he who is free from the pairs of opposites is easily released from bondage.

That is, not renunciation of action but of attachment to the pairs determines true renunciation. A man who is always in action may be a good sannyasa (renouncer) and another who may be doing no work may well be a hypocrite. See III. 6.

4. It is the ignorant who speak of sankhya and yoga as different, not so those who have knowledge. He who is rightly established even in one wins to the fruit of both.

The yogi engrossed in sankhya (knowledge)lives even in thought for the good of the world and attains the fruit of karmayoga by the sheer power of his thought. The karmayogi ever engrossed in unattached action naturally enjoys the peace of the jnanayogi.

5. The goal that the sankhyas attain is also reached by the yogins. He sees truly who sees both sankhya and yoga as one.

6. But renunciation, O Mahabahu, is hard to attain except by yoga; the ascetic equipped with yoga attains Brahman ere long.

7. The yogi who has cleared himself, has gained mastery over his mind and all his senses, who has become one with the Atman in all creation, although he acts he remains unaffected.

8. The yogi who has seen the Truth knows that it is not he that acts whilst seeing, hearing, touching, smelling, eating, walking, sleeping, or breathing,

9. Talking, letting go, holding fast, opening or closing the eyes—in the conviction that is the senses that are moving in their respective spheres.

So long as 'self' endures, this detachment cannot be achieved. A sensual man therefore may not shelter himself under the pretence that it is not he but his senses that are acting. Such a mischievous interpretation betrays a gross ignorance of the Gita and right conduct. The next shloka makes this clear.

10. He who dedicates his actions to Brahman and performs them without attachment is not smeared by sin, as the lotus-leaf by water.

11. Only with the body, mind and intellect and also with the senses, do the yogins perform action without attachment for the sake of self-purification.

12. A man of yoga obtains everlasting peace by abandoning the fruit of action; the man ignorant of yoga, selfishly attached to fruit, remains bound.

13. Renouncing with the mind all actions, the dweller in the body, who is master of himself, rests happily in his city of nine gates, neither doing nor getting anything done.

The principal gates of the body are the two eyes, the two nostrils, the two ears, the mouth, and the two organs of excretion—though really speaking the countless pores of the skin are no less gates. If the gatekeeper always remains on the alert and performs his task, letting in or out only the objects that deserve ingress or egress, then of him it can truly be said that he has no part in the ingress or egress, but that he is a passive witness. He thus does nothing nor gets any thing done.

14. The Lord creates neither agency nor action for the world; neither does he connect action with its fruit. It is nature that is at work.

God is no doer. The inexorable law of karma prevails, and in the very fulfillment of the law—giving everyone his deserts, making everyone reap what he sows—lies God's abounding mercy and justice. In undiluted justice is mercy. Mercy which is inconsistent with justice is not mercy but its opposite. But man is not a judge knowing past, present, and future. So for him the law is reversed and mercy or forgiveness is the purest justice. Being himself ever liable to be judged he must accord to others what he would accord to himself, viz. forgiveness. Only by cultivating the spirit of forgiveness can he reach the state of a yogi, whom no actions bind, the man of even-mindedness, the man skilled in action.

15. The Lord does not take upon Himself anyone's vice or virtue; it is ignorance that veils knowledge and deludes all creatures.

The delusion lies in man arrogating to himself the authorship of action and the attributing to God the consequences thereof—punishment or reward as the case may be.

16. But to them whose ignorance is destroyed by the knowledge of Atman, this their knowledge, like the sun, reveals the Supreme.

17. Those whose intellect is suffused with That, whose self has become one with That, who abide in That, and whose end and aim is that, wipe out their sins with knowledge, and go whence there is no return.

18. The men of Self-realization look with an equal eye on a brahmana possessed of learning and humility, a cow, an elephant, a dog and even a dog-eater.

That is to say, they serve every one of them alike, according to the needs of each. Treating a brahmana and shwapaka (dog-eater) alike means that the wise man will suck the poison off a snake-bitten shwapaka with as much eagerness and readiness as he would from a snake-bitten brahmana.

19. In this very body they have conquered the round of birth and death, whose mind is anchored in sameness; for perfect Brahman is same to all, therefore in Brahman they rest.

As a man thinks, so he becomes, and therefore those whose minds are bent on being the same to all achieve that sameness and become one with Brahman.

20. He whose understanding is secure, who is undeluded, who knows Brahman and who rests in Brahman, will neither be glad to get what is pleasant, nor sad to get what is unpleasant.

21. He who has detached himself from contacts without, finds bliss in Atman; having achieved union with Brahman he enjoys eternal bliss.

He who has weaned himself from outward objects to the inner Atman is fitted for union with Brahman and the highest bliss. To withdraw oneself from contacts without and to bask in the sunshine of union with Brahman are two aspects of the same state, two sides of the same coin.

22. For the joys derived from sense-contacts are nothing but mines of misery; they have beginning and end, O Kaunteya; the wise man does not revel therein.

23. The man who is able even here on earth, ere he is released from the body, to hold out against the floodtide of lust and wrath,—he is a yogi, he is happy.

As a corpse has no likes and dislikes, no sensibility to pleasure and pain, even so he who though alive is dead to these, he truly lives, he is truly happy.

24. He who finds happiness only within, rest only within, light only within,—that yogi, having become one with nature, attains to oneness with Brahman.

25. They win oneness with Brahman—the seers whose sins are wiped out, whose doubts are resolved, who have mastered themselves, and who are engrossed in the welfare of all beings.

26. Rid of lust and wrath, masters of themselves, the ascetics who have realized Atman find oneness with Brahman everywhere around them.

27-28. That ascetic is ever free—who, having shut out the outward sense-contacts, sits with his gaze fixed between the brows, outward and inward breathing in the nostrils made equal; his senses, mind, and reason held in check; rid of longing, fear and wrath; and intent on Freedom.

These shlokas refer to some of the yogic practices laid down in the Yoga-sutras. A word of caution is necessary regarding these practices. They serve for the yogin the same purpose as athletics and gymnastics do for the bhogin (who pursues worldly pleasures). His physical exercises help the latter to keep his senses of enjoyment in full vigour. The yogic practices help the yogin to keep his body in condition and his senses in subjection. Men versed in these practices are rare in these days, and few of them turn them to good account. He who has achieved the preliminary stage on the path to self-discipline, he who has a passion for Freedom, and who having rid himself of the pairs of opposites has conquered fear, would do well to go in for these practices which will surely help him. It is such a disciplined man alone who can, through these practices, render his body a holy temple of God. Purity both of the mind and body is a sine qua non, without which these processes are likely, in the first instance, to lead a man astray and then drive him deeper into the slough of delusion. That this has been the result in some cases many know from actual experience. That is why that prince of yogins, Patanjali gave the first place to yamas (cardinal vows) and niyamas (casual vows), and held as eligible for yogic practices only those who have gone through the preliminary discipline.

The five cardinal vows are: non-violence, truth, non-stealing, celibacy, non-possession. The five casual vows are: bodily purity, contentment, the study of the scriptures, austerity, and meditation of God.

29. Knowing Me as the Acceptor of sacrifice and austerity, the great Lord of all the worlds, the Friend of all creation, the yogi attains to peace.

This shloka may appear to be in conflict with shlokas 14 and 15 of this discourse and similar ones in other discourses. It is not really so. Almighty God is Doer and non-Doer, Enjoyer and non-Enjoyer both. He is indescribably, beyond the power of human speech. Man somehow strives to have a glimpse of Him and in so doing invests Him with diverse and even contradictory attributes.

Thus ends the fifth discourse, entitled 'Sannyasa Yoga' in the converse of Lord Krishna and Arjuna, on the science of Yoga, as part of the knowledge of Brahman, in the Upanishad called the Bhagawadgita.

Discourse VI

This discourse deals with some of the means for the accomplishment of Yoga or the discipline of the mind and its activities.

The Lord Said:

1. He who performs all obligatory action, without depending on the fruit thereof, is a sannyasin and a yogin—not the man who neglects the sacrificial fire nor he who neglects action.

Fire here may be taken to mean all possible instruments of action. Fire was needed when sacrifices used to be performed with its help. Assuming that spinning were a means of universal service in this age, a man by neglecting the spinning wheel would not become a sannyasi.

2. What is called sannyasa, know thou to be yoga, O Pandava; for none can become a yogin who has not renounced selfish purpose.

3. For the man who seeks to scale the heights of yoga, action is said to be the means; for the same man, when he has scaled those heights, repose is said to be the means.

He who has purged himself of all impurities and who has achieved even-mindedness will easily achieve Self-realization. But this does not mean that he who has scaled the heights of yoga will disdain to work for the guidance of the world. On the contrary that work will be to him not only the breath of his nostrils, but also as natural to him as breathing. He will do so by the sheer force of will. See V. 4.

4. When a man is not attached either to the objects of sense or to actions and sheds all selfish purpose, then he is said to have scaled the heights of yoga.

5. By one's Self should one raise oneself, and not allow oneself to fall; for Atman (Self) alone is the friend of self, and Self alone is self's foe.

6. His Self alone is friend, who has conquered himself by his Self: but to him who has not conquered himself and is thus inimical to himself, even his Self behaves as foe.

7. Of him who has conquered himself and who rests in perfect calm the self is completely composed, in cold and heat, in pleasure and pain, in honour and dishonour.

8. The yogin who is filled with the contentment of wisdom and discriminative knowledge, who is firm as a rock, who has mastered his senses, and to whom a clod of earth, a stone and gold are the same, is possessed of yoga.

9. He excels who regards alike the boon companion, the friend, the enemy, the stranger, the mediator, the alien and the ally, as also the saint and the sinner.

10. Let the yogi constantly apply his thought to Atman remaining alone in a scheduled place, his mind and body in control, rid of desires and possessions.

11. Fixing for himself, in a pure spot, a firm seat, neither too high nor yet too low, covered with kusha grass, thereon a deerskin, and thereon a cloth;

12. Sitting on that seat, with mind concentrated, the functions of thought and sense of control, he should set himself to the practice of yoga for the sake of self-purification.

13. Keeping himself steady, holding the trunk, the neck and the head in a straight line and motionless, fixing his eye on the tip of his nose, and looking not around.

14. Tranquil in spirit, free from fear, steadfast in the vow of brahmacharya, holding his mind in control, the yogi should sit, with all his thoughts on Me, absorbed in Me.

Brahmacharya (usually translated 'celibacy') means not only sexual continence but observance of all the cardinal vows for the attainment of Brahman.

15. The yogi, who ever thus, with mind controlled, unites himself to Atman, wins the peace which culminates in Nirvana, the peace that is in Me.

16. Yoga is not for him who eats too much, nor for him who fasts too much, neither for him who sleeps too much, nor yet for him who is too wakeful.

17. To him who is disciplined in food and recreation, in effort in all activities, and in sleep and waking, yoga (discipline) becomes a relief from all ills.

18. When one's thought, completely controlled, rests steadily on only Atman, when one is free from longing for all objects of desire, then one is called a yogin.

19. As a taper in a windless spot flickers not, even so is a yogin, with his thought controlled, seeking to unite himself with Atman.

20. Where thought curbed by the practice of yoga completely ceases, where a man sits content within himself, Atman having seen Atman;

21. Where he experiences that endless bliss beyond the senses which can be grasped by reason alone; wherein established he swerves not from the Truth;

22. Where he holds no other gain greater than that which he has gained; and where, securely seated, he is not shaken by any calamity however great;

23. That state should be known as yoga (union with the Supreme), the disunion from all union with pain. This yoga must one practice with firm resolve and unwearying zeal.

24. Shaking oneself completely free from longings born of selfish purpose; reining in the whole host of senses, from all sides, with the mind itself;

25. With reason held securely by the will, he should gradually attain calm and with the mind established in Atman think of nothing.

26. Wherever the fickle and unsteady mind wanders, thence should it be reined and brought under the sole sway of Atman.

28. The yogin, cleansed of all stain, unites himself ever thus to Atman, easily enjoys the endless bliss of contact with Brahman.

29. The man equipped with yoga looks on all with an impartial eye, seeing Atman in all beings and all beings in Atman.

30. He who sees Me everywhere and everything in Me, never vanishes from Me nor I from him.

31. The yogin who, anchored in unity, worships Me abiding in all beings, lives and moves in me, no matter how he live and move.

So long as 'self' subsists, the Supreme Self is absent; when 'self' is extinguished, the Supreme Self is seen everywhere. Also see note on XIII. 23.

32. He who, by likening himself with others, senses pleasure and pain equally for all as for himself, is deemed to be the highest yogi, O Arjuna.

Arjuna Said:

33. I do not see, O Madhusudana, how this yoga, based on the equal-mindedness that Thou hast expounded to me, can steadily endure, because of fickleness (of the mind).

34. For fickle is the mind, O Krishna, unruly, overpowering and stubborn; to curb it is, I think, as hard as to curb the wind.

The Lord Said:

35. Undoubtedly, O Mahabahu, the mind is fickle and hard to curb; yet, O Kaunteya, it can be held in check by constant practice and dispassion.

36. Without self-restraint, yoga, I hold, is difficult to attain; but the self-governed soul can attain it by proper means, if he strives for it.

Arjuna Said:

37. If one, possessed of faith, but slack of effort, because of his mind straying from yoga, reach not perfection in yoga, what end does he come to, O Krishna?

38. Without a foothold, and floundering in the path to Brahman fallen from both, is he indeed not lost, O Mahabahu, like a dissipated cloud?

39. This my doubt, O Krishna, do thou dispel utterly; for there is to be found none other than thou to banish this doubt.

The Lord Said:

40. Neither in this world, nor in the next, can there be ruin for him, O Partha; no well-doer, oh loved one, meets with a sad end.

41. Fallen from yoga, a man attains the worlds of righteous souls, and having dwelt there for numberless years is then born in a house of pure and gentle blood.

42. Or he may even be born into a family of yogins, though such birth as this is all too rare in this world.

43. There, O Kurunandana, he discovers the intellectual stage he had reached in previous birth, and thence he stretches forward again towards perfection.

44. By virtue of that previous practice he is borne on, whether he will it or not, even he with a desire to know yoga passes beyond the Vedic ritual.

45. But the yogi who perseveres in his striving, cleansed of sin, perfected through many births, reaches the highest state.

46. The yogin is deemed higher than the man of austerities; he is deemed also higher than the man of knowledge; higher is he than the man engrossed in ritual; therefore be thou a yogin, O Arjuna!

47. And among all yogins, he who worships Me with faith, his inmost self all rapt in Me, is deemed by me to be the best yogin.

Thus ends the sixth discourse entitled 'Dhyana Yoga' in the converse of Lord Krishna and Arjuna, on the science of Yoga, as part of the knowledge of Brahman in the Upanishad called the Bhagawadgita.

Discourse VII

With this discourse begins an exposition of the nature of Reality and the secret of devotion.

The Lord Said:

1. Hear, O Partha, how, with thy mind rivetted on me, by practicing yoga and making me the sole refuge, thou shalt, without doubt, know me fully.

2. I will declare to thee, in its entirety, this knowledge, combined with discriminative knowledge, which when thou hast known there remains here nothing more to be known.

3. Among thousands of men hardly one strives after perfection; among those who strive hardly one knows Me in truth.

4. Earth, Water, Fire, Air, Ether, Mind, Reason and Ego—thus eightfold is my prakriti divided.

The eightfold prakriti is substantially the same as the field described in XIII. 5 and the perishable Being in XV. 16.

5. This is My lower aspect; but know thou My other aspect, the higher—which is Jiva (the Vital Essence) by which, O Mahabahu, this world is sustained.

6. Know that these two compose the source from which all beings spring; I am the origin and end of the entire universe.

7. There is nothing higher than I, O Dhananjaya; all this is strung on Me as a row of gems upon a thread.

8. In water I am the savour, O Kaunteya; in the sun and the moon I am the light; the syllable AUM in all the Vedas; the sound in ether, and manliness in men.

9. I am the sweet fragrance in earth; the brilliance in fire; the life in all beings; and the austerity in ascetics.

10. Know Me, O Partha, to be the primeval seed of all beings; I am the reason of rational beings and the splendour of the splendid.

11. Of the strong, I am the strength, divorced from lust and passion; in beings I am desire undivorced from righteousness.

12. Know that all the manifestations of the three gunas, sattva, rajas, and tamas, proceed from none but Me; yet I am not in them; they are in Me.

God is not dependent on them, they are dependent on Him. Without Him those various manifestations would be impossible.

13. Befogged by these manifestations of the three gunas, the entire world fails to recognize Me, the imperishable, as transcending them.

14. For this My divine delusive mystery made up of the three gunas is hard to pierce; but those who make Me their sole refuge pierce the veil.

15. The deluded evil-doers, lowest of men, do not see refuge in Me; for, by reason of this delusive mystery, they are bereft of knowledge and given to devilish ways.

16. Four types of well-doers are devoted to Me, O Arjuna; they are, O Bharatarshabha, the afflicted, the spiritual seeker, the material seeker, and the enlightened.

17. Of these the enlightened, ever attached to Me in single-minded devotion, is the best; for to the enlightened I am exceedingly dear and he is dear to Me.

18. All these are estimable indeed, but the enlightened I hold to be My very self; for he, the true yogi, is stayed on Me alone, the supreme goal.

19. At the end of many births the enlightened man finds refuge in Me; rare indeed is this great soul to whom 'Vasudeva is all'.

20. Men, bereft of knowledge by reason of various longings, seek refuge in other gods, pinning their faith on diverse rites, guided by their own nature.

21. Whatever form one desires to worship in faith and devotion, in that very form I make that faith of his secure.

22. Possessed of that faith he seeks a propitiate that one, and obtains therethrough his longings, dispensed in truth by none but Me.

23. But limited is the fruit that falls to those shortsighted ones; those who worship the gods go to the gods, those who worship Me come unto Me.

24. Not knowing My transcendent, imperishable, supreme character, the undiscerning think Me who am unmanifest to have become manifest.

25. Veiled by the delusive mystery created by My unique power, I am not manifest to all; this bewildered world does not recognize Me, birthless and changeless.

Having the power to create this world of sense and yet unaffected by it, He is described as having unique power.

26. I know, O Arjuna, all creatures past, present and to be; but no one knows Me.

27. All creatures in this universe are bewildered, O Parantapa, by virtue of the delusion of the pairs of opposite sprung from likes and dislikes, O Bharata.

28. But those virtuous men whose sin has come to an end, freed from delusion and of the pairs of opposites, worship Me in steadfast faith.

29. Those who endeavour for freedom from age and death by taking refuge in Me, know in full that Brahman, Adhyatma and all Karma.

30. Those who know Me, including Adhibhuta, Adhidaiva, Adhiyajna, possessed of even-mindedness, they know Me even at the time of passing away.

The terms in italics are defined in the next discourse the subject of which is indicated in 29-30. The sense is that every nook and cranny of the universe is filled with Brahman, that He is the sole Agent of all action, and that the man who imbued to Him, becomes one with Him at the time of passing hence. All his desires are extinguished in his vision of Him and he wins his freedom.

Thus ends the seventh discourse, entitled 'Jananvijnana Yoga' in the converse of Lord Krishna and Arjuna, on the science of Yoga, as part of the knowledge of Brahman in the Upanishad called the Bhagawadgita.

Discourse VIII

The nature of the Supreme is further expounded in this discourse.

Arjuna Said:

1. What is that Brahman? What is Adhyatma? What Karma, O Purushottama? What is called Adhibhuta? And what Adhidaiva?

2. And who here in this body is Adhiyajna and how? And how at the time of death art Thou to be known by the self-controlled?

The Lord Said:

3. The Supreme, the Imperishable is Brahman; its manifestation is Adhyatma; the creative process whereby all beings are created is called Karma.

4. Adhibhuta is My perishable form; Adhidaivata is the individual self in that form; and O best among the embodied, Adhiyajna am I in this body, purified by sacrifice.

That is, from Imperishable Unmanifest down to the perishable atom everything in the universe is the Supreme and an expression of the Supreme. Why then should mortal man arrogate to himself authorship of anything rather than do His bidding and dedicate all action to Him?

5. And he who, at the last hour remembering Me only, departs leaving the body, enters into Me; of that there is no doubt.

6. Or whatever form a man continually contemplates, that same he remembers in the hour of death, and to that very form he goes, O Kaunteya.

7. Therefore at all times remember Me and fight on; thy mind and reason thus on Me fixed thou shalt surely come to Me.

8. With thought steadied by constant practice, and wandering nowhere, he who meditates on the Supreme Celestial Being, O Partha, goes to Him.

9-10. Whoso, at the time of death, with unwavering mind, with devotion, and fixing the breath rightly between the brows by the power of yoga, meditates on the Sage, the Ancient, the Ruler, subtler than the subtlest, the Supporter of all, the Inconceivable, glorious as the sun beyond the darkness,—he goes to that Supreme Celestial Being.

11. That which the knowers of the Vedas call the Imperishable (or that word which the knowers of the Vedas repeat), wherein the ascetics freed from passion enter and desiring which they practice brahmacharya, that Goal (or Word) I will declare to thee in brief.

12. Closing all the gates, locking up the mind in the hridaya, fixing his breath within the head, rapt in yogic meditation;

13. Whoso departs leaving the body uttering AUM—Brahman in one syllable—repeatedly thinking on Me, he reaches the highest state.

14. That yogi easily wins to Me, O Partha, who, ever attached to Me, constantly remembers Me with undivided mind.

15. Great souls, having come to Me, reach the highest perfection; they come not again to birth, unlasting and (withal) an abode of misery.

16. From the world of Brahma down, all the worlds are subject to return, O Arjuna; but on coming to Me there is no rebirth.

17. Those men indeed know what is Day and what is Night, who know that Brahma's day lasts a thousand yugas and that his night too is a thousand yugas long.

That is to say, our day and night of a dozen hours each are less than the infinitesimal fraction of a moment in that vast cycle of time. Pleasures pursued during these incalculably small moments are as illusory as a mirage. Rather than waste these brief moments, we should devote them to serving God through service of mankind. On the other hand, our time is such a small drop in the ocean of eternity that if we fail of our object here, viz. Self-realization, we need not despair. She should bide our time.

18. At the coming of Day all the manifest spring forth from the Unmanifest, and at the coming of Night they are dissolved into that same Unmanifest.

Knowing this too, man should understand that he has very little power over things, the round of birth and death is ceaseless.

19. This same multitude of creatures come to birth, O Partha, again and again; they are dissolved at the coming of Night, whether they will or not; and at the break of Day they are re-born.

20. But higher than the Unmanifest is another Unmanifest Being, everlasting, which perisheth not when all creatures perish.

21. This Unmanifest, named the Imperishable, is declared to be the highest goal. For those who reach it there is no return. That is my highest abode.

22. This Supreme Being, O Partha, may be won by undivided devotion; in It all beings dwell, by It all is pervaded.

23. Now I will tell thee, Bharatarshabha, the conditions which determine the exemption from return, as also the return, of yogins after they pass away hence.

24. Fire, Light, Day, the Bright Fortnight, the six months of the Northern Solstice—through these departing men knowing Brahman go to Brahman.

25. Smoke, Night, the Dark Fortnight, the six months of the Southern Solstice—Therethrough the yogin attains to the lunar light and thence returns.

I do not understand the meaning of these two shlokas. They do not seem to me to be consistent with the teaching of the Gita. The Gita teaches that he whose heart is meek with devotion, who is devoted to unattached action and has seen the Truth must win salvation, no matter when he dies. These shlokas seem to run counter to this. They may perhaps be stretched to mean broadly that a man of sacrifice, a man of light, a man who has known Brahman finds release from birth if he retains that enlightenment at the time of death, and that on the contrary the man who has none of these attributes goes to the world of the moon—not at all lasting—and returns to birth. The moon, after all, shines with borrowed light.

26. These two paths—bright and dark—are deemed to be the eternal paths of the world; by the one a man goes to return not, by the other he returns again.

The Bright one may be taken to mean the path of knowledge and the dark one that of ignorance.

27. The Yogin knowing these two paths falls not into delusion, O Partha; therefore, at all times, O Arjuna, remain steadfast in yoga.

"Will not fall into delusion" means that he who knows the two paths and has known the secret of even-mindedness will not take the path of ignorance.

28. Whatever fruit of good deeds is laid down as accruing from (a study of) the Vedas, from sacrifices, austerities, and acts of charity—all that the yogin transcends, on knowing this, and reaches the Supreme and Primal Abode.

He who has achieved even-mindedness by dint of devotion, knowledge and service not only obtains the fruit of all his good actions, but also wins salvation.

Thus ends the eighth discourse entitled 'Brahma Yoga' in the converse of Lord Krishna and Arjuna, on the science of Yoga, as part of the knowledge of Brahman in the Upanishad called the Bhagawadgita.

Discourse IX

This discourse reveals the glory of devotion.

The Lord Said:

1. I will now declare to thee, who art uncensorious, this mysterious knowledge, together with discriminative knowledge, knowing which thou shalt be released from ill.

2. This is the king of sciences, the king of mysteries, pure and sovereign, capable of direct comprehension, the essence of dharma, easy to practice, changeless.

3. Men who have no faith in this doctrine, O Parantapa, far from coming to Me, return repeatedly to the path of this world of death.

4. By Me, unmanifest in form, this whole world is pervaded; all beings are in Me, I am not in them.

5. And yet those beings are not in Me. That indeed is My unique power as Lord! Sustainer of all beings, I am not in them; My Self brings them into existence.

The sovereign power of God lies in this mystery, this miracle, that all beings are in Him and yet not in Him, He in them and yet not in them. This is the description of God in the language of mortal man. Indeed He soothes man by revealing to him all His aspects by using all kinds of paradoxes. All beings are in him inasmuch as all creation is His; but as He transcends it all, as He really is not the author of it all, it may be said with equal truth that the beings are not in Him. He really is in all His true devotees, He is not, according to them, in those who deny Him. What is this if not a mystery, a miracle of God?

6. As the mighty wind, moving everywhere, is ever contained in ether, even so know that all beings are contained in Me.

7. All beings, O Kaunteya, merge into my prakriti, at the end of a kalpa, and I send them forth again when a kalpa begins.

8. Resorting to my prakriti, I send forth again and again this multitude of beings, powerless under the sway of prakriti.

9. But all this activity, O Dhananjaya, does not bind Me, seated as one indifferent, unattached to it.

10. With me as Presiding Witness, prakriti gives birth to all that moves and does not move; and because of this, O Kaunteya, the wheel of the world keeps going.

11. Not knowing My transcendent nature as the sovereign Lord of all beings, fools condemn Me incarnated as man.

For they deny the existence of God and do not recognize the Director in the human body.

12. Vain are the hopes, actions and knowledge of those witless ones who have resorted to the delusive nature of monsters and devils.

13. But those great souls who resort to the divine nature, O Partha, know Me as the Imperishable Source of all beings and worship Me with an undivided mind.

14. Always declaring My glory, striving in steadfast faith, they do Me devout homage; ever attached to Me, they worship Me.

15. Yet others, with knowledge-sacrifice, worship Me, who am to be seen everywhere, as one, as different or as many.

16. I am the sacrificial vow; I am the sacrifice; I the ancestral oblation; I the herb; I the sacred text; I the clarified butter; I the fire; I the burnt offering.

17. Of this universe I am the Father, Mother, Creator, Grandsire: I am what is to be known, the sacred syllable AUM; the rig, the Saman and the Yajus;

18. I am the Goal, the Sustainer, the Lord, the Witness, the Abode, the Refuge, the Friend; the Origin, the End the Preservation, the Treasurehouse, the Imperishable Seed.

19. I give heat; I hold back and pour forth rain; I am deathlessness and also death. O Arjuna, Being and not-Being as well.

20. Followers of the three Vedas, who drink the soma juice and are purged of sin, worship Me with sacrifice and pray for going to heaven; they reach the holy world of the gods and enjoy in heaven the divine joys of the gods.

The reference is to the sacrificial ceremonies and rites in vogue in the days of the Gita. We cannot definitely say what they were like nor what the soma juice exactly was.

21. They enjoy the vast world of heaven, and their merit spent, they enter the world of the mortals; thus those who, following the Vedic law, long for the fruit of their action earn but the round of birth and death.

22. As for those who worship Me, thinking on Me alone and nothing else, ever attached to Me, I bear the burden of getting them what they need.

There are thus three unmistakable marks of a true yogi or bhakta—even-mindedness, skill in action, undivided devotion. These three must be completely harmonized in a yogi. Without devotion there is no even-mindedness, without even-mindedness no devotion, and without skill in action devotion and even-minded might well be a pretense.

23. Even those who, devoted to other gods, worship them in full faith, even they, O Kaunteya, worship none but Me, though not according to the rule.

'Not according to the rule' means not knowing Me as the Impersonal and the Absolute.

24. For I am the Acceptor and the Director of all sacrifices; but not recognizing Me as I am, they go astray.

25. Those who worship the gods go to the gods; those who worship the manes go to the manes; those who worship the spirits go to the spirits; but those who worship Me come to Me.

26. Any offering of leaf, flower, fruit or water, made to Me in devotion, by an earnest soul, I lovingly accept.

That is to say, it is the Lord in every being whom we serve with devotion who accepts the service.

27. Whatever thou doest, whatever thou eatest, whatever thou offerest as sacrifice or gift, whatever austerity thou dost perform, O kaunteya, dedicate all to Me.

28. So doing thou shalt be released from the bondage of action, yielding good and evil fruit; having accomplished both renunciation and performance, thou shalt be released (from birth and death) and come unto Me.

29. I am the same to all beings; with Me there is non disfavoured, none favoured; but those who worship Me with devotion are in Me and I in them.

30. A sinner, howsoever great, if he turns to Me with undivided devotion, must indeed be counted a saint; for he has a settled resolve.

The undivided devotion subdues both his passions and his evil deeds.

31. For soon he becomes righteous and wins everlasting peace; know for a certainty, O kaunteya, that my bhakta never perishes.

32. For finding refuge in Me, even those who though are born of the womb of sin, women, vaishyas, and shudras too, reach the supreme goal.

33. How much more then, the pure brahmanas and seer-kings who are my devotees? Do thou worship Me, therefore, since thou hast come to this fleeting and joyless world.

34. On Me fix thy mind, to Me bring thy devotion, to Me offer thy sacrifice, to Me make thy obeisance; thus having attached thyself to Me and made Me thy end and aim, to Me indeed shalt thou come.

Thus ends the ninth discourse entitled 'Rajavidya-rajaguhya Yoga' in the converse of Lord Krishna and Arjuna, on the science of Yoga, as part of the knowledge of Brahman in the Upanishad called the Bhagawadgita.

Discourse X

For the benefit of His devotees, the Lord gives in this discourse a glimpse of His divine manifestations.

The Lord Said:

1. Yet once more, O Mahabahu, here My supreme word, which I will utter to thee, gratified one, for thy benefit.

2. Neither the gods nor the great seers know My origin; for I am, every way, the origin of them both.

3. He who knows Me, the great lord of the worlds, as birthless and without beginning, he among mortals, undeluded, is released from sins.

4. Discernment, knowledge, freedom from delusion, long suffering, truth, self-restraint, inward calm, pleasure, pain, birth, death, fear and fearlessness;

5. Non-violence, even-mindedness, contentment, austerity, beneficence, good and ill fame,—all these various attributes of creatures proceed verily from Me.

6. The seven great seers, the ancient four, and the Manus too were born of Me and of My mind, and of them were born all the creatures in the world.

7. He who knows in truth My immanence and My yoga becomes gifted with unshakable yoga; of this there is no doubt.

8. I am the source of all, all proceeds from me; knowing this, the wise worship Me with hearts full of devotion.

9. With me in their thoughts, their whole soul devoted to Me, teaching one another, with me ever on their lips, they live in contentment and joy.

10. To these, ever in tune with Me worshipping me with affectionate devotion, I give the power of selfless action, whereby they come to Me.

11. Out of every compassion for them, I who dwell in their hearts, destroy the darkness, born of ignorance, with the refulgent lamp of knowledge.

Arjuna Said:

12. Lord! Thou art the supreme Brahman, the supreme Abode, the supreme Purifier! Everlasting Celestial Being, the Primal God, Unborn, All-pervading.

13. Thus have all the seers—the divine seer Narada, Asita, Devala, Vyasa—declared Thee; and Thou Thyself dost tell me so.

14. All that Thou tellest me is true, I know, O Keshava, verily, Lord, neither the gods nor the demons know Thy manifestation.

15. Thyself alone Thou knowest by Thyself, O Purushottama, O Source and Lord of all beings, God of Gods, O Ruler of the universe.

16. Indeed Thou oughtest to tell me of all Thy manifestations, without a remainder, whereby Thou dost pervade the worlds.

17. O Yogin! constantly meditating on Thee, how am I to know Thee? In what various aspects am I to think of Thee, O Lord?

18. Recount to me yet again, in full detail, Thy unique power and Thy immanence, O Janardana! For my ears cannot be sated with listening to Thy life-giving words.

The Lord Said:

19. Yea, I will unfold to thee, O Kurushreshtha, My divine manifestations,—the chiefest only; for there is no limit to their extent.

20. I am the Atman, O Gudakesha, seated in the heart of every being; I am the beginning, the middle and the end of all beings.

21. Of the Adityas I am Vishnu; of luminaries, the radiant Sun; of Maruts, I am Marichi; of constellations, the moon.

22. Of the Vedas I am the Sama Veda; of the gods Indra; of the senses I am the mind; of beings I am the consciousness.

23. Of Rudras I am Shankara; of Yakshas and Rakshasas Kubera; of Vasus I am the Fire; of mountains Meru.

24. Of priests, O Partha, know Me to be the chief Brihaspati; of army captains I am Kartikeya; and of waters the ocean.

25. Of the great seers I am Bhrigu; of words I am the one syllable 'AUM'; of sacrifices I am the Japa sacrifice; of things immovable, the Himalaya.

26. Of all trees I am Ashvattha; of the divine seers, Narada; of the heavenly choir I am Chitraratha; of the perfected I am Kapila the ascetic.

27. Of horses, Know Me to be the Uchchaihshravas born with Amrita; of mighty elephants I am Airavata; of men, the monarch.

28. Of weapons, I am Vajra; of cows, Kamadhenu; I am Kandarpa, the god of generation; of serpants I am Vasuki.

29. Of cobras I am Anata; of water-dwellers I am Varuna; of the manes I am Aryaman; and of the chastisers, Yama.

30. Of demons I am Prahlada; of reckoners, the time; of beasts I am the lion; and of birds, Garuda.

31. Of cleansing agents I am the Wind; of wielders of weapons, Rama; of fishes I am the crocodile; of rivers the Ganges.

32. Of creations I am the beginning, end and middle, O Arjuna; of sciences, the science of spiritual knowledge; of debators, the right argument.

33. Of letters, the letter A; of compounds I am the dvandva; I am the imperishable Time; I am the creator to be seen everywhere.

34. All-seizing Death am I, as the source of things to be; in feminine virtues I am Kirti (glory), Shri (beauty), Vak (speech), Smriti (memory), Medha (intelligence), Dhriti (constancy) and Kshama (forgiveness).

35. Of Saman hymns I am Brihat Saman; of metres, Gayatri; of months I am Margashirsha; of seasons, the spring.

36. Of deceivers I am the dice-play; of the splendid the splendour; I am victory, I am resolution, I am the goodness of the good.

The 'dice-play of deceivers' need not alarm one. For the good and evil nature of things in not the matter in question, it is the directing and immanent power of God that is being described. Let the deceivers also know that they are under God's rule and judgment and put away their pride and deceit.

37. Of Vrishnis I am Vasudeva; of Pandavas Dhananjaya; of ascetics I am Vyasa; and of seers, Ushanas.

38. I am the rod of those that punish; the strategy of those seeking victory; of secret things I am silence, and the knowledge of those that know.

39. Whatever is the seed of every being, O Arjuna, that am I; there is nothing, whether moving or fixed, that can be without Me.

40. there is no end to my divine manifestations; what extent of them I have told thee now is only by way of illustration.

41. Whatever is glorious, beautiful and mighty know thou that all such has issued from a fragment of My splendour.

42. But why needest thou to learn this at great length, O Arjuna? With but a part of Myself I stand upholding this universe.

Thus ends the tenth discourse, entitled 'Vibhuti Yoga' in the converse of Lord Krishna and Arjuna, on the science of Yoga, as part of the knowledge of Brahman, in the Upanishad called the Bhagawadgita.

Discourse XI

In this discourse the Lord reveals to Arjuna's vision what Arjuna has heard with his ears—the Universal Form of the Lord. This discourse is a favourite with the Bhaktas. Here there is no argument, there is pure poetry. Its solemn music[1] reverberates in one's ears and it is not possible to tire of reading it again and again.

Arjuna Said:

1. Out of Thy grace towards me, thou hast told me the supreme mystery revealing the knowledge of the Supreme; it has banished my delusion.

2. Of the origin and destruction of beings I have heard from Thee in full detail, as also Thy imperishable ajesty [sic], O Kamala-patraksha!

3. Thou art indeed as Thou hast described Thyself, Parameshvara! I do crave to behold, now, that form of Thine as Ishvara.

4. If, Lord, thou thinkest it possible for me to bear the sight, reveal to me, O Yogeshvara, Thy imperishable form.

The Lord Said:

5. Behold, O Partha, my forms divine in their hundreds and thousands, infinitely diverse, infinitely various in color and aspect.

6. Behold the Adityas, the Vasus, the Rudras, the two Ashwins, the Maruts; behold, O Bharata, numerous marvels never revealed before.

7. Behold today, O Gudakesha, in my body, the whole universe, moving and unmoving, all in one, and whatever else thou cravest to see.

8. But thou canst not see Me with these thine own eyes. I give thee the eye divine; behold My sovereign power!

Sanjaya Said:

9. With these words, O King, the great Lord of Yoga, Hari, then revealed to Partha His supreme form as Ishvara.

10. With many mouths and many eyes, many wondrous aspects, many divine ornaments, and many brandished weapons divine.

11. Wearing divine garlands and vestments, annointed with divine perfumes, it was the form of God, all-marvellous [sic], infinite, seen everywhere.

12. Were the splendour of a thousand suns to shoot forth all at once in the sky that might perchance resemble the splendour of that Mighty One.

13. Then did Pandava see the whole universe in its manifold divisions gathered as one in the body of that God of gods.

14. Then Dhananjaya, wonderstruck and thrilled in every fibre of his being, bowed low his head before the Lord, addressing Him thus with folded hands.

Arjuna Said:

15. With Thy form, O Lord, I see all the gods and the diverse multitudes of beings, the Lord Brahma, on his lotus-throne and all the seers and serpents divine.

16. With many arms and bellies, mouths and eyes, I see Thy infinite form everywhere. Neither Thy end, nor middle, nor beginning, do I see, O Lord of the Universe, Universal-formed!

17. With crown and mace and disc, a mass of effulgence, gleaming everywhere I see Thee, so dazzling to the sight, bright with the splendour of the fiery sun blazing from all sides,—incomprehensible.

18. Thou art the Supreme Imperishable worthy to be known; Thou art the final resting place of this universe; Thou art the changeless guardian of the Eternal Dharma; Thou art, I believe, the Everlasting Being.

19. Thou hast no beginning, middle nor end; infinite is Thy might; arms innumerable; for eyes, the sun and the moon; Thy mouth a blazing fire, overpowering the universe with Thy radiance.

20. By Thee alone are filled the spaces between heaven and earth and all the quarters; at the sight of this Thy wondrous terrible form, the three worlds are sore oppressed, O Mahatman!

21. Here, too, the multitudes of gods are seen to enter Thee; some awe-struck praise Thee with folded arms; the hosts of great seers and siddhas, 'All Hail' on their lips, hymn Thee with songs of praise.

22. The Rudras, Adityas, Vasus, Sadhyas, all the gods, the twin Ashwins, Maruts, Manes, the hosts of Gandharvas, Yakshas, Asuras and Siddhas—all gaze on Thee in wonderment.

23. At the sight of thy mighty form, O Mahabahu, many-mouthed, with eyes, arms, thighs and feet innumerable, with many vast bellies, terrible with many jaws, the worlds feel fearfully oppressed, and so do I.

24. For as I behold Thee touching the sky, glowing, numerous-hued with gaping mouths and wide resplendent eyes, I feel oppressed in my innermost being; no peace nor quiet I find, O Vishnu!

25. As I see Thy mouths with fearful jaws, resembling the Fire of Doom, I lose all sense of direction, and find no relief. Be gracious, O Devesha, O Jagannivasa!

26. All the sons of Dhritarashtra, and with them the crowd of kings, Bhishma, Drona, and that Karna too, as also our chief warriors—

27. Are hastening into the fearful jaws of Thy terrible mouths. Some indeed, caught between Thy teeth, are seen, their heads being crushed to atoms.

28. As rivers, in their numerous torrents, run head-long to the sea, even so the heroes of the world of men rush into Thy flaming mouths.

29. As moths, fast-flying, plunge into blazing fire, straight to their doom, even so these rush headlong into Thy mouths, to their destruction.

30. Devouring all these from all sides, Thou lappest them with Thy flaming tongues; Thy fierce rays blaze forth, filling the whole universe with their lustre.

31. Tell me, Lord, who Thou art so dread of form! Hail to Thee, O Devavara! Be gracious! I desire to know Thee, Primal Lord; for I comprehend not what Thou dost.

The Lord Said:

32. Doom am I, full-ripe, dealing death to the worlds, engaged in devouring mankind. Even without slaying them not one of the warriors, ranged for battle against thee, shall survive.

33. Therefore, do thou arise, and win renown! Defeat thy foes and enjoy a thriving kingdom. By Me have these already been destroyed; be thou no more than an instrument, O Savyasachin!

34. Drona, Bhishma, Jayadratha and Karna, as also the other warrior chiefs—already slain by Me—slay thou! Fight! Victory is thine over the foes in the field.

Sanjaya Said:

35. Hearing this world of Keshava, crown-wearer Arjuna folded his hands, and trembling made obeisance. Bowing and all hesitant, in faltering accents, he proceeded to address Krishna once more.

Arjuna Said:

36. Right proper it is, O Hrishikesha, that Thy praise should stir the world to gladness and tender emotion; the Rakshasas in fear fly to every quarter and all the hosts of Siddhas do reverent homage.

37. And why should they not bow down to Thee, O Mahatma? Thou art the First Creator, greater even than Brahma. O Ananta, O Devesha, O Jagannivasa, Thou art the Imperishable, Being, not-Being, and That which transcends even these.

38. Thou art the Primal God, the Ancient Being; Thou art the Final Resting Place of this Universe; Thou art the Knower, the 'to-be-known', the Supreme Abode; by Thee, O Myriad-formed, is the universe pervaded.

39. Thou art Vayu, Yama, Agni, Varuna, Shashanka, Prajapati, and Prapitamaha! All Hail to Thee, a thousand times all hail! Again and yet again all hail to Thee!

40. All hail to Thee from before and behind! all hail to Thee from every side, O All; Thy prowess is infinite, Thy might is measureless! Thou holdest all; therefore Thou art all.

41. If ever in carelessness, thinking of Thee as comrade, I addressed Thee saying, 'O Krishna!', 'O Yadava!' not knowing Thy greatness, in negligence or in affection,

42. If ever I have been rude to Thee in jest, whilst at play, at rest-time, or at meals, whilst alone or in company, O Achyuta, forgive Thou my fault—I beg of Thee, O Incomprehensible!

43. Thou art Father of this world, of the moving and the un-moving; thou art its adored, its worthiest, Master; there is none equal to Thee; how then any greater than Thee? Thy power is matchless in the three worlds.

44. Therefore, I prostrate myself before Thee, and beseech Thy grace, O Lord adorable! As father with son, as comrade with comrade, so shouldst Thou bear, beloved Lord, with me, Thy loved one.

45. I am filled with joy to see what never was seen before, and yet my heart is oppressed with fear. Show me that original form of Thine, O Lord! Be gracious, Devesha, O Jagannivasa!

46. I crave to see Thee even as Thou wast, with crown, with mace, and disc in hand; wear Thou, once more, that four-armed form, O thousand-armed Vishvamurti!

The Lord Said:

47. It is to favour thee, O Arjuna, that I have revealed to thee, by My own unique power, this My form Supreme, Resplendent, Universal, Infinite, Primal—which none save thee has ever seen.

48. Not by the study of the Vedas, not by sacrifice, not by the study of other scriptures, not by gifts, nor yet by performance of rites or of fierce austerities can I, in such a form, be seen by any one save thee in the world of men, O Kurupravira!

49. Be thou neither oppressed nor bewildered to look on this awful form of Mine. Banish thy fear, ease thy mind, and lo! behold Me once again as I was.

Sanjaya Said.

50. So said Vasudeva to Arjuna, and revealed to him once more His original form. Wearing again His form benign, the Mahatma consoled him terrified.

Arjuna Said.

51. Beholding again thy benign human form I am come to myself and once more in my normal state.

The Lord Said:

52. Very hard to behold is that form of Mine which thou hast seen; even the gods always yearn to see it.

53. Not by the Vedas, not by penance, nor by gifts, nor yet by sacrifice, can any behold Me in the form that thou hast seen.

54. But by single-minded devotion, O Arjuna, I may in this form be known and seen, and truly entered into, O Parantapa!

55. He alone comes to me, O Pandava, who does My work, who has made Me his goal, who is My devotee, who has renounced attachment, who has ill-will toward none.

Thus ends the eleventh discourse, entitled 'Vishvarupadarshana Yoga' in the converse of Lord Krishna and Arjuna, on the science of Yoga as part of the knowledge of Brahman in the Upanishad called the Bhagawadgita.

[1]The music, of course, of the original! In translation, 'the glory is gone'. For a very free rendering which brings out some at least of the haunting music of the original the reader must go to Sir Edwin Arnold's flowing stanzas.

Discourse XII

Thus we see that vision of God is possible only through single-minded devotion. Contents of devotion must follow as a matter of course. This twelfth discourse should be learnt by hard even if all discourses are not. It is one of the shortest. The marks of a devotee should be carefully noted.

Arjuna Said:

1. Of the devotees who thus worship Thee, incessantly attached, and those who worship the Imperishable Unmanifest, which are the better yogins?

The Lord Said:

2. Those I regard as the best yogins who, riveting their minds on Me, ever attached, worship Me, with the highest faith.

3. But those who worship the Imperishable, the indefinable, the Unmanifest, the Omnipresent, the Unthinkable, the Rock-seated, the Immovable, the Unchanging,

4. Keeping the whole host of senses in complete control, looking on all with an impartial eye, engrossed in the welfare of all beings—these come indeed to Me.

5. Greater is the travail of those whose mind is fixed on the Unmanifest; for it is hard for embodied mortals to gain the Unmanifest—Goal.

Mortal man can only imagine the Unmanifest, the Impersonal, and as his language fails him he often negatively describes It as 'Neti', 'Neti' (Not That, Not That). And so even iconoclasts are at bottom no better than idol-worshippers. To worship a book, to go to church, or to pray with one's face in a particular direction—all these are forms of worshipping the Formless in an image or idol. And yet, both the idol-breaker and the idol-worshipper cannot lose sight of the fact that there is something which is beyond all form, Unthinkable, Formless, Impersonal, Changeless. The highest goal of the devotee is to become one with the object of his devotion. The bhakta extinguishes himself and merges into, becomes, Bhagvan. This state can best be reached by devoting oneself to some form, and so it is said that the short cut to the Unmanifest is really the longest and the most difficult.

6. But those who casting all their actions on Me, making Me their all in all, worship Me with the meditation of undivided devotion,

7. Of such, whose thoughts are centered on Me, O Partha, I become ere long the Deliverer from the ocean of this world of death.

8. On Me set thy mind, on Me rest thy conviction; thus without doubt shalt thou remain only in Me hereafter.

9. If thou canst not set thy mind steadily on Me, then by the method of constant practice seek to win Me, O Dhananjaya.

10. If thou art also unequal to this method of constant practice, concentrate on service for Me; even thus serving Me thou shalt attain perfection.

11. If thou art unable even to do this, then dedicating all to Me, with mind controlled, abandon the fruit of action.

12. Better is knowledge than practice, better than knowledge is concentration, better than concentration is renunciation of the fruit of all action, from which directly issues peace.

'Practice' (abhyasa) is the practice of the yoga of meditation and control of psychic processes; 'knowledge' (jnana) is intellectual effort; 'concentration' (dhyana) is devoted worship. If as a result of all this there is no renunciation of the fruit of action, 'practice' is no 'practice', 'knowledge' is no 'knowledge', and 'concentration' is no 'concentration'.

13. Who has ill-will towards none, who is friendly and compassionate, who has shed all thought of 'mine' or 'I', who regards pain and pleasure alike, who is long-suffering;

14. Who is ever content, gifted with yoga, self-restrained, of firm conviction, who has dedicated his mind and reason to Me—that devotee (bhakta) of Mine is dear to Me.

15. Who gives no trouble to the world, to whom the world causes no trouble, who is free from exultation, resentment, fear and vexation,—that man is dear to Me.

16. Who expects naught, who is pure, resourceful, unconcerned, untroubled, who indulges in no undertakings,—that devotee of Mine is dear to Me.

17. Who rejoices not, neither frets nor grieves, who covets not, who abandons both good and ill—that devotee of Mine is dear to Me.

18. Who is same to foe and friend, who regards alike respect and disrespect, cold and heat, pleasure and pain, who is free from attachment;

19. Who weighs in equal scale blame and praise, who is silent, content with whatever his lot, who owns no home, who is of steady mind,—that devotee of Mine is dear to Me.

20. They who follow this essence of dharma, as I have told it, with faith, keeping Me as their goal,—those devotees are exceeding dear to Me.

Thus ends the twelfth discourse entitled 'Bhakti Yoga' in the converse of Lord Krishna and Arjuna, on the science of Yoga, as part of the knowledge of Brahman in the Upanishad called the Bhagawadgita.

Discourse XIII

This discourse treats of the distinction between the body (not-Self) and the Atman (the Self).

The Lord Said:

1. This body, O Kaunteya, is called the Field; he who knows it is called the knower of the Field by those who know.

2. And understand Me to be, O Bharata, the knower of the Field in all the Fields; and the knowledge of the Field and the knower of the Field, I hold, is true knowledge.

3. What the Field is, what its nature, what its modifications, and whence is what, as also who He is, and what His power—hear this briefly from Me.

4. This subject has been sung by seers distinctively and in various ways, in different hymns as also in aphoristic texts about Brahman well reasoned and unequivocal.

5. The great elements, Individuation, Reason, the Unmanifest, the ten senses, and the one (mind), and the five spheres of the senses;

6. Desire, dislike, pleasure, pain, association, consciousness, cohesion—this, in sum, is what is called the Field with its modifications.

The great elements are Earth, Water, Fire, Air and Ether. 'Individuation' is the thought of I, or that the body is 'I'; the 'Unmanifest' is prakriti or maya; the ten senses are the five senses of perception—smell, taste, sight, touch and hearing, and the five organs of action, viz.: the hands, the feet, the tongue, and the two organs of excretion. The five spheres or objects of the senses are smell, savour, form, touch, and sound. 'Association' is the property of the different organs to co-operate. Dhriti is not patience or constancy but cohesion, i.e. the property of all the atoms in the body to hold together; from 'individuation' springs this cohesion. Individuation is inherent in the unmanifest prakriti. The undeluded man is he who can cast off the individuation or ego, and having done so the shock of an inevitable thing like death and pairs of opposites caused by sense-contacts fail to affect him. The Field, subject to all its modifications, has to be abandoned in the end by the enlightened and the unenlightened alike.

7. Freedom from pride and pretentiousness, nonviolence, forgiveness, uprightness, service of the Master, purity, steadfastenes, self-restraint;

8. Aversion from sense-objects, absence of conceit, realization of the painfulness and evil of birth, death, age and disease;

9. Absence of attachment, refusal to be wrapped up in one's children, wife, home and family, even-mindedness whether good or ill befall;

10. Unwavering and all-exclusive devotion to Me, resort to secluded spots, distaste for the haunts of men;

11. Settled conviction of the nature of the Atman, perception of the goal of the knowledge of Truth,—

All this is declared to be Knowledge and the reverse of it is ignorance.

12. I will (now) expound to thee that which is to be known and knowing which one enjoys immortality; it is the supreme Brahman which has no beginning, which is called neither Being nor non-Being.

The Supreme can be described neither as Being nor as non-Being. It is beyond definition or description, above all attributes.

13. Everywhere having hands and feet, everywhere having eyes, heads, mouths, everywhere having ears, It abides embracing everything in the universe.

14. Seeming to possess the functions of the senses, It is devoid of all the senses; It touches naught, upholds all; having no gunas, It experiences the gunas.

15. Without all beings, yet within; immovable yet moving, so subtle that It cannot be perceived; so far and yet so near It is.

He who knows It is within It, close to It; mobility and immobility, peace and restlessness, we owe to It, for It has motion and yet is motionless.

16. Undivided, It seems to subsist divided in all beings; this Brahman—That which is to be known as the Sustainer of all, yet It is their Devourer and Creator.

17. Light of all lights, It is said to be beyond darkness; It is knowledge, the object of knowledge, to be gained only by knowledge; It is seated in the hearts of all.

18. Thus have I expounded in brief the Field, Knowledge and That which is to be known; My devotee, when he knows this, is worthy to become one with Me.

19. Know that Prakriti and Purusha are both without beginning; know that all the modifications and gunas are born of Prakriti.

20. Prakriti is described as the cause in the creation of effects from causes; Purusha is described as the cause of the experiencing of pleasure and pain.

21. For the Purusha, residing in Prakriti, experiences the gunas born in Prakriti; attachment to these gunas is the cause of his birth in good or evil wombs.

Prakriti in common parlance is Maya. Purusha is the Jiva. Jiva acting in accordance with his nature experiences the fruit of actions arising out of the three gunas.

22. What is called in this body the Witness, the Assentor, the Sustainer, the Experiencer, the Great Lord and also the Supreme Atman, is Supreme Being.

23. He who thus knows Purusha and Prakriti with its gunas, is not born again, no matter how he live and move.

Read in the light of discourses II, IX and XII this shloka may not be taken to support any kind of libertinism. It shows the virtue of self-surrender and selfless devotion. All actions bind the self, but if all are dedicated to the Lord they do not bind, rather they release him. He who has thus extinguished the 'self or the thought of 'I' and who acts as ever in the great witness' eye, will never sin nor err. the self-sense is at the root of all error or sin. Where the 'I' has ben extinguished, there is no sin. This shloka shows how to steer clear of all sin.

24. Some through meditation hold the Atman by themselves in their own self; others by Sankhya Yoga, and others by Karma Yoga.

25. Yet others, not knowing (Him) thus, worship (Him) having heard from others; they too pass beyond death, because of devoted adherence to what they have heard.

26. Wherever something is born, animate or inanimate, know thou Bharatarshabha, that it issues from the union of the Field and the Knower of the Field.

27. Who sees abiding in all beings the same Parameshvara, imperishable in the perishable, he sees indeed.

28. When he sees the same Ishvara abiding everywhere alike, he does not hurt himself by himself and hence he attains the highest goal.

He who sees the same God everywhere merges in Him and sees naught else; he thus does not yield to passion, does not become his own foe and thus attains Freedom.

29. Who sees that it is Prakriti that performs all actions and thus (knows) that Atman performs them not, he sees indeed.

Just as, in the case of a man who is asleep, his "Self" is not the agent of sleep, but Prakriti, even so the enlightened man will detach his "Self" from all activities. to the pure everything is pure. Prakriti is not unchaste, it is when arrogant man takes her as wife that of these twain passion is born.

30. When he sees the diversity of beings as founded in unity and the whole expanse issuing therefrom, then he attains to Brahman.

To realize that everything rests in Brahman is to attain to the state of Brahman. Then Jiva becomes Shiva.

31. This imperishable Supreme Atman, O Kaunteya, though residing in the body, acts not and is not stained, for he has no beginning and no gunas.

32. As the all-pervading ether, by reason of its subtlety, is not soiled even so Atman pervading every part of the body is not soiled.

33. As the one Sun illumines the whole universe, even so the Master of the Field illumines the whole field, O Bharata!

34. Those who, with the eyes of knowledge, thus perceive the distinction between the Field and the Knower of the Field, and (the secret) of the release o beings from Prakriti, they attain to the Supreme.

Thus ends the thirteenth discourse, entitled 'Kshetra-kshetrajnavibhaga Yoga' in the converse of Lord Krishna and Arjuna, on the science of Yoga, as part of the knowledge of Brahman in the Upanishad called the Bhagawadgita.

Discourse XIV

The description of Prakriti naturally leads on to that of its constituents, the Gunas, which from the subject of this discourse. And that, in turn, leads to a description of the marks of him who has passed beyond the three gunas. These are practically the same as those of the man of secure understanding (II. 54-72) as also those of the ideal Bhakta (XII. 12-20).

The Lord Said:

1. Yet again I will expound the highest and the best of all knowledge, knowing which all the sages passed hence to the highest perfection.

2. By having recourse to this knowledge they became one with Me. They need not come to birth even at a creation, nor do they suffer at a dissolution.

3. The great prakriti is for me the womb in which I deposit the germ; from it all beings come to birth, O Bharata.

4. Whatever forms take birth in the various species, the great prakriti is their Mother and I the seed-giving Father.

5. Sattva, rajas and tamas are the gunas sprung from prakriti; it is they, O Mahabahu, that keep the imperishable Dweller bound to the body.

6. Of these sattva, being stainless, is light-giving and healing; it binds with the bond of happiness and the bond of knowledge, O sinless one.

7. Rajas, know thou, is of the nature of passion, the source of thirst and attachment; it keeps man bound with the bond of action.

8. Tamas, know thou, born of ignorance, is mortal man's delusion; it keeps him bound with heedlessness, sloth and slumber, O Bharata.

9. Sattva attaches man to happiness, rajas to action, and tamas, shrouding knowledge, attaches him to heedlessness.

10. Sattva prevails, O Bharata, having overcome rajas and tamas; rajas, when it has overpowered sattva and tamas; likewise tamas reigns when sattva and rajas are crushed.

11. When the light—knowledge—shines forth from al the gates of this body, then it may be known that the sattva thrives.

12. Greed, activity, assumption of undertakings, restlessness, craving—these are in evidence when rajas flourishes, O Bharatarshabha.

13. Ignorance, dullness, heedlessness, and delusion—these are in evidence when tamas reigns, O Kurunandana.

14. If the embodied one meets his end whilst sattva prevails, then he attains to the spotless worlds of the knowers of the Highest.

15. If he dies during the reign within him of rajas, he is born among men attached to action; and if he dies in tamas, he is born in species not endowed with reason.

16. The fruit of sattvika action is said to be stainless merit. That of rajas is pain and that of tamas ignorance.

18. Those abiding in sattva rise upwards, those in rajas stay midway, those in tamas sink downwards.

19. when the seer perceives no agent other than the gunas, and knows Him who is above the gunas, he attains to My being.

As soon as a man realizes that he is not the doer, but the gunas are the agent, the 'self' vanishes, and he goes through all his actions spontaneously, just to sustain the body. And as the body is meant to subserve the highest end, all his actions will even reveal detachment and dispassion. Such a seer can easily have a glimpse of the One who is above the gunas and offer his devotion to Him.

20. When the embodied one transcends these three gunas which are born of his contact with the body, he is released from the pain of birth, death and age and attains deathlessness.

Arjuna Said:

21. What, O Lord, are the marks of him who has transcended the three gunas? How does he conduct himself? How does he transcend the three gunas?

The Lord Said:

22. He, O Pandava, who does not disdain light, activity, and delusion when they come into being, nor desires them when they vanish;

23. He, who seated as one indifferent, is not shaken by the gunas, and stays still and moves not, knowing it is gunas playing their parts;

24. He who holds pleasure and pain alike, who is sedate, who regards as same earth, stone and gold, who is wise and weighs in equal scale things pleasant and unpleasant, who is even-minded in praise and blame;

25. Who holds alike respect and disrespect, who is the same to friend and foe, who indulges in no undertakings—That man is called gunatita.

Shls. 22-25 must be read and considered together. Light activity and delusion, as we have seen in the foregoing shlokas, are the products or indications of sattva, rajas and tamas respectively. The inner meaning of these verses is that he who has transcended the gunas will be unaffected by them. A stone does not desire light, nor does it disdain activity or inertness; it is still, without having the will to be so. If someone puts it into motion, it does not fret; if again, it is allowed to lie still, it does not feel that inertness or delusion has seized it. The difference between a stone and a gunatita is that the latter has full consciousness and with full knowledge he shakes himself free from the bonds that bind an ordinary mortal. He has, as a result of his knowledge, achieved the purpose of a stone. Like the stone he is witness, but not the doer, of the activities of the gunas or prakriti. Of such jnani one may say that he is sitting still, unshaken in the knowledge that it is the gunas playing their parts. We who are every moment of our lives acting as though we are the doers can only imagine the state, we can hardly experience it. But we can hitch our waggon to that star and work our way closer and closer towards it by gradually withdrawing the self from our actions. A gunatita has experience of his own condition but he cannot describe it, for he who can describe it ceases to be one. The moment he proceeds to do so, 'self' peeps in. The peace and light and bustle and inertness of our common experience are illusory. The Gita itself has made it clear in so many words that the sattvika state is the one nearest that of a gunatita. Therefore every one should strive to develop more and more sattva in himself, believing that some day he will reach the goal of the state of gunatita.

26. He who serves me in an unwavering and exclusive bhaktiyoga transcends these gunas and is worthy to become one with Brahman.

27. For I am the very image of Brahman, changeless and deathless, as also of everlasting dharma and perfect bliss.

Thus ends the fourteenth discourse, entitled 'Gunatrayavibhaga Yoga' in the converse of Lord Krishna and Arjuna, on the science of Yoga, as part of the knowledge of Brahman, in the Upanishad called the Bhagawadgita.

Discourse XV

This discourse deals with the supreme form of the Lord, transcending Kshara (perishable) and Akshara (imperishable).

The Lord Said:

1. With the root above and branches below, the ashvattha tree, they say, is impossible; it has Vedic hymns for its leaves; he who knows it knows the Vedas.

Shvah means tomorrow, and ashvattha (na shvopi sthata) means that which will not last even until tomorrow, i.e. the world of sense which is every moment in a state of flux. But even though it is perpetually changing, as its root is Brahman or the Supreme, it is imperishable. It has for its protection and support the leaves of the Vedic hymns, i.e. dharma. He who knows the world of sense as such and who knows dharma is the real jnani, that man has really known the Vedas.

2. Above all and below its branches spread, blossoming because of the gunas, having for their shoots the sense-objects; deep down in the world of men are ramified its roots, in the shape of the consequences of action.

This is the description of the tree of the world of sense as the unenlightened see it. They fail to discover its Root above in Brahman and so they are always attached to the objects of sense. They water the tree with the three gunas and remain bound to Karman in the world of men.

3. Its form as such is not here perceived, neither is its end, nor beginning, nor basis. Let man first hew down this deep-rooted Ashvattha with the sure weapon of detachment;

4. Let him pray to win to that haven from which there is no return and seek to find refuge in the primal Being from whom has emanated this ancient world of action.

'Detachment in shl. 3 here means dispassion, aversion to the objects of the senses. Unless man is determined to cut himself off from the temptations of the world of sense he will go deeper into the mire every day. These verses show that one dare not play with the objects of the senses with impunity.

5. To that imperishable haven those enlightened souls go—who are without pride and delusion, who have triumphed over the taints of attachment, who are ever in tune with the Supreme, whose passions have died, who are exempt from the pairs of opposites, such as pleasure and pain.

6. Neither the sun, nor the moon, nor fire illumine it; men who arrive there return not—that is My supreme abode.

7. As part indeed of Myself which has been the eternal Jiva in this world of life, attracts the mind and the five senses from their place in prakriti.

8. When the master (of the body) acquires a body and discards it he carries these with him wherever he goes, even as the wind carries scents from flower beds.

9. Having settled himself in the senses—ear, eye, touch, taste, and smell—as well as the mind, through them he frequents their objects.

These objects are the natural objects of the senses. The frequenting or enjoyment of these would be tainted if there were the sense of 'I' about it; otherwise it is pure, even as a child's enjoyment of these objects is innocent.

10. The deluded perceive Him not as He leaves or settles in (a body) or enjoys (sense objects) in association with the gunas; it is those endowed with the eye of knowledge who alone see Him.

11. Yogins who strive see Him seated in themselves; the witless ones who have not cleansed themselves to see Him not, even though they strive.

This does not conflict with the covenant that God has made even with the sinner in discourse 9. Akritatman (who has not cleansed himself) means one who has no devotion in him, who has not made up his mind to purify himself. The most confirmed sinner, if he has humility enough to seek refuge in surrender to God, purifies himself and succeeds in finding Him. Those who do not care to observe the cardinal and the casual vows and expect to find God through bare intellectual exercise are witless, Godless; they will not find Him.

12. The light in the sun which illumines the whole universe and which is in the moon and in fire—that light, know thou, is Mine;

13. It is I, who penetrating the earth uphold all beings with My strength, and becoming the moon—the essence of all sap—nourish all the herbs;

14. It is I who becoming the Vaishvanara Fire and entering the bodies of all that breathe, assimilate the four kinds of food with the help of the outward and the inward breaths.

15. And I am seated in the hearts of all, from Me proceed memory, knowledge and the dispelling of doubts; it is I who am to be known in all the Vedas, I, the author of Vedanta and the knower of the Vedas.

16. There are two Beings in the world: kshara (perishable) and akshara (imperishable). Kshara embraces all creatures and their permanent basis is akshara.

17. The Supreme Being is surely another—called Paramatman who is the Imperishable Ishvara pervades and supports the three worlds.

18. Because I transcend the kshara and am also higher than the akshara, I am known in the world and in the Vedas as Purushottama (the Highest Being).

19. He who, undeluded, knows Me as Purushottama, knows all, he worships Me with all his heart, O Bharata.

20. Thus I have revealed to thee, sinless one, this most mysterious shastra; he who understands this, O Bharata, is a man of understanding, he has fulfilled his life's mission.

Thus ends the fifteenth discourse, entitled 'purushottama Yoga' in the converse of Lord krishna and Arjuna, on the science of Yoga, as part of the knowledge of Brahman in the Upanishad called the Bhagawadgita.

Discourse XVI

This discourse treats of the divine and the devilish heritage.

The Lord Said:

1. Fearlessness, purity of heart, steadfastness in jnana and yoga—knowledge and action, beneficence, self-restraint, sacrifice, spiritual study, austerity, and uprightness;

2. Non-violence, truth, slowness to wrath, the spirit of dedication, serenity, aversion to slander, tenderness to all that lives, freedom from greed, gentleness, modesty, freedom from levity;

3. Spiritedness, forgiveness, fortitude, purity, freedom from ill-will and arrogance—these are to be found in one born with the divine heritage, O Bharata.

4. Pretentiousness, arrogance, self-conceit, wrath, coarseness, ignorance—these are to be found in one born with the devilish heritage.

5. The divine heritage makes for Freedom, the devilish for bondage. Grieve not, O Partha; thou art born with a divine heritage.

6. There are two orders of created beings in this world—the divine and the devilish; the divine order has been described in detail, hear from Me now of the devilish, O Partha.

7. Men of the devil do not know what they may do and what they may not do; neither is there any purity, nor right conduct, nor truth to be found in them.

8. 'Without truth, without basis, without God is the universe,' they say; 'born of the union of the sexes, prompted by naught but lust.'

9. Holding this view, these depraved souls, of feeble understanding and of fierce deeds, come forth as enemies of the world to destroy it.

10. Given to insatiable lust, possessed by pretentiousness, arrogance and conceit, they seize wicked purposes in their delusion, and go about pledged to uncleaned deeds.

11. Given to boundless cares that end only with their death, making indulgence or lust their sole goal, convinced that that is all;

12. Caught in a myriad snares of hope, slaves to lust and wrath, they speak unlawfully to amass wealth for the satisfaction of their appetites.

13. 'This have I gained today; this aspiration shall I now attain; this wealth is mine; this likewise shall be mine hereafter;

14. 'This enemy I have already slain, others also I shall slay; lord of all am I; enjoyment is mine, perfection is mine, strength is mine, happiness is mine;

15. 'Wealthy am I, and high-born. What other is like unto me? I shall perform a sacrifice! I shall give alms! I shall be merry!' Thus think they, by ignorance deluded;

16. And tossed about by diverse fancies, caught in the net of delusion, stuck deep in the indulgence of appetites, into foul hell they fall.

17. Wise in their own conceit, stubborn, full of the intoxication of pelf and pride, they offer nominal sacrifices for show, contrary to the rule.

18. Given to pride, force, arrogance, lust and wrath they are deriders indeed, scorning Me in their own and other' bodies.

19. These cruel scorners, lowest of mankind and vile, I hurl down again and again, into devilish wombs.

20. Doomed to devilish wombs, these deluded ones, far from ever coming to Me, sink lower and lower in birth after birth.

21. Three-fold is the gate of hell, leading man to perdition—Lust, Wrath, and Greed; these three, therefore, should be shunned.

22. The man who escapes these three gates of Darkness, O Kaunteya, works out his welfare and thence reaches the highest state.

23. He who forsakes the rule of shastra and does but the bidding of his selfish desires, gains neither perfection, nor happiness, nor the highest state.

Shastra does not mean the rites and formulae laid down in the so-called dharmashastra, but the path of self-restraint laid down by the seers and the saints.

24. Therefore let shastra be thy authority for determining what ought to be done and what ought not to be done; ascertain thou the rule of the shastra and do thy task here (accordingly).

Shastra here too has the same meaning as in the preceding shloka. Let no one be a law unto himself, but take as his authority the law laid down by men who have known and lived religion.

Thus ends the sixteenth discourse, entitled 'Daivasurasampadvibhaga Yoga' in the converse of Lord Krishna and Arjuna, on the science of Yoga, as part of the knowledge of Brahman in the Upanishad called the Bhagawadgita.

Discourse XVII

On being asked to consider shastra (conduct of the worthy) as the authority, Arjuna is faced with a difficulty. What is the position of those who may not be able to accept the authority of Shastra but who may act in faith? An answer to the question is attempted in this discourse. Krishna rests content with pointing out the rocks and shoals on the path of the one who forsakes the beaconlight of Shastra (conduct of the worthy). In doing so he deals with the faith and sacrifice, austerity and charity, performed with faith, and their divisions according to the spirit in which they are performed. He also sings the greatness of the mystic syllables AUM TAT SAT—a formula of dedication of all work to God.

Arjuna Said:

1. What, then, O Krishna, is the position of those who forsake the rule of Shastra and yet worship with faith? Do they act from sattva or rajas or tamas?

The Lord Said:

2. Threefold is the faith of men, an expression of their nature in each case; it is sattvika, rajas or tamasa. Hear thou of it.

3. The faith of every man is in accord with his innate character; man is made up of faith; whatever his object of faith, even so is he.

4. Sattvika persons worship the gods; rajas ones, the Yakshas and Rakshasas; and others—men of tamas—worship manes and spirits.

5. Those men who, wedded to pretentiousness and arrogance, possessed by the violence of lust and passion, practice fierce austerity not ordained by shastra;

6. They, whilst they torture the several elements that make up their bodies, torture Me too dwelling in them; know them to be of unholy resolves.

7. Of three kinds again is the food that is dear to each; so also are sacrifice, austerity, and charity. Hear how they differ.

8. Victuals that add to one's years, vitality, strength, health, happiness and appetite; are savoury, rich, substantial and inviting, are dear to the sattvika.

9. Victuals that are bitter, sour, salty, over-hot, spicy, dry, burning, and causing pain, bitterness and disease, are dear to rajasa.

10. Food which has become cold, insipid, putrid, stale, discarded and unfit for sacrifice, is dear to the tamasa.

11. That sacrifice is sattvika which is willingly offered as a duty without desire for fruit and according to the rule.

12. But when sacrifice is offered with an eye to fruit and for vain glory, know, O Bharatashreshtha, that it is rajasa.

13. Sacrifice which is contrary to the rule, which produces no food, which lacks the sacred text, which involves no giving up, which is devoid of faith is said to be tamasa.

14. Homage to the gods, to Brahmanas, to gurus and to wise men; cleanliness, uprightness, brahmacharya and non-violence—these constitute austerity (tapas) of the body.

15. Words that cause no hurt, that are true loving and helpful, and spiritual study constitute austerity of speech.

16. Serenity, benignity, silence, self-restraint, and purity of the spirit—these constitute austerity of the mind.

17. This threefold austerity practiced in perfect faith by men not desirous of fruit, and disciplined, is said to be sattvika.

18. Austerity which is practiced with an eye to gain praise, honour and homage and for ostentation is said to be rajasa; it is fleeting and unstable.

19. Austerity which is practiced from any foolish obsession, either to torture oneself or to procure another's ruin, is called tamasa.

20. Charity, given as a matter of duty, without expectation of any return, at the right place and time, and to the right person is said to be sattvika.

21. Charity, which is given either in hope of receiving in return, or with a view of winning merit, or grudgingly, is declared to be rajasa.

22. Charity given at the wrong place and time, and to the undeserving recipient disrespectfully and with contempt is declared to be tamasa.

23. AUM TAT SAT has been declared to be the threefold name of Brahman and by that name were created of old the Brahmanas, the Vedas and sacrifices.

24. Therefore, with AUM ever on their lips, are all the rites of sacrifice, charity and austerity, performed always to the rule, by Brahmavadins.

25. With the utterance of TAT and without the desire for fruit are the several rites of sacrifice, austerity and charity performed by those seeking Freedom.

26. SAT is employed in the sense of 'real' and 'good'; O Partha, SAT is also applied to beautiful deeds.

27. Constancy in sacrifice, austerity and charity, is called SAT; and all work for those purposes is also SAT.

The substance of the last four shlokas is that every action should be done in a spirit of complete dedication to God. For AUM alone is the only Reality. That only which is dedicated to It counts.

28. Whatever is done, O Partha, by way of sacrifice, charity or austerity or any other work, is called Asat if done without faith. It counts for naught hereafter as here.

Thus ends the seventeenth discourse, entitled 'Sharaddhatrayavibhaga Yoga' in the converse of Lord Krishna and Arjuna, on the science of Yoga, as part of the knowledge of Brahman in the Upanishad called the Bhagawadgita.

Discourse XVIII

This concluding discourse sums up the teaching of the Gita. It may be said to be summed up in the following: "Abandon all duties and come to Me, the only Refuge" (66). That is true renunciation. But abandonment of all duties does not mean abandonment of actions; it means abandonment of the desire for fruit. Even the highest act of service must be dedicated to Him, without the desire. That is Tyaga (abandonment), that is Sannyasa (renunciation).

Arjuna Said:

1. Mahabahu! I would fain learn severally the secret of sannyasa and of tyaga, O Hrishikesha, O Keshinishudana.

The Lord Said:

2. Renunciation of actions springing from selfish desire is known as sannyasa by the seers; abandonment of the fruit of all action is called tyaga by the wise.

3. Some thoughtful persons say: 'All action should be abandoned as an evil'; others say: 'Action for sacrifice, charity and austerity should not be relinquished'.

4. Hear my decision in this matter of tyaga, O Bharatasattama; for tyaga, too, O mightiest of men, has been described to be of three kinds.

5. Action for sacrifice, charity and austerity may not be abandoned; it must needs be performed. Sacrifice, charity and austerity are purifiers of the wise.

6. But even these actions should be performed abandoning all attachment and fruit; such, O Partha, is my best and considered opinion.

7. It is not right to renounce one's allotted task; its abandonment, from delusion, is said to be tamasa.

8. He who abandons action, deeming it painful and for fear of straining his limbs, he will never gain the fruit of abandonment, for his abandonment is rajasa.

9. But when an allotted task is performed from a sense of duty and with abandonment of attachment and fruit, O Arjuna, that abandonment is deemed to be sattvika.

10. Neither does he disdain unpleasant action, nor does he cling to pleasant action—this wise man full of sattva, who practices abandonment, and who has shaken off all doubts.

11. For the embodied one cannot completely abandon action; but he who abandons the fruit of action is named a tyagi.

12. To those who do not practice abandonment accrues, when they pass away, the fruit of action which is of three kinds: disagreeable, agreeable, mixed; but never to the sannyasins.

13. Learn, from me, O Mahabahu, the five factors mentioned in the Sankhyan doctrine for the accomplishment of all action:

14. The field, the doer, the various means, the several different operations, the fifth and the last, the Unseen.

15. Whatever action, right or wrong, a man undertakes to do with the body, speech or mind, these are the five factors thereof.

16. This being so, he who, by reason of unenlightened intellect, sees the unconditioned Atman as the agent—such a man is dense and unseeing.

17. He who is free from all sense of 'I', whose motive is untainted, slays not nor is bound, even though he slay all these worlds.

This shloka though seemingly somewhat baffling is not really so. The Gita on many occasions presents the ideal to attain which the aspirant has to strive but which may not be possible completely to realize in the world. It is like definitions in geometry. A perfect straight line does not exist, but it is necessary to imagine it in order to prove the various propositions. Even so, it is necessary to hold up ideals of this nature as standards for imitation in matters of conduct. This then would seem to be the meaning of this shloka: He who has made ashes of 'self', whose motive is untainted, may slay the whole world, if he will. But in reality he who has annihilated 'self' has annihilated his flesh too, and he whose motive is untainted sees the past, present and future. Such a being can be one and only one—God. He acts and yet is no doer, slays and yet is no slayer. For mortal man and royal road—the conduct of the worthy—is ever before him, viz. ahimsa—holding all life sacred.

18. Knowledge, the object of knowledge, and the knower compose the threefold urge to action; the means, the action and the doer compose the threefold sum of action.

19. Knowledge, action, and the doer are of three kinds according to their different gunas; hear thou these, just as they have been described in the science of the gunas.

20. Know that knowledge whereby one sees in all beings immutable entity—a unity in diversity—to be sattvika.

21. That knowledge which perceives separately in all beings several entities of diverse kinds, know thou to be rajasa.

22. And knowledge which, without reason, clings to one single thing, as though it were everything, which misses the true essence and is superficial is tamasa.

23. That action is called sattvika which, being one's allotted task, is performed without attachment, without like or dislike, and without a desire for fruit.

24. That action which is prompted by the desire for fruit, or by the thought of 'I', and which involves much dissipation of energy is called rajasa.

25. That action which is blindly undertaken without any regard to capacity and consequences, involving loss and hurt, is called tamasa.

26. That doer is called sattvika who has shed all attachment, all thought of 'I', who is filled with firmness and zeal, and who recks neither success nor failure.

27. That doer is said to be rajasa who is passionate, desirous of the fruit of action, greedy, violent, unclean, and moved by joy and sorrow.

28. That doer is called tamasa who is undisciplined, vulgar, stubborn, knavish, spiteful, indolent, woebegone, and dilatory.

29. Hear now, O Dhananjaya, detailed fully and severally, the threefold division of understanding and will, according to their gunas.

30. That understanding, O Partha, is sattvika which knows action from inaction, what ought to be done from what ought not to be done, fear from fearlessness and bondage from release.

31. That understanding, O Partha, is rajasa, which decides erroneously between right and wrong, between what ought to be done and what ought not to be done.

32. That understanding, O Partha, is tamasa, which, shrouded in darkness, thinks wrong to be right and mistakes everything for its reverse.

33. That will, O Partha, is sattvika which maintains an unbroken harmony between the activities of the mind, the vital energies and the senses.

34. That will, O Partha, is rajasa which clings, with attachment, to righteousness, desire and wealth, desirous of fruit in each case.

35. That will, O Partha, is tamasa, whereby insensate man does not abandon sleep, fear, grief, despair and self-conceit.

36. Hear now from Me, O Bharatarshabha, the three kinds of pleasure.

Pleasure which is enjoyed only by repeated practice, and which puts an end to pain,

37. Which, in its inception, is as poison, but in the end as nectar, born of the serene realization of the true nature of Atman—that pleasure is said to be sattvika.

38. That pleasure is called rajasa which, arising from the contact of the senses with their objects, is at first as nectar but in the end like poison.

39. That pleasure is called tamasa which arising from sleep and sloth and heedlessness, stupefies the soul both at first and in the end.

40. There is no being, either on earth or in heaven among the gods, that can be free from these three gunas born of prakriti.

41. The duties of Brahmanas, Kshatriyas, Vaishyas, and Shudras, are distributed according to their innate qualifications, O Parantapa.

42. Serenity, self-restraint, austerity, purity, forgiveness, uprightness, knowledge and discriminative knowledge, faith in God are the Brahmana's natural duties.

43. Valour, spiritedness, constancy, resourcefulness, not fleeing from battle, generosity, and the capacity to rule are the natural duties of a Kshatriya.

44. Tilling the soil, protection of the cow and commerce are the natural functions of a Vaishya, while service is the natural duty of a Shudra.

45. Each man, by complete absorption in the performance of his duty, wins perfection. Hear now how he wins such perfection by devotion to that duty.

46. By offering the worship of his duty to Him who is the moving spirit of all beings, and by whom all this is pervaded, man wins perfection.

47. Better one's own duty, though uninviting, than another's which may be more easily performed; doing duty which accords with one's nature, one incurs no sin.

The central teaching of the Gita is detachment—abandonment of the fruit of action. And there would be no room for this abandonment if one were to prefer another's duty to one's own. Therefore one's own duty is said to be better than another's. It is the spirit in which duty is done that matters, and its unattached performance is its own reward.

48. One should not abandon, O Kaunteya, that duty to which one is born, imperfect though it be; for all action, in its inception, is enveloped in imperfection, as fire in smoke.

49. He who has weaned himself of all kinds, who is master of himself, who is dead to desire, attains through renunciation the perfection of freedom from action.

50. Learn now from Me, in brief, O Kaunteya, how he who has gained this perfection, attains to Brahman, the supreme consummation of knowledge.

51. Equipped with purified understanding, restraining the self with firm will, abandoning sound and other objects of the senses, putting aside likes and dislikes,

52. Living in solitude, spare in diet, restrained in speech, body and mind, ever absorbed in dhyanayoga, anchored in dispassion,

53. Without pride, violence, arrogance, lust, wrath, possession, having shed all sense of 'mine' and at peace with himself, he is fit to become one with Brahman.

54. One with Brahman and at peace with himself, he grieves not, nor desires; holding all beings alike, he achieves supreme devotion to Me.

55. By devotion, he realizes in truth how great I am, who I am; and having known Me in reality he enters into Me.

56. Even whilst always performing actions, he who makes Me his refuge wins, by My grace, the eternal and imperishable haven.

57. Casting, with thy mind, all actions on Me, make Me thy goal, and resorting to the yoga of even-mindedness fix thy thought ever on Me.

58. Fixing his thy thought on Me, thou shalt surmount all obstacles by My grace; but if possessed by the sense of 'I' thou listen not, thou shalt perish.

59. If obsessed by the sense of 'I', thou thinkest, 'I will not fight', vain is thy obsession; (thy) nature will compel thee.

60. What thou wilt not do, O Kaunteya, because of thy delusion, thou shalt do, even against thy will, bound as thou art by the duty to which thou art born.

61. God, O Arjuna, dwells in the heart of every being and by His delusive mystery whirls them all, (as though) set on a machine.

62. In Him alone seek thy refuge with all thy heart, O Bharata. By His grace shalt thou win to the eternal haven of supreme peace.

63. Thus have I expounded to thee the most mysterious of all knowledge; ponder over it fully, then act as thou wilt.

64. Hear again My supreme word, the most mysterious of all; dearly beloved thou art of Me, hence I desire to declare thy welfare.

65. On Me fix thy mind, to Me bring thy devotion, to Me offer thy sacrifice, to Me make thy obeisance; to Me indeed shalt thou come—solemn is My promise to thee, thou art dear to Me.

66. Abandon all duties and come to Me the only refuge. I will release thee from all sins; grieve not!

67. Utter this never to him who knows no austerity, has no devotion, nor any desire to listen, nor yet to him who scoffs at Me.

68. He who will propound this supreme mystery to My devotees, shall, by that act of highest devotion to Me, surely come to Me.

69. Nor among men is there any who renders dearer service to Me than he; nor shall there be on earth any more beloved by Me than he.

It is only he who has himself gained the knowledge and lived it in his life that can declare it to others. These two shlokas cannot possibly have any reference to him, who no matter how he conducts himself, can give flawless reading and interpretation of the Gita.

70. And the man of faith who, scorning not, will but listen to it,—even he shall be released and will go to the happy worlds of men of virtuous deeds.

72. Hast thou heard this, O Partha, with a concentrated mind? Has thy delusion, born of ignorance, been destroyed, O Dhananjaya?

Arjuna Said:

73. Thanks to Thy grace, O Achyuta, my delusion is destroyed, my understanding has returned. I stand secure, my doubts all dispelled; I will do thy bidding.

Sanjaya Said:

74. Thus did I hear this marvellous and thrilling discourse between Vasudeva and the great-souled Partha.

75. It was by Vyasa's favor that I listened to this supreme and mysterious Yoga as expounded by the lips of the Master of Yoga, Krishna Himself.

76. O King, as often as I recall that marvellous and purifying discourse between Keshava and Arjuna, I am filled with recurring rapture.

77. And as often as I recall that marvellous form of Hari, my wonder knows no bounds and I rejoice again and again.

78. Wheresoever Krishna, the Master of Yoga, is, and wheresoever is Partha the Bowman, there rest assured are Fortune, Victory, Prosperity, and Eternal Right.

Thus ends the eighteenth discourse, entitled 'Sannyasa Yoga' in the converse of Lord Krishna and Arjuna, on the science of Yoga, as part of the knowledge of Brahman in the Upanishad called the Bhagawadgita.

Bhagavad-Gita
Translated from the Sanskrit by Sir Edwin Arnold

Table of Contents

Preface

This famous and marvellous Sanskrit poem occurs as an episode of the Mahabharata, in the sixth—or "Bhishma"—Parva of the great Hindoo epic. It enjoys immense popularity and authority in India, where it is reckoned as one of the "Five Jewels,"—pancharatnani—of Devanagiri literature. In plain but noble language it unfolds a philosophical system which remains to this day the prevailing Brahmanic belief, blending as it does the doctrines of Kapila, Patanjali, and the Vedas. So lofty are many of its declarations, so sublime its aspirations, so pure and tender its piety, that Schlegel, after his study of the poem, breaks forth into this outburst of delight and praise towards its unknown author: "Magistrorum reverentia a Brachmanis inter sanctissima pietatis officia refertur. Ergo te primum, Vates sanctissime, Numinisque hypopheta! quisquis tandem inter mortales dictus tu fueris, carminis bujus auctor,, cujus oraculis mens ad excelsa quaeque,quaeque,, aeterna atque divina, cum inenarraoih quddam delectatione rapitur-te primum, inquam, salvere jubeo, et vestigia tua semper adore." Lassen re-echoes this splendid tribute; and indeed, so striking are some of the moralities here inculcated, and so close the parallelism—ofttimes actually verbal— between its teachings and those of the New Testament, that a controversy has arisen between Pandits and Missionaries on the point whether the author borrowed from Christian sources, or the Evangelists and Apostles from him.

This raises the question of its date, which cannot be positively settled. It must have been inlaid into the ancient epic at a period later than that of the original Mahabharata, but Mr Kasinath Telang has offered some fair arguments to prove it anterior to the Christian era. The weight of evidence, however, tends to place its composition at about the third century after Christ; and perhaps there are really echoes in this Brahmanic poem of the lessons of Galilee, and of the Syrian incarnation.

Its scene is the level country between the Jumna and the Sarsooti rivers-now Kurnul and Jheend. Its simple plot consists of a dialogue held by Prince Arjuna, the brother of King Yudhisthira, with Krishna, the Supreme Deity, wearing the disguise of a charioteer. A great battle is impending between the armies of the Kauravas and Pandavas, and this conversation is maintained in a war-chariot drawn up between the opposing hosts.

The poem has been turned into French by Burnouf, into Latin by Lassen, into Italian by Stanislav Gatti, into Greek by Galanos, and into English by Mr. Thomson and Mr Davies, the prose transcript of the last-named being truly beyond praise for its fidelity and clearness. Mr Telang has also published at Bombay a version in colloquial rhythm, eminently learned and intelligent, but not conveying the dignity or grace of the original. If I venture to offer a translation of the wonderful poem after so many superior scholars, it is in grateful recognition of the help derived from their labours, and because English literature would certainly be incomplete without possessing in popular form a poetical and philosophical work so dear to India.

There is little else to say which the "Song Celestial" does not explain for itself. The Sanskrit original is written in the Anushtubh metre, which cannot be successfully reproduced for Western ears. I have therefore cast it into our flexible blank verse, changing into lyrical measures where the text itself similarly breaks. For the most part, I believe the sense to be faithfully preserved in the following pages; but Schlegel himself had to say: "In reconditioribus me semper poetafoster mentem recte divinasse affirmare non ausim."

EDWIN ARNOLD

The Distress of Arjuna

Dhritirashtra:
Ranged thus for battle on the sacred plain—
On Kurukshetra—say, Sanjaya! say
What wrought my people, and the Pandavas?

Sanjaya:
When he beheld the host of Pandavas,
Raja Duryodhana to Drona drew,
And spake these words: "Ah, Guru! see this line,
How vast it is of Pandu fighting-men,
Embattled by the son of Drupada,
Thy scholar in the war! Therein stand ranked
Chiefs like Arjuna, like to Bhima chiefs,
Benders of bows; Virata, Yuyudhan,
Drupada, eminent upon his car,
Dhrishtaket, Chekitan, Kasi's stout lord,
Purujit, Kuntibhoj, and Saivya,
With Yudhamanyu, and Uttamauj
Subhadra's child; and Drupadi's;-all famed!
All mounted on their shining chariots!
On our side, too,—thou best of Brahmans! see
Excellent chiefs, commanders of my line,
Whose names I joy to count: thyself the first,
Then Bhishma, Karna, Kripa fierce in fight,
Vikarna, Aswatthaman; next to these
Strong Saumadatti, with full many more
Valiant and tried, ready this day to die
For me their king, each with his weapon grasped,
Each skilful in the field. Weakest-meseems-
Our battle shows where Bhishma holds command,
And Bhima, fronting him, something too strong!
Have care our captains nigh to Bhishma's ranks
Prepare what help they may! Now, blow my shell!"

Then, at the signal of the aged king,
With blare to wake the blood, rolling around
Like to a lion's roar, the trumpeter
Blew the great Conch; and, at the noise of it,

Trumpets and drums, cymbals and gongs and horns
Burst into sudden clamour; as the blasts
Of loosened tempest, such the tumult seemed!
Then might be seen, upon their car of gold
Yoked with white steeds, blowing their battle-shells,
Krishna the God, Arjuna at his side:
Krishna, with knotted locks, blew his great conch
Carved of the "Giant's bone;" Arjuna blew
Indra's loud gift; Bhima the terrible—
Wolf-bellied Bhima-blew a long reed-conch;
And Yudhisthira, Kunti's blameless son,
Winded a mighty shell, "Victory's Voice;"
And Nakula blew shrill upon his conch
Named the "Sweet-sounding," Sahadev on his
Called"Gem-bedecked," and Kasi's Prince on his.
Sikhandi on his car, Dhrishtadyumn,
Virata, Satyaki the Unsubdued,
Drupada, with his sons, (O Lord of Earth!)
Long-armed Subhadra's children, all blew loud,
So that the clangour shook their foemen's hearts,
With quaking earth and thundering heav'n.

Then 'twas-
Beholding Dhritirashtra's battle set,
Weapons unsheathing, bows drawn forth, the war
Instant to break-Arjun, whose ensign-badge
Was Hanuman the monkey, spake this thing
To Krishna the Divine, his charioteer:
"Drive, Dauntless One! to yonder open ground
Betwixt the armies; I would see more nigh
These who will fight with us, those we must slay
To-day, in war's arbitrament; for, sure,
On bloodshed all are bent who throng this plain,
Obeying Dhritirashtra's sinful son."

Thus, by Arjuna prayed, (O Bharata!)
Between the hosts that heavenly Charioteer
Drove the bright car, reining its milk-white steeds
Where Bhishma led,and Drona,and their Lords.
"See!" spake he to Arjuna, "where they stand,
Thy kindred of the Kurus:" and the Prince

Marked on each hand the kinsmen of his house,
Grandsires and sires, uncles and brothers and sons,
Cousins and sons-in-law and nephews, mixed
With friends and honoured elders; some this side,
Some that side ranged: and, seeing those opposed,
Such kith grown enemies-Arjuna's heart
Melted with pity, while he uttered this:

Arjuna.
Krishna! as I behold, come here to shed
Their common blood, yon concourse of our kin,
My members fail, my tongue dries in my mouth,
A shudder thrills my body, and my hair
Bristles with horror; from my weak hand slips
Gandiv, the goodly bow; a fever burns
My skin to parching; hardly may I stand;
The life within me seems to swim and faint;
Nothing do I foresee save woe and wail!
It is not good, O Keshav! nought of good
Can spring from mutual slaughter! Lo, I hate
Triumph and domination, wealth and ease,
Thus sadly won! Aho! what victory
Can bring delight, Govinda! what rich spoils
Could profit; what rule recompense; what span
Of life itself seem sweet, bought with such blood?
Seeing that these stand here, ready to die,
For whose sake life was fair, and pleasure pleased,
And power grew precious:-grandsires, sires, and sons,
Brothers, and fathers-in-law, and sons-in-law,
Elders and friends! Shall I deal death on these
Even though they seek to slay us? Not one blow,
O Madhusudan! will I strike to gain

The rule of all Three Worlds; then, how much less
To seize an earthly kingdom! Killing these
Must breed but anguish, Krishna! If they be
Guilty, we shall grow guilty by their deaths;
Their sins will light on us, if we shall slay
Those sons of Dhritirashtra, and our kin;
What peace could come of that, O Madhava?
For if indeed, blinded by lust and wrath,

These cannot see, or will not see, the sin
Of kingly lines o'erthrown and kinsmen slain,
How should not we, who see, shun such a crime—
We who perceive the guilt and feel the shame—
O thou Delight of Men, Janardana?
By overthrow of houses perisheth
Their sweet continuous household piety,
And-rites neglected, piety extinct—
Enters impiety upon that home;
Its women grow unwomaned, whence there spring
Mad passions, and the mingling-up of castes,
Sending a Hell-ward road that family,
And whoso wrought its doom by wicked wrath.
Nay, and the souls of honoured ancestors
Fall from their place of peace, being bereft
Of funeral-cakes and the wan death-water.[1]
So teach our holy hymns. Thus, if we slay
Kinsfolk and friends for love of earthly power,
Ahovat! what an evil fault it were!
Better I deem it, if my kinsmen strike,
To face them weaponless, and bare my breast
To shaft and spear, than answer blow with blow.

So speaking, in the face of those two hosts,
Arjuna sank upon his chariot-seat,
And let fall bow and arrows, sick at heart.

The Book of Doctrines

Sanjaya.
Him, filled with such compassion and such grief,
With eyes tear-dimmed, despondent, in stern words
The Driver, Madhusudan, thus addressed:

Krishna.
How hath this weakness taken thee? Whence springs
The inglorious trouble, shameful to the brave,
Barring the path of virtue? Nay, Arjun!
Forbid thyself to feebleness! it mars
Thy warrior-name! cast off the coward-fit!
Wake! Be thyself! Arise, Scourge of thy Foes!

Arjuna.
How can I, in the battle, shoot with shafts
On Bhishma, or on Drona-O thou Chief!—
Both worshipful, both honourable men?

Better to live on beggar's bread
  With those we love alive,
Than taste their blood in rich feasts spread,
  And guiltily survive!
Ah! were it worse-who knows?—to be
  Victor or vanquished here,
When those confront us angrily
  Whose death leaves living drear?
In pity lost, by doubtings tossed,
  My thoughts-distracted-turn
To Thee, the Guide I reverence most,
  That I may counsel learn:
I know not what would heal the grief
  Burned into soul and sense,
If I were earth's unchallenged chief—
  A god—and these gone thence!

Sanjaya.
So spake Arjuna to the Lord of Hearts,
And sighing,"I will not fight!" held silence then.

To whom, with tender smile, (O Bharata!)
While the Prince wept despairing 'twixt those hosts,
Krishna made answer in divinest verse:

Krishna.
Thou grievest where no grief should be! thou speak'st
Words lacking wisdom! for the wise in heart
Mourn not for those that live, nor those that die.
Nor I, nor thou, nor any one of these,
Ever was not, nor ever will not be,
For ever and for ever afterwards.
All, that doth live, lives always! To man's frame
As there come infancy and youth and age,
So come there raisings-up and layings-down
Of other and of other life-abodes,
Which the wise know, and fear not. This that irks—
Thy sense-life, thrilling to the elements—
Bringing thee heat and cold, sorrows and joys,
'Tis brief and mutable! Bear with it, Prince!
As the wise bear. The soul which is not moved,
The soul that with a strong and constant calm
Takes sorrow and takes joy indifferently,
Lives in the life undying! That which is
Can never cease to be; that which is not
Will not exist. To see this truth of both
Is theirs who part essence from accident,
Substance from shadow. Indestructible,
Learn thou! the Life is, spreading life through all;
It cannot anywhere, by any means,
Be anywise diminished, stayed, or changed.
But for these fleeting frames which it informs
With spirit deathless, endless, infinite,
They perish. Let them perish, Prince! and fight!
He who shall say, "Lo! I have slain a man!"
He who shall think, "Lo! I am slain!" those both
Know naught! Life cannot slay. Life is not slain!
Never the spirit was born; the spirit shall cease to be never;
Never was time it was not; End and Beginning are dreams!
Birthless and deathless and changeless remaineth the spirit for ever;
Death hath not touched it at all, dead though the house of it seems!

Who knoweth it exhaustless, self-sustained,
Immortal, indestructible,—shall such
Say, "I have killed a man, or caused to kill?"

Nay, but as when one layeth
  His worn-out robes away,
And taking new ones, sayeth,
  "These will I wear to-day!"
So putteth by the spirit
  Lightly its garb of flesh,
And passeth to inherit
  A residence afresh.

I say to thee weapons reach not the Life;
Flame burns it not, waters cannot o'erwhelm,
Nor dry winds wither it. Impenetrable,
Unentered, unassailed, unharmed, untouched,
Immortal, all-arriving, stable, sure,
Invisible, ineffable, by word
And thought uncompassed, ever all itself,
Thus is the Soul declared! How wilt thou, then,—
Knowing it so,—grieve when thou shouldst not grieve?
How, if thou hearest that the man new-dead
Is, like the man new-born, still living man—
One same, existent Spirit—wilt thou weep?
The end of birth is death; the end of death
Is birth: this is ordained! and mournest thou,
Chief of the stalwart arm! for what befalls
Which could not otherwise befall? The birth
Of living things comes unperceived; the death
Comes unperceived; between them, beings perceive:
What is there sorrowful herein, dear Prince?

Wonderful, wistful, to contemplate!
  Difficult, doubtful, to speak upon!
Strange and great for tongue to relate,
  Mystical hearing for every one!
Nor wotteth man this, what a marvel it is,
  When seeing, and saying, and hearing are done!

This Life within all living things, my Prince!

Hides beyond harm; scorn thou to suffer, then,
For that which cannot suffer. Do thy part!
Be mindful of thy name, and tremble not!
Nought better can betide a martial soul
Than lawful war; happy the warrior
To whom comes joy of battle—comes, as now,
Glorious and fair, unsought; opening for him
A gateway unto Heav'n. But, if thou shunn'st
This honourable field—a Kshattriya—
If, knowing thy duty and thy task, thou bidd'st
Duty and task go by—that shall be sin!
And those to come shall speak thee infamy
From age to age; but infamy is worse
For men of noble blood to bear than death!
The chiefs upon their battle-chariots
Will deem 'twas fear that drove thee from the fray.
Of those who held thee mighty-souled the scorn
Thou must abide, while all thine enemies
Will scatter bitter speech of thee, to mock
The valour which thou hadst; what fate could fall
More grievously than this? Either—being killed—
Thou wilt win Swarga's safety, or—alive
And victor—thou wilt reign an earthly king.
Therefore, arise, thou Son of Kunti! brace
Thine arm for conflict, nerve thy heart to meet—
As things alike to thee—pleasure or pain,
Profit or ruin, victory or defeat:
So minded, gird thee to the fight, for so
Thou shalt not sin!

Thus far I speak to thee
As from the "Sankhya"—unspiritually—
Hear now the deeper teaching of the Yog,
Which holding, understanding, thou shalt burst
Thy Karmabandh, the bondage of wrought deeds.
Here shall no end be hindered, no hope marred,
No loss be feared: faith—yea, a little faith—
Shall save thee from the anguish of thy dread.
Here, Glory of the Kurus! shines one rule—
One steadfast rule—while shifting souls have laws
Many and hard. Specious, but wrongful deem

The speech of those ill-taught ones who extol
The letter of their Vedas, saying, "This
Is all we have, or need;" being weak at heart
With wants, seekers of Heaven: which comes—they say—
As "fruit of good deeds done;" promising men
Much profit in new births for works of faith;
In various rites abounding; following whereon
Large merit shall accrue towards wealth and power;
Albeit, who wealth and power do most desire
Least fixity of soul have such, least hold
On heavenly meditation. Much these teach,
From Veds, concerning the "three qualities;"
But thou, be free of the "three qualities,"
Free of the "pairs of opposites,"[2] and free
From that sad righteousness which calculates;
Self-ruled, Arjuna! simple, satisfied![3]
Look! like as when a tank pours water forth
To suit all needs, so do these Brahmans draw
Text for all wants from tank of Holy Writ.
But thou, want not! ask not! Find full reward
Of doing right in right! Let right deeds be
Thy motive, not the fruit which comes from them.
And live in action! Labour! Make thine acts
Thy piety, casting all self aside,
Contemning gain and merit; equable
In good or evil: equability
Is Yog, is piety!

Yet, the right act
Is less, far less, than the right-thinking mind.
Seek refuge in thy soul; have there thy heaven!
Scorn them that follow virtue for her gifts!
The mind of pure devotion—even here—
Casts equally aside good deeds and bad,
Passing above them. Unto pure devotion
Devote thyself: with perfect meditation
Comes perfect act, and the right-hearted rise—
More certainly because they seek no gain—
Forth from the bands of body, step by step,
To highest seats of bliss. When thy firm soul
Hath shaken off those tangled oracles

Which ignorantly guide, then shall it soar
To high neglect of what's denied or said,
This way or that way, in doctrinal writ.
Troubled no longer by the priestly lore,
Safe shall it live, and sure; steadfastly bent
On meditation. This is Yog—and Peace!

Arjuna.
What is his mark who hath that steadfast heart,
Confirmed in holy meditation? How
Know we his speech, Kesava? Sits he, moves he
Like other men?

Krishna.
When one, O Pritha's Son!
Abandoning desires which shake the mind—
Finds in his soul full comfort for his soul,
He hath attained the Yog—that man is such!
In sorrows not dejected, and in joys
Not overjoyed; dwelling outside the stress
Of passion, fear, and anger; fixed in calms
Of lofty contemplation;—such an one
Is Muni, is the Sage, the true Recluse!
He who to none and nowhere overbound
By ties of flesh, takes evil things and good
Neither desponding nor exulting, such
Bears wisdom's plainest mark! He who shall draw
As the wise tortoise draws its four feet safe
Under its shield, his five frail senses back
Under the spirit's buckler from the world
Which else assails them, such an one, my Prince!
Hath wisdom's mark! Things that solicit sense
Hold off from the self-governed; nay, it comes,
The appetites of him who lives beyond
Depart,—aroused no more. Yet may it chance,
O Son of Kunti! that a governed mind
Shall some time feel the sense-storms sweep, and wrest
Strong self-control by the roots. Let him regain
His kingdom! let him conquer this, and sit
On Me intent. That man alone is wise
Who keeps the mastery of himself! If one

Ponders on objects of the sense, there springs
Attraction; from attraction grows desire,
Desire flames to fierce passion, passion breeds
Recklessness; then the memory—all betrayed—
Lets noble purpose go, and saps the mind,
Till purpose, mind, and man are all undone.
But, if one deals with objects of the sense
Not loving and not hating, making them
Serve his free soul, which rests serenely lord,
Lo! such a man comes to tranquillity;
And out of that tranquillity shall rise
The end and healing of his earthly pains,
Since the will governed sets the soul at peace.
The soul of the ungoverned is not his,
Nor hath he knowledge of himself; which lacked,
How grows serenity? and, wanting that,
Whence shall he hope for happiness?

The mind
That gives itself to follow shows of sense
Seeth its helm of wisdom rent away,
And, like a ship in waves of whirlwind, drives
To wreck and death. Only with him, great Prince!
Whose senses are not swayed by things of sense—
Only with him who holds his mastery,
Shows wisdom perfect. What is midnight-gloom
To unenlightened souls shines wakeful day
To his clear gaze; what seems as wakeful day
Is known for night, thick night of ignorance,
To his true-seeing eyes. Such is the Saint!

And like the ocean, day by day receiving
   Floods from all lands, which never overflows
Its boundary-line not leaping, and not leaving,
   Fed by the rivers, but unswelled by those;—

So is the perfect one! to his soul's ocean
   The world of sense pours streams of witchery;
They leave him as they find, without commotion,
   Taking their tribute, but remaining sea.

Yea! whoso, shaking off the yoke of flesh
Lives lord, not servant, of his lusts; set free
From pride, from passion, from the sin of "Self,"
Toucheth tranquillity! O Pritha's Son!
That is the state of Brahm! There rests no dread
When that last step is reached! Live where he will,
Die when he may, such passeth from all 'plaining,
To blest Nirvana, with the Gods, attaining.

Virtue in Work

Arjuna.
Thou whom all mortals praise, Janardana!
If meditation be a nobler thing
Than action, wherefore, then, great Kesava!
Dost thou impel me to this dreadful fight?
Now am I by thy doubtful speech disturbed!
Tell me one thing, and tell me certainly;
By what road shall I find the better end?

Krishna.
I told thee, blameless Lord! there be two paths
Shown to this world; two schools of wisdom.

First
The Sankhya's, which doth save in way of works
Prescribed[4] by reason; next, the Yog, which bids
Attain by meditation, spiritually:
Yet these are one! No man shall 'scape from act
By shunning action; nay, and none shall come
By mere renouncements unto perfectness.
Nay, and no jot of time, at any time,
Rests any actionless; his nature's law
Compels him, even unwilling, into act;
[For thought is act in fancy]. He who sits
Suppressing all the instruments of flesh,
Yet in his idle heart thinking on them,
Plays the inept and guilty hypocrite:
But he who, with strong body serving mind,
Gives up his mortal powers to worthy work,
Not seeking gain, Arjuna! such an one
Is honourable. Do thine allotted task!
Work is more excellent than idleness;
The body's life proceeds not, lacking work.
There is a task of holiness to do,
Unlike world-binding toil, which bindeth not
The faithful soul; such earthly duty do
Free from desire, and thou shalt well perform
Thy heavenly purpose. Spake Prajapati—

In the beginning, when all men were made,
And, with mankind, the sacrifice— "Do this!
Work! sacrifice! Increase and multiply
With sacrifice! This shall be Kamaduk,
Your 'Cow of Plenty,' giving back her milk
Of all abundance. Worship the gods thereby;
The gods shall yield thee grace. Those meats ye crave
The gods will grant to Labour, when it pays
Tithes in the altar-flame. But if one eats
Fruits of the earth, rendering to kindly Heaven
No gift of toil, that thief steals from his world."

Who eat of food after their sacrifice
Are quit of fault, but they that spread a feast
All for themselves, eat sin and drink of sin.
By food the living live; food comes of rain,
And rain comes by the pious sacrifice,
And sacrifice is paid with tithes of toil;
Thus action is of Brahma, who is One,
The Only, All-pervading; at all times
Present in sacrifice. He that abstains
To help the rolling wheels of this great world,
Glutting his idle sense, lives a lost life,
Shameful and vain. Existing for himself,
Self-concentrated, serving self alone,
No part hath he in aught; nothing achieved,
Nought wrought or unwrought toucheth him; no hope
Of help for all the living things of earth
Depends from him.[5] Therefore, thy task prescribed
With spirit unattached gladly perform,
Since in performance of plain duty man
Mounts to his highest bliss. By works alone
Janak and ancient saints reached blessedness!
Moreover, for the upholding of thy kind,
Action thou should'st embrace. What the wise choose
The unwise people take; what best men do
The multitude will follow. Look on me,
Thou Son of Pritha! in the three wide worlds
I am not bound to any toil, no height
Awaits to scale, no gift remains to gain,
Yet I act here! and, if I acted not—

Earnest and watchful—those that look to me
For guidance, sinking back to sloth again
Because I slumbered, would decline from good,
And I should break earth's order and commit
Her offspring unto ruin, Bharata!
Even as the unknowing toil, wedded to sense,
So let the enlightened toil, sense-freed, but set
To bring the world deliverance, and its bliss;
Not sowing in those simple, busy hearts
Seed of despair. Yea! let each play his part
In all he finds to do, with unyoked soul.
All things are everywhere by Nature wrought
In interaction of the qualities.
The fool, cheated by self, thinks, "This I did"
And "That I wrought; "but—ah, thou strong-armed Prince!—
A better-lessoned mind, knowing the play
Of visible things within the world of sense,
And how the qualities must qualify,
Standeth aloof even from his acts. Th' untaught
Live mixed with them, knowing not Nature's way,
Of highest aims unwitting, slow and dull.
Those make thou not to stumble, having the light;
But all thy dues discharging, for My sake,
With meditation centred inwardly,
Seeking no profit, satisfied, serene,
Heedless of issue—fight! They who shall keep
My ordinance thus, the wise and willing hearts,
Have quittance from all issue of their acts;
But those who disregard My ordinance,
Thinking they know, know nought, and fall to loss,
Confused and foolish. 'Sooth, the instructed one
Doth of his kind, following what fits him most:
And lower creatures of their kind; in vain
Contending 'gainst the law. Needs must it be
The objects of the sense will stir the sense
To like and dislike, yet th' enlightened man
Yields not to these, knowing them enemies.
Finally, this is better, that one do
His own task as he may, even though he fail,
Than take tasks not his own, though they seem good.
To die performing duty is no ill;

But who seeks other roads shall wander still.

Arjuna.
Yet tell me, Teacher! by what force doth man
Go to his ill, unwilling; as if one
Pushed him that evil path?

Krishna.
Kama it is!
Passion it is! born of the Darknesses,
Which pusheth him. Mighty of appetite,
Sinful, and strong is this!—man's enemy!
As smoke blots the white fire, as clinging rust
Mars the bright mirror, as the womb surrounds
The babe unborn, so is the world of things
Foiled, soiled, enclosed in this desire of flesh.
The wise fall, caught in it; the unresting foe
It is of wisdom, wearing countless forms,
Fair but deceitful, subtle as a flame.
Sense, mind, and reason—these, O Kunti's Son!
Are booty for it; in its play with these
It maddens man, beguiling, blinding him.
Therefore, thou noblest child of Bharata!
Govern thy heart! Constrain th' entangled sense!
Resist the false, soft sinfulness which saps
Knowledge and judgment! Yea, the world is strong,
But what discerns it stronger, and the mind
Strongest; and high o'er all the ruling Soul.
Wherefore, perceiving Him who reigns supreme,
Put forth full force of Soul in thy own soul!
Fight! vanquish foes and doubts, dear Hero! slay
What haunts thee in fond shapes, and would betray!

The Religion of Knowledge

Krishna.
This deathless Yoga, this deep union,
I taught Vivaswata,[6] the Lord of Light;
Vivaswata to Manu gave it; he
To Ikshwaku; so passed it down the line
Of all my royal Rishis. Then, with years,
The truth grew dim and perished, noble Prince!
Now once again to thee it is declared—
This ancient lore, this mystery supreme—
Seeing I find thee votary and friend.

Arjuna.
Thy birth, dear Lord, was in these later days,
And bright Vivaswata's preceded time!
How shall I comprehend this thing thou sayest,
"From the beginning it was I who taught?"

Krishna.
Manifold the renewals of my birth
Have been, Arjuna! and of thy births, too!
But mine I know, and thine thou knowest not,
O Slayer of thy Foes! Albeit I be
Unborn, undying, indestructible,
The Lord of all things living; not the less—
By Maya, by my magic which I stamp
On floating Nature-forms, the primal vast—
I come, and go, and come. When Righteousness
Declines, O Bharata! when Wickedness
Is strong, I rise, from age to age, and take
Visible shape, and move a man with men,
Succouring the good, thrusting the evil back,
And setting Virtue on her seat again.
Who knows the truth touching my births on earth
And my divine work, when he quits the flesh
Puts on its load no more, falls no more down
To earthly birth: to Me he comes, dear Prince!
Many there be who come! from fear set free,
From anger, from desire; keeping their hearts

Fixed upon me—my Faithful—purified
By sacred flame of Knowledge. Such as these
Mix with my being. Whoso worship me,
Them I exalt; but all men everywhere
Shall fall into my path; albeit, those souls
Which seek reward for works, make sacrifice
Now, to the lower gods. I say to thee
Here have they their reward. But I am He
Made the Four Castes, and portioned them a place
After their qualities and gifts. Yea, I
Created, the Reposeful; I that live
Immortally, made all those mortal births:
For works soil not my essence, being works
Wrought uninvolved.[7] Who knows me acting thus
Unchained by action, action binds not him;
And, so perceiving, all those saints of old
Worked, seeking for deliverance. Work thou
As, in the days gone by, thy fathers did.

Thou sayst, perplexed, It hath been asked before
By singers and by sages, "What is act,
And what inaction? "I will teach thee this,
And, knowing, thou shalt learn which work doth save
Needs must one rightly meditate those three—
Doing,—not doing,—and undoing. Here
Thorny and dark the path is! He who sees
How action may be rest, rest action—he
Is wisest 'mid his kind; he hath the truth!
He doeth well, acting or resting. Freed
In all his works from prickings of desire,
Burned clean in act by the white fire of truth,
The wise call that man wise; and such an one,
Renouncing fruit of deeds, always content.
Always self-satisfying, if he works,
Doth nothing that shall stain his separate soul,
Which—quit of fear and hope—subduing self—
Rejecting outward impulse—yielding up
To body's need nothing save body, dwells
Sinless amid all sin, with equal calm
Taking what may befall, by grief unmoved,
Unmoved by joy, unenvyingly; the same

In good and evil fortunes; nowise bound
By bond of deeds. Nay, but of such an one,
Whose crave is gone, whose soul is liberate,
Whose heart is set on truth—of such an one
What work he does is work of sacrifice,
Which passeth purely into ash and smoke
Consumed upon the altar! All's then God!
The sacrifice is Brahm, the ghee and grain
Are Brahm, the fire is Brahm, the flesh it eats
Is Brahm, and unto Brahm attaineth he
Who, in such office, meditates on Brahm.
Some votaries there be who serve the gods
With flesh and altar-smoke; but other some
Who, lighting subtler fires, make purer rite
With will of worship. Of the which be they
Who, in white flame of continence, consume
Joys of the sense, delights of eye and ear,
Forgoing tender speech and sound of song:
And they who, kindling fires with torch of Truth,
Burn on a hidden altar-stone the bliss
Of youth and love, renouncing happiness:
And they who lay for offering there their wealth,
Their penance, meditation, piety,
Their steadfast reading of the scrolls, their lore
Painfully gained with long austerities:
And they who, making silent sacrifice,
Draw in their breath to feed the flame of thought,
And breathe it forth to waft the heart on high,
Governing the ventage of each entering air
Lest one sigh pass which helpeth not the soul:
And they who, day by day denying needs,
Lay life itself upon the altar-flame,
Burning the body wan. Lo! all these keep
The rite of offering, as if they slew
Victims; and all thereby efface much sin.
Yea! and who feed on the immortal food
Left of such sacrifice, to Brahma pass,
To The Unending. But for him that makes
No sacrifice, he hath nor part nor lot
Even in the present world. How should he share
Another, O thou Glory of thy Line?

In sight of Brahma all these offerings
Are spread and are accepted! Comprehend
That all proceed by act; for knowing this,
Thou shalt be quit of doubt. The sacrifice
Which Knowledge pays is better than great gifts
Offered by wealth, since gifts' worth—O my Prince!
Lies in the mind which gives, the will that serves:
And these are gained by reverence, by strong search,
By humble heed of those who see the Truth
And teach it. Knowing Truth, thy heart no more
Will ache with error, for the Truth shall show
All things subdued to thee, as thou to Me.
Moreover, Son of Pandu! wert thou worst
Of all wrong-doers, this fair ship of Truth
Should bear thee safe and dry across the sea
Of thy transgressions. As the kindled flame
Feeds on the fuel till it sinks to ash,
So unto ash, Arjuna! unto nought
The flame of Knowledge wastes works' dross away!
There is no purifier like thereto
In all this world, and he who seeketh it
Shall find it—being grown perfect—in himself.
Believing, he receives it when the soul
Masters itself, and cleaves to Truth, and comes—
Possessing knowledge—to the higher peace,
The uttermost repose. But those untaught,
And those without full faith, and those who fear
Are shent; no peace is here or other where,
No hope, nor happiness for whoso doubts.
He that, being self-contained, hath vanquished doubt,
Disparting self from service, soul from works,
Enlightened and emancipate, my Prince!
Works fetter him no more! Cut then atwain
With sword of wisdom, Son of Bharata!
This doubt that binds thy heart-beats! cleave the bond
Born of thy ignorance! Be bold and wise!
Give thyself to the field with me! Arise!

Religion of Renouncing Works

Arjuna.
Yet, Krishna! at the one time thou dost laud
Surcease of works, and, at another time,
Service through work. Of these twain plainly tell
Which is the better way?

Krishna.
To cease from works
Is well, and to do works in holiness
Is well; and both conduct to bliss supreme;
But of these twain the better way is his
Who working piously refraineth not.

That is the true Renouncer, firm and fixed,
Who—seeking nought, rejecting nought—dwells proof
Against the "opposites."[8] O valiant Prince!
In doing, such breaks lightly from all deed:
'Tis the new scholar talks as they were two,
This Sankhya and this Yoga: wise men know
Who husbands one plucks golden fruit of both!
The region of high rest which Sankhyans reach
Yogins attain. Who sees these twain as one
Sees with clear eyes! Yet such abstraction, Chief!
Is hard to win without much holiness.
Whoso is fixed in holiness, self-ruled,
Pure-hearted, lord of senses and of self,
Lost in the common life of all which lives—
A "Yogayukt"—he is a Saint who wends
Straightway to Brahm. Such an one is not touched
By taint of deeds. "Nought of myself I do!"
Thus will he think-who holds the truth of truths—
In seeing, hearing, touching, smelling; when
He eats, or goes, or breathes; slumbers or talks,
Holds fast or loosens, opes his eyes or shuts;
Always assured "This is the sense-world plays
With senses."He that acts in thought of Brahm,
Detaching end from act, with act content,
The world of sense can no more stain his soul

Than waters mar th' enamelled lotus-leaf.
With life, with heart, with mind,-nay, with the help
Of all five senses—letting selfhood go—
Yogins toil ever towards their souls' release.
Such votaries, renouncing fruit of deeds,
Gain endless peace: the unvowed, the passion-bound,
Seeking a fruit from works, are fastened down.
The embodied sage, withdrawn within his soul,
At every act sits godlike in "the town
Which hath nine gateways,"[9] neither doing aught
Nor causing any deed. This world's Lord makes
Neither the work, nor passion for the work,
Nor lust for fruit of work; the man's own self
Pushes to these! The Master of this World
Takes on himself the good or evil deeds
Of no man—dwelling beyond! Mankind errs here
By folly, darkening knowledge. But, for whom
That darkness of the soul is chased by light,
Splendid and clear shines manifest the Truth
As if a Sun of Wisdom sprang to shed
Its beams of dawn. Him meditating still,
Him seeking, with Him blended, stayed on Him,
The souls illuminated take that road
Which hath no turning back—their sins flung off
By strength of faith. [Who will may have this Light;
Who hath it sees.] To him who wisely sees,
The Brahman with his scrolls and sanctities,
The cow, the elephant, the unclean dog,
The Outcast gorging dog's meat, are all one.

The world is overcome—aye! even here!
By such as fix their faith on Unity.
The sinless Brahma dwells in Unity,
And they in Brahma. Be not over-glad
Attaining joy, and be not over-sad
Encountering grief, but, stayed on Brahma, still
Constant let each abide! The sage whose sou
Holds off from outer contacts, in himself
Finds bliss; to Brahma joined by piety,
His spirit tastes eternal peace. The joys
Springing from sense-life are but quickening wombs

Which breed sure griefs: those joys begin and end!
The wise mind takes no pleasure, Kunti's Son!
In such as those! But if a man shall learn,
Even while he lives and bears his body's chain,
To master lust and anger, he is blest!
He is the Yukta; he hath happiness,
Contentment, light, within: his life is merged
In Brahma's life; he doth Nirvana touch!
Thus go the Rishis unto rest, who dwell
With sins effaced, with doubts at end, with hearts
Governed and calm. Glad in all good they live,
Nigh to the peace of God; and all those live
Who pass their days exempt from greed and wrath,
Subduing self and senses, knowing the Soul!

The Saint who shuts outside his placid soul
All touch of sense, letting no contact through;
Whose quiet eyes gaze straight from fixed brows,
Whose outward breath and inward breath are drawn
Equal and slow through nostrils still and close;
That one-with organs, heart, and mind constrained,
Bent on deliverance, having put away
Passion, and fear, and rage;—hath, even now,
Obtained deliverance, ever and ever freed.
Yea! for he knows Me Who am He that heeds
The sacrifice and worship, God revealed;
And He who heeds not, being Lord of Worlds,
Lover of all that lives, God unrevealed,
Wherein who will shall find surety and shield!

Religion by Self-Restraint

Krishna.
Therefore, who doeth work rightful to do,
Not seeking gain from work, that man, O Prince!
Is Sanyasi and Yogi—both in one
And he is neither who lights not the flame
Of sacrifice, nor setteth hand to task.

Regard as true Renouncer him that makes
Worship by work, for who renounceth not
Works not as Yogin. So is that well said:
"By works the votary doth rise to faith,
And saintship is the ceasing from all works;
Because the perfect Yogin acts—but acts
Unmoved by passions and unbound by deeds,
Setting result aside.

Let each man raise
The Self by Soul, not trample down his Self,
Since Soul that is Self's friend may grow Self's foe.
Soul is Self's friend when Self doth rule o'er Self,
But Self turns enemy if Soul's own self
Hates Self as not itself.[10]

The sovereign soul
Of him who lives self-governed and at peace
Is centred in itself, taking alike
Pleasure and pain; heat, cold; glory and shame.
He is the Yogi, he is Yukta, glad
With joy of light and truth; dwelling apart
Upon a peak, with senses subjugate
Whereto the clod, the rock, the glistering gold
Show all as one. By this sign is he known
Being of equal grace to comrades, friends,
Chance-comers, strangers, lovers, enemies,
Aliens and kinsmen; loving all alike,
Evil or good.

Sequestered should he sit,

Steadfastly meditating, solitary,
His thoughts controlled, his passions laid away,
Quit of belongings. In a fair, still spot
Having his fixed abode,—not too much raised,
Nor yet too low,—let him abide, his goods
A cloth, a deerskin, and the Kusa-grass.
There, setting hard his mind upon The One,
Restraining heart and senses, silent, calm,
Let him accomplish Yoga, and achieve
Pureness of soul, holding immovable
Body and neck and head, his gaze absorbed
Upon his nose-end,[11] rapt from all around,
Tranquil in spirit, free of fear, intent
Upon his Brahmacharya vow, devout,
Musing on Me, lost in the thought of Me.
That Yojin, so devoted, so controlled,
Comes to the peace beyond,—My peace, the peace
Of high Nirvana!

But for earthly needs
Religion is not his who too much fasts
Or too much feasts, nor his who sleeps away
An idle mind; nor his who wears to waste
His strength in vigils. Nay, Arjuna! call
That the true piety which most removes
Earth-aches and ills, where one is moderate
In eating and in resting, and in sport;
Measured in wish and act; sleeping betimes,
Waking betimes for duty.

When the man,
So living, centres on his soul the thought
Straitly restrained—untouched internally
By stress of sense—then is he Yukta. See!
Steadfast a lamp burns sheltered from the wind;
Such is the likeness of the Yogi's mind
Shut from sense-storms and burning bright to Heaven.
When mind broods placid, soothed with holy wont;
When Self contemplates self, and in itself
Hath comfort; when it knows the nameless joy
Beyond all scope of sense, revealed to soul—

Only to soul! and, knowing, wavers not,
True to the farther Truth; when, holding this,
It deems no other treasure comparable,
But, harboured there, cannot be stirred or shook
By any gravest grief, call that state "peace,"
That happy severance Yoga; call that man
The perfect Yogin!

Steadfastly the will
Must toil thereto, till efforts end in ease,
And thought has passed from thinking. Shaking off
All longings bred by dreams of fame and gain,
Shutting the doorways of the senses close
With watchful ward; so, step by step, it comes
To gift of peace assured and heart assuaged,
When the mind dwells self-wrapped, and the soul broods
Cumberless. But, as often as the heart
Breaks—wild and wavering—from control, so oft
Let him re-curb it, let him rein it back
To the soul's governance; for perfect bliss
Grows only in the bosom tranquillised,
The spirit passionless, purged from offence,
Vowed to the Infinite. He who thus vows
His soul to the Supreme Soul, quitting sin,
Passes unhindered to the endless bliss
Of unity with Brahma. He so vowed,
So blended, sees the Life-Soul resident
In all things living, and all living things
In that Life-Soul contained. And whoso thus
Discerneth Me in all, and all in Me,
I never let him go; nor looseneth he
Hold upon Me; but, dwell he where he may,
Whate'er his life, in Me he dwells and lives,
Because he knows and worships Me, Who dwell
In all which lives, and cleaves to Me in all.
Arjuna! if a man sees everywhere—
Taught by his own similitude—one Life,
One Essence in the Evil and the Good,
Hold him a Yogi, yea! well-perfected!

Arjuna.

Slayer of Madhu! yet again, this Yog,
This Peace, derived from equanimity,
Made known by thee—I see no fixity
Therein, no rest, because the heart of men
Is unfixed, Krishna! rash, tumultuous,
Wilful and strong. It were all one, I think,
To hold the wayward wind, as tame man's heart.

Krishna.
Hero long-armed! beyond denial, hard
Man's heart is to restrain, and wavering;
Yet may it grow restrained by habit, Prince!
By wont of self-command. This Yog, I say,
Cometh not lightly to th' ungoverned ones;
But he who will be master of himself
Shall win it, if he stoutly strive thereto.

Arjuna.
And what road goeth he who, having faith,
Fails, Krishna! in the striving; falling back
From holiness, missing the perfect rule?
Is he not lost, straying from Brahma's light,
Like the vain cloud, which floats 'twixt earth and heaven
When lightning splits it, and it vanisheth?
Fain would I hear thee answer me herein,
Since, Krishna! none save thou can clear the doubt.

Krishna.
He is not lost, thou Son of Pritha! No!
Nor earth, nor heaven is forfeit, even for him,
Because no heart that holds one right desire
Treadeth the road of loss! He who should fail,
Desiring righteousness, cometh at death
Unto the Region of the Just; dwells there
Measureless years, and being born anew,
Beginneth life again in some fair home
Amid the mild and happy. It may chance
He doth descend into a Yogin house
On Virtue's breast; but that is rare! Such birth
Is hard to be obtained on this earth, Chief!
So hath he back again what heights of heart

He did achieve, and so he strives anew
To perfectness, with better hope, dear Prince!
For by the old desire he is drawn on
Unwittingly; and only to desire
The purity of Yog is to pass
Beyond the Sabdabrahm, the spoken Ved.
But, being Yogi, striving strong and long,
Purged from transgressions, perfected by births
Following on births, he plants his feet at last
Upon the farther path. Such as one ranks
Above ascetics, higher than the wise,
Beyond achievers of vast deeds! Be thou
Yogi Arjuna! And of such believe,
Truest and best is he who worships Me
With inmost soul, stayed on My Mystery!

Religion by Discernment

Krishna.
Learn now, dear Prince! how, if thy soul be set
Ever on Me—still exercising Yog,
Still making Me thy Refuge—thou shalt come
Most surely unto perfect hold of Me.
I will declare to thee that utmost lore,
Whole and particular, which, when thou knowest,
Leaveth no more to know here in this world.

Of many thousand mortals, one, perchance,
Striveth for Truth; and of those few that strive—
Nay, and rise high—one only—here and there—
Knoweth Me, as I am, the very Truth.

Earth, water, flame, air, ether, life, and mind,
And individuality—those eight
Make up the showing of Me, Manifest.

These be my lower Nature; learn the higher,
Whereby, thou Valiant One! this Universe
Is, by its principle of life, produced;
Whereby the worlds of visible things are born
As from a Yoni. Know! I am that womb:
I make and I unmake this Universe:
Than me there is no other Master, Prince!
No other Maker! All these hang on me
As hangs a row of pearls upon its string.
I am the fresh taste of the water; I
The silver of the moon, the gold o' the sun,
The word of worship in the Veds, the thrill
That passeth in the ether, and the strength
Of man's shed seed. I am the good sweet smell
Of the moistened earth, I am the fire's red light,
The vital air moving in all which moves,
The holiness of hallowed souls, the root
Undying, whence hath sprung whatever is;
The wisdom of the wise, the intellect
Of the informed, the greatness of the great.

The splendour of the splendid. Kunti's Son!
These am I, free from passion and desire;
Yet am I right desire in all who yearn,
Chief of the Bharatas! for all those moods,
Soothfast, or passionate, or ignorant,
Which Nature frames, deduce from me; but all
Are merged in me—not I in them! The world—
Deceived by those three qualities of being—
Wotteth not Me Who am outside them all,
Above them all, Eternal! Hard it is
To pierce that veil divine of various shows
Which hideth Me; yet they who worship Me
Pierce it and pass beyond.

I am not known
To evil-doers, nor to foolish ones,
Nor to the base and churlish; nor to those
Whose mind is cheated by the show of things,
Nor those that take the way of Asuras.[12]

Four sorts of mortals know me: he who weeps,
Arjuna! and the man who yearns to know;
And he who toils to help; and he who sits
Certain of me, enlightened.

Of these four,
O Prince of India! highest, nearest, best
That last is, the devout soul, wise, intent
Upon "The One." Dear, above all, am I
To him; and he is dearest unto me!
All four are good, and seek me; but mine own,
The true of heart, the faithful—stayed on me,
Taking me as their utmost blessedness,
They are not "mine,"but I—even I myself!
At end of many births to Me they come!
Yet hard the wise Mahatma is to find,
That man who sayeth, "All is Vasudev!"[13]

There be those, too, whose knowledge, turned aside
By this desire or that, gives them to serve
Some lower gods, with various rites, constrained

By that which mouldeth them. Unto all such—
Worship what shrine they will, what shapes, in faith—
'Tis I who give them faith! I am content!
The heart thus asking favour from its God,
Darkened but ardent, hath the end it craves,
The lesser blessing—but 'tis I who give!
Yet soon is withered what small fruit they reap:
Those men of little minds, who worship so,
Go where they worship, passing with their gods.
But Mine come unto me! Blind are the eyes
Which deem th' Unmanifested manifest,
Not comprehending Me in my true Self!
Imperishable, viewless, undeclared,
Hidden behind my magic veil of shows,
I am not seen by all; I am not known—
Unborn and changeless—to the idle world.
But I, Arjuna! know all things which were,
And all which are, and all which are to be,
Albeit not one among them knoweth Me!

By passion for the "pairs of opposites,"
By those twain snares of Like and Dislike, Prince!
All creatures live bewildered, save some few
Who, quit of sins, holy in act, informed,
Freed from the "opposites,"and fixed in faith,
Cleave unto Me.

Who cleave, who seek in Me
Refuge from birth[14] and death, those have the Truth!
Those know Me BRAHMA; know Me Soul of Souls,
The ADHYATMAN; know KARMA, my work;
Know I am ADHIBHUTA, Lord of Life,
And ADHIDAIVA, Lord of all the Gods,
And ADHIYAJNA, Lord of Sacrifice;
Worship Me well, with hearts of love and faith,
And find and hold me in the hour of death.

Religion by Service of the Supreme

Arjuna.
Who is that BRAHMA? What that Soul of Souls,
The ADHYATMAN? What, Thou Best of All!
Thy work, the KARMA? Tell me what it is
Thou namest ADHIBHUTA? What again
Means ADHIDAIVA? Yea, and how it comes
Thou canst be ADHIYAJNA in thy flesh?
Slayer of Madhu! Further, make me know
How good men find thee in the hour of death?

Krishna.
I BRAHMA am! the One Eternal GOD,
And ADHYATMAN is My Being's name,
The Soul of Souls! What goeth forth from Me,
Causing all life to live, is KARMA called:
And, Manifested in divided forms,
I am the ADHIBHUTA, Lord of Lives;
And ADHIDAIVA, Lord of all the Gods,
Because I am PURUSHA, who begets.
And ADHIYAJNA, Lord of Sacrifice,
I—speaking with thee in this body here—
Am, thou embodied one! (for all the shrines
Flame unto Me!) And, at the hour of death,
He that hath meditated Me alone,
In putting off his flesh, comes forth to Me,
Enters into My Being—doubt thou not!
But, if he meditated otherwise
At hour of death, in putting off the flesh,
He goes to what he looked for, Kunti's Son!
Because the Soul is fashioned to its like.

Have Me, then, in thy heart always! and fight!
Thou too, when heart and mind are fixed on Me,
Shalt surely come to Me! All come who cleave
With never-wavering will of firmest faith,
Owning none other Gods: all come to Me,
The Uttermost, Purusha, Holiest!

Whoso hath known Me, Lord of sage and singer,
   Ancient of days; of all the Three Worlds Stay,
Boundless,—but unto every atom Bringer
   Of that which quickens it: whoso, I say,

Hath known My form, which passeth mortal knowing;
   Seen my effulgence—which no eye hath seen—
Than the sun's burning gold more brightly glowing,
   Dispersing darkness,—unto him hath been

Right life! And, in the hour when life is ending,
   With mind set fast and trustful piety,
Drawing still breath beneath calm brows unbending,
   In happy peace that faithful one doth die,—

In glad peace passeth to Purusha's heaven.
   The place which they who read the Vedas name
AKSHARAM, "Ultimate;" whereto have striven
   Saints and ascetics—their road is the same.

That way—the highest way—goes he who shuts
The gates of all his senses, locks desire
Safe in his heart, centres the vital airs
Upon his parting thought, steadfastly set;
And, murmuring OM, the sacred syllable—
Emblem of BRAHM—dies, meditating Me.

For who, none other Gods regarding, looks
Ever to Me, easily am I gained
By such a Yogi; and, attaining Me,
They fall not—those Mahatmas—back to birth,
To life, which is the place of pain, which ends,
But take the way of utmost blessedness.

The worlds, Arjuna!—even Brahma's world—
Roll back again from Death to Life's unrest;
But they, O Kunti's Son! that reach to Me,
Taste birth no more. If ye know Brahma's Day
Which is a thousand Yugas; if ye know
The thousand Yugas making Brahma's Night,
Then know ye Day and Night as He doth know!

When that vast Dawn doth break, th' Invisible
Is brought anew into the Visible;
When that deep Night doth darken, all which is
Fades back again to Him Who sent it forth;
Yea! this vast company of living things—
Again and yet again produced—expires
At Brahma's Nightfall; and, at Brahma's Dawn,
Riseth, without its will, to life new-born.
But—higher, deeper, innermost—abides
Another Life, not like the life of sense,
Escaping sight, unchanging. This endures
When all created things have passed away:
This is that Life named the Unmanifest,
The Infinite! the All! the Uttermost.
Thither arriving none return. That Life
Is Mine, and I am there! And, Prince! by faith
Which wanders not, there is a way to come
Thither. I, the PURUSHA, I Who spread
The Universe around me—in Whom dwell
All living Things—may so be reached and seen![14]

Richer than holy fruit on Vedas growing,
  Greater than gifts, better than prayer or fast,
Such wisdom is! The Yogi, this way knowing,
  Comes to the Utmost Perfect Peace at last.

Religion by the Kingly Knowledge and the Kingly Mystery

Krishna.
Now will I open unto thee—whose heart
Rejects not—that last lore, deepest-concealed,
That farthest secret of My Heavens and Earths,
Which but to know shall set thee free from ills,—
A royal lore! a Kingly mystery!
Yea! for the soul such light as purgeth it
From every sin; a light of holiness
With inmost splendour shining; plain to see;
Easy to walk by, inexhaustible!

They that receive not this, failing in faith
To grasp the greater wisdom, reach not Me,
Destroyer of thy foes! They sink anew
Into the realm of Flesh, where all things change!

By Me the whole vast Universe of things
Is spread abroad;—by Me, the Unmanifest!
In Me are all existences contained;
Not I in them!

Yet they are not contained,
Those visible things! Receive and strive to embrace
The mystery majestical! My Being—
Creating all, sustaining all—still dwells
Outside of all!

See! as the shoreless airs
Move in the measureless space, but are not space,
[And space were space without the moving airs];
So all things are in Me, but are not I.

At closing of each Kalpa, Indian Prince!
All things which be back to My Being come:
At the beginning of each Kalpa, all
Issue new-born from Me.

By Energy
And help of Prakriti my outer Self,
Again, and yet again, I make go forth
The realms of visible things—without their will—
All of them—by the power of Prakriti.

Yet these great makings, Prince! involve Me not
Enchain Me not! I sit apart from them,
Other, and Higher, and Free; nowise attached!

Thus doth the stuff of worlds, moulded by Me,
Bring forth all that which is, moving or still,
Living or lifeless! Thus the worlds go on!

The minds untaught mistake Me, veiled in form;—
Naught see they of My secret Presence, nought
Of My hid Nature, ruling all which lives.
Vain hopes pursuing, vain deeds doing; fed
On vainest knowledge, senselessly they seek
An evil way, the way of brutes and fiends.
But My Mahatmas, those of noble soul
Who tread the path celestial, worship Me
With hearts unwandering,—knowing Me the Source,
Th' Eternal Source, of Life. Unendingly
They glorify Me; seek Me; keep their vows
Of reverence and love, with changeless faith
Adoring Me. Yea, and those too adore,
Who, offering sacrifice of wakened hearts,
Have sense of one pervading Spirit's stress,
One Force in every place, though manifold!
I am the Sacrifice! I am the Prayer!
I am the Funeral-Cake set for the dead!
I am the healing herb! I am the ghee,
The Mantra, and the flame, and that which burns!
I am-of all this boundless Universe-
The Father, Mother, Ancestor, and Guard!
The end of Learning! That which purifies
In lustral water! I am OM! I am
Rig-Veda, Sama-Veda, Yajur-Ved;
The Way, the Fosterer, the Lord, the Judge,
The Witness; the Abode, the Refuge-House,

The Friend, the Fountain and the Sea of Life
Which sends, and swallows up; Treasure of Worlds
And Treasure-Chamber! Seed and Seed-Sower,
Whence endless harvests spring! Sun's heat is mine;
Heaven's rain is mine to grant or to withhold;
Death am I, and Immortal Life I am,
Arjuna! SAT and ASAT, Visible Life,
And Life Invisible!

Yea! those who learn
  The threefold Veds, who drink the Soma-wine,
Purge sins, pay sacrifice—from Me they earn
  Passage to Swarga; where the meats divine

Of great gods feed them in high Indra's heaven.
  Yet they, when that prodigious joy is o'er,
Paradise spent, and wage for merits given,
  Come to the world of death and change once more.

They had their recompense! they stored their treasure,
  Following the threefold Scripture and its writ;
Who seeketh such gaineth the fleeting pleasure
  Of joy which comes and goes! I grant them it!

But to those blessed ones who worship Me,
Turning not otherwhere, with minds set fast,
I bring assurance of full bliss beyond.

Nay, and of hearts which follow other gods
In simple faith, their prayers arise to me,
O Kunti's Son! though they pray wrongfully;
For I am the Receiver and the Lord
Of every sacrifice, which these know not
Rightfully; so they fall to earth again!
Who follow gods go to their gods; who vow
Their souls to Pitris go to Pitris; minds
To evil Bhuts given o'er sink to the Bhuts;
And whoso loveth Me cometh to Me.
Whoso shall offer Me in faith and love
A leaf, a flower, a fruit, water poured forth,
That offering I accept, lovingly made

With pious will. Whate'er thou doest, Prince!
Eating or sacrificing, giving gifts,
Praying or fasting, let it all be done
For Me, as Mine. So shalt thou free thyself
From Karmabandh, the chain which holdeth men
To good and evil issue, so shalt come
Safe unto Me-when thou art quit of flesh—
By faith and abdication joined to Me!

I am alike for all! I know not hate,
I know not favour! What is made is Mine!
But them that worship Me with love, I love;
They are in Me, and I in them!

Nay, Prince!
If one of evil life turn in his thought
Straightly to Me, count him amidst the good;
He hath the high way chosen; he shall grow
Righteous ere long; he shall attain that peace
Which changes not. Thou Prince of India!
Be certain none can perish, trusting Me!
O Pritha's Son! whoso will turn to Me,
Though they be born from the very womb of Sin,
Woman or man; sprung of the Vaisya caste
Or lowly disregarded Sudra,—all
Plant foot upon the highest path; how then
The holy Brahmans and My Royal Saints?
Ah! ye who into this ill world are come—
Fleeting and false—set your faith fast on Me!
Fix heart and thought on Me! Adore Me! Bring
Offerings to Me! Make Me prostrations! Make
Me your supremest joy! and, undivided,
Unto My rest your spirits shall be guided.

Religion by the Heavenly Perfections

Krishna.[16]
Hear farther yet, thou Long-Armed Lord! these latest words I say—
Uttered to bring thee bliss and peace, who lovest Me alway—
Not the great company of gods nor kingly Rishis know
My Nature, Who have made the gods and Rishis long ago;
He only knoweth-only he is free of sin, and wise,
Who seeth Me, Lord of the Worlds, with faith-enlightened eyes,
Unborn, undying, unbegun. Whatever Natures be
To mortal men distributed, those natures spring from Me!
Intellect, skill, enlightenment, endurance, self-control,
Truthfulness, equability, and grief or joy of soul,
And birth and death, and fearfulness, and fearlessness, and shame,
And honour, and sweet harmlessness,[17] and peace which is the same
Whate'er befalls, and mirth, and tears, and piety, and thrift,
And wish to give, and will to help,—all cometh of My gift!
The Seven Chief Saints, the Elders Four, the Lordly Manus set—
Sharing My work—to rule the worlds, these too did I beget;
And Rishis, Pitris, Manus, all, by one thought of My mind;
Thence did arise, to fill this world, the races of mankind;
Wherefrom who comprehends My Reign of mystic Majesty—
That truth of truths—is thenceforth linked in faultless faith to Me:
Yea! knowing Me the source of all, by Me all creatures wrought,
The wise in spirit cleave to Me, into My Being brought;
Hearts fixed on Me; breaths breathed to Me; praising Me, each to each,
So have they happiness and peace, with pious thought and speech;
And unto these—thus serving well, thus loving ceaselessly—
I give a mind of perfect mood, whereby they draw to Me;
And, all for love of them, within their darkened souls I dwell,
And, with bright rays of wisdom's lamp, their ignorance dispel.

Arjuna.
Yes! Thou art Parabrahm! The High Abode!
The Great Purification! Thou art God
Eternal, All-creating, Holy, First,
Without beginning! Lord of Lords and Gods!
Declared by all the Saints—by Narada,
Vyasa Asita, and Devalas;
And here Thyself declaring unto me!

What Thou hast said now know I to be truth,
O Kesava! that neither gods nor men
Nor demons comprehend Thy mystery
Made manifest, Divinest! Thou Thyself
Thyself alone dost know, Maker Supreme!
Master of all the living! Lord of Gods!
King of the Universe! To Thee alone
Belongs to tell the heavenly excellence
Of those perfections wherewith Thou dost fill
These worlds of Thine; Pervading, Immanent!
How shall I learn, Supremest Mystery!
To know Thee, though I muse continually?
Under what form of Thine unnumbered forms
Mayst Thou be grasped? Ah! yet again recount,
Clear and complete, Thy great appearances,
The secrets of Thy Majesty and Might,
Thou High Delight of Men! Never enough
Can mine ears drink the Amrit[18] of such words!

Krishna.
Hanta! So be it! Kuru Prince! I will to thee unfold
Some portions of My Majesty, whose powers are manifold!
I am the Spirit seated deep in every creature's heart;
From Me they come; by Me they live; at My word they depart!
Vishnu of the Adityas I am, those Lords of Light;
Maritchi of the Maruts, the Kings of Storm and Blight;
By day I gleam, the golden Sun of burning cloudless Noon;
By Night, amid the asterisms I glide, the dappled Moon!
Of Vedas I am Sama-Ved, of gods in Indra's Heaven
Vasava; of the faculties to living beings given
The mind which apprehends and thinks; of Rudras Sankara;
Of Yakshas and of Rakshasas, Vittesh; and Pavaka
Of Vasus, and of mountain-peaks Meru; Vrihaspati
Know Me 'mid planetary Powers; 'mid Warriors heavenly
Skanda; of all the water-floods the Sea which drinketh each,
And Bhrigu of the holy Saints, and OM of sacred speech;
Of prayers the prayer ye whisper;[19] of hills Himala's snow,
And Aswattha, the fig-tree, of all the trees that grow;
Of the Devarshis, Narada; and Chitrarath of them
That sing in Heaven, and Kapila of Munis, and the gem
Of flying steeds, Uchchaisravas, from Amrit-wave which burst;

Of elephants Airavata; of males the Best and First;
Of weapons Heav'n's hot thunderbolt; of cows white Kamadhuk,
From whose great milky udder-teats all hearts' desires are strook;
Vasuki of the serpent-tribes, round Mandara entwined;
And thousand-fanged Ananta, on whose broad coils reclined
Leans Vishnu; and of water-things Varuna; Aryam
Of Pitris, and, of those that judge, Yama the Judge I am;
Of Daityas dread Prahlada; of what metes days and years,
Time's self I am; of woodland-beasts-buffaloes, deers, and bears-
The lordly-painted tiger; of birds the vast Garud,
The whirlwind 'mid the winds; 'mid chiefs Rama with blood imbrued,
Makar 'mid fishes of the sea, and Ganges 'mid the streams;
Yea! First, and Last, and Centre of all which is or seems
I am, Arjuna! Wisdom Supreme of what is wise,
Words on the uttering lips I am, and eyesight of the eyes,
And "A" of written characters, Dwandwa[20] of knitted speech,
And Endless Life, and boundless Love, whose power sustaineth each;
And bitter Death which seizes all, and joyous sudden Birth,
Which brings to light all beings that are to be on earth;
And of the viewless virtues, Fame, Fortune, Song am I,
And Memory, and Patience; and Craft, and Constancy:
Of Vedic hymns the Vrihatsam, of metres Gayatri,
Of months the Margasirsha, of all the seasons three
The flower-wreathed Spring; in dicer's-play the conquering
Double-Eight;
The splendour of the splendid, and the greatness of the great,
Victory I am, and Action! and the goodness of the good,
And Vasudev of Vrishni's race, and of this Pandu brood
Thyself!—Yea, my Arjuna! thyself; for thou art Mine!
Of poets Usana, of saints Vyasa, sage divine;
The policy of conquerors, the potency of kings,
The great unbroken silence in learning's secret things;
The lore of all the learned, the seed of all which springs.
Living or lifeless, still or stirred, whatever beings be,
None of them is in all the worlds, but it exists by Me!
Nor tongue can tell, Arjuna! nor end of telling come
Of these My boundless glories, whereof I teach thee some;
For wheresoe'er is wondrous work, and majesty, and might,
From Me hath all proceeded. Receive thou this aright!
Yet how shouldst thou receive, O Prince! the vastness of this word?
I, who am all, and made it all, abide its separate Lord!

The Manifesting of the One and Manifold

Arjuna.
This, for my soul's peace, have I heard from Thee,
The unfolding of the Mystery Supreme
Named Adhyatman; comprehending which,
My darkness is dispelled; for now I know—
O Lotus-eyed![21]—whence is the birth of men,
And whence their death, and what the majesties
Of Thine immortal rule. Fain would I see,
As thou Thyself declar'st it, Sovereign Lord!
The likeness of that glory of Thy Form
Wholly revealed. O Thou Divinest One!
If this can be, if I may bear the sight,
Make Thyself visible, Lord of all prayers!
Show me Thy very self, the Eternal God!

Krishna.
Gaze, then, thou Son of Pritha! I manifest for thee
Those hundred thousand thousand shapes that clothe my Mystery:
I show thee all my semblances, infinite, rich, divine,
My changeful hues, my countless forms. See! in this face of mine,
Adityas, Vasus, Rudras, Aswins, and Maruts; see
Wonders unnumbered, Indian Prince! revealed to none save thee.
Behold! this is the Universe!—Look! what is live and dead
I gather all in one—in Me! Gaze, as thy lips have said,
On GOD ETERNAL, VERY GOD! See Me! see what thou prayest!

Thou canst not!—nor, with human eyes, Arjuna! ever mayest!
Therefore I give thee sense divine. Have other eyes, new light!
And, look! This is My glory, unveiled to mortal sight!

Sanjaya.
Then, O King! the God, so saying,
Stood, to Pritha's Son displaying
All the splendour, wonder, dread
Of His vast Almighty-head.
Out of countless eyes beholding,
Out of countless mouths commanding,
Countless mystic forms enfolding

In one Form: supremely standing
Countless radiant glories wearing,
Countless heavenly weapons bearing,
Crowned with garlands of star-clusters,
Robed in garb of woven lustres,
Breathing from His perfect Presence
Breaths of every subtle essence
Of all heavenly odours; shedding
Blinding brilliance; overspreading—
Boundless, beautiful—all spaces
With His all-regarding faces;
So He showed! If there should rise
Suddenly within the skies
Sunburst of a thousand suns
Flooding earth with beams undeemed-of,
Then might be that Holy One's
Majesty and radiance dreamed of!

So did Pandu's Son behold
All this universe enfold
All its huge diversity
Into one vast shape, and be
Visible, and viewed, and blended
In one Body—subtle, splendid,
Nameless—th' All-comprehending
God of Gods, the Never-Ending
Deity!

But, sore amazed,
Thrilled, o'erfilled, dazzled, and dazed,
Arjuna knelt; and bowed his head,
And clasped his palms; and cried, and said:

Arjuna.
Yea! I have seen! I see!
Lord! all is wrapped in Thee!
The gods are in Thy glorious frame! the creatures
Of earth, and heaven, and hell
In Thy Divine form dwell,
And in Thy countenance shine all the features

Of Brahma, sitting lone
Upon His lotus-throne;
Of saints and sages, and the serpent races
Ananta, Vasuki;
Yea! mightiest Lord! I see
Thy thousand thousand arms, and breasts, and faces,
And eyes,—on every side
Perfect, diversified;
And nowhere end of Thee, nowhere beginning,
Nowhere a centre! Shifts—
Wherever soul's gaze lifts—
Thy central Self, all-wielding, and all-winning!

Infinite King! I see
The anadem on Thee,
The club, the shell, the discus; see Thee burning
In beams insufferable,
Lighting earth, heaven, and hell
With brilliance blazing, glowing, flashing; turning

Darkness to dazzling day,
Look I whichever way;
Ah, Lord! I worship Thee, the Undivided,
The Uttermost of thought,
The Treasure-Palace wrought
To hold the wealth of the worlds; the Shield provided

To shelter Virtue's laws;
The Fount whence Life's stream draws
All waters of all rivers of all being:
The One Unborn, Unending:
Unchanging and Unblending!
With might and majesty, past thought, past seeing!

Silver of moon and gold
Of sun are glories rolled
From Thy great eyes; Thy visage, beaming tender
Throughout the stars and skies,
Doth to warm life surprise
Thy Universe. The worlds are filled with wonder

Of Thy perfections! Space
Star-sprinkled, and void place
From pole to pole of the Blue, from bound to bound,
Hath Thee in every spot,
Thee, Thee!—Where Thou art not,
O Holy, Marvellous Form! is nowhere found!

O Mystic, Awful One!
At sight of Thee, made known,
The Three Worlds quake; the lower gods draw nigh Thee;
They fold their palms, and bow
Body, and breast, and brow,
And, whispering worship, laud and magnify Thee!

Rishis and Siddhas cry
"Hail! Highest Majesty!"
From sage and singer breaks the hymn of glory
In dulcet harmony,
Sounding the praise of Thee;
While countless companies take up the story,

Rudras, who ride the storms,
Th' Adityas' shining forms,
Vasus and Sadhyas, Viswas, Ushmapas;
Maruts, and those great Twins
The heavenly, fair, Aswins,
Gandharvas, Rakshasas, Siddhas, and Asuras,[22]—

These see Thee, and revere
In sudden-stricken fear;
Yea! the Worlds,—seeing Thee with form stupendous,
With faces manifold,
With eyes which all behold,
Unnumbered eyes, vast arms, members tremendous,

Flanks, lit with sun and star,
Feet planted near and far,
Tushes of terror, mouths wrathful and tender;—
The Three wide Worlds before Thee
Adore, as I adore Thee,
Quake, as I quake, to witness so much splendour!

I mark Thee strike the skies
With front, in wondrous wise
Huge, rainbow-painted, glittering; and thy mouth
Opened, and orbs which see
All things, whatever be
In all Thy worlds, east, west, and north and south.

O Eyes of God! O Head!
My strength of soul is fled,
Gone is heart's force, rebuked is mind's desire!
When I behold Thee so,
With awful brows a-glow,
With burning glance, and lips lighted by fire

Fierce as those flames which shall
Consume, at close of all,
Earth, Heaven! Ah me! I see no Earth and Heaven!
Thee, Lord of Lords! I see,
Thee only-only Thee!
Now let Thy mercy unto me be given,

Thou Refuge of the World!
Lo! to the cavern hurled
Of Thy wide-opened throat, and lips white-tushed,
I see our noblest ones,
Great Dhritarashtra's sons,
Bhishma, Drona, and Karna, caught and crushed!

The Kings and Chiefs drawn in,
That gaping gorge within;
The best of both these armies torn and riven!
Between Thy jaws they lie
Mangled full bloodily,
Ground into dust and death! Like streams down-driven

With helpless haste, which go
In headlong furious flow
Straight to the gulfing deeps of th' unfilled ocean,
So to that flaming cave
Those heroes great and brave
Pour, in unending streams, with helpless motion!

Like moths which in the night
Flutter towards a light,
Drawn to their fiery doom, flying and dying,
So to their death still throng,
Blind, dazzled, borne along
Ceaselessly, all those multitudes, wild flying!

Thou, that hast fashioned men,
Devourest them again,
One with another, great and small, alike!
The creatures whom Thou mak'st,
With flaming jaws Thou tak'st,
Lapping them up! Lord God! Thy terrors strike

From end to end of earth,
Filling life full, from birth
To death, with deadly, burning, lurid dread!
Ah, Vishnu! make me know
Why is Thy visage so?
Who art Thou, feasting thus upon Thy dead?

Who? awful Deity!
I bow myself to Thee,
Namostu Te, Devavara! Prasid![23]
O Mightiest Lord! rehearse
Why hast Thou face so fierce?
Whence doth this aspect horrible proceed?

Krishna.
Thou seest Me as Time who kills,
Time who brings all to doom,
The Slayer Time, Ancient of Days, come hither to consume;
Excepting thee, of all these hosts of hostile chiefs arrayed,
There stands not one shall leave alive the battlefield! Dismayed
No longer be! Arise! obtain renown! destroy thy foes!
Fight for the kingdom waiting thee when thou hast vanquished those.
By Me they fall—not thee! the stroke of death is dealt them now,
Even as they show thus gallantly; My instrument art thou!
Strike, strong-armed Prince, at Drona! at Bhishma strike! deal death
On Karna, Jyadratha; stay all their warlike breath!
'Tis I who bid them perish! Thou wilt but slay the slain;

Fight! they must fall, and thou must live, victor upon this plain!

Sanjaya.
Hearing mighty Keshav's word,
Tremblingly that helmed Lord
Clasped his lifted palms, and—praying
Grace of Krishna—stood there, saying,
With bowed brow and accents broken,
These words, timorously spoken:

Arjuna.
Worthily, Lord of Might!
The whole world hath delight
In Thy surpassing power, obeying Thee;
The Rakshasas, in dread
At sight of Thee, are sped
To all four quarters; and the company

Of Siddhas sound Thy name.
How should they not proclaim
Thy Majesties, Divinest, Mightiest?
Thou Brahm, than Brahma greater!
Thou Infinite Creator!
Thou God of gods, Life's Dwelling-place and Rest!

Thou, of all souls the Soul!
The Comprehending Whole!
Of being formed, and formless being the Framer;
O Utmost One! O Lord!
Older than eld, Who stored
The worlds with wealth of life! O Treasure-Claimer,

Who wottest all, and art
Wisdom Thyself! O Part
In all, and All; for all from Thee have risen
Numberless now I see
The aspects are of Thee!
Vayu[24] Thou art, and He who keeps the prison

Of Narak, Yama dark;
And Agni's shining spark;

Varuna's waves are Thy waves. Moon and starlight
Are Thine! Prajapati
Art Thou, and 'tis to Thee
They knelt in worshipping the old world's far light,

The first of mortal men.
Again, Thou God! again
A thousand thousand times be magnified!
Honour and worship be—
Glory and praise,—to Thee
Namo, Namaste, cried on every side;

Cried here, above, below,
Uttered when Thou dost go,
Uttered where Thou dost come! Namo! we call;
Namostu! God adored!
Namostu! Nameless Lord!
Hail to Thee! Praise to Thee! Thou One in all;

For Thou art All! Yea, Thou!
Ah! if in anger now
Thou shouldst remember I did think Thee Friend,
Speaking with easy speech,
As men use each to each;
Did call Thee "Krishna," "Prince," nor comprehend

Thy hidden majesty,
The might, the awe of Thee;
Did, in my heedlessness, or in my love,
On journey, or in jest,
Or when we lay at rest,
Sitting at council, straying in the grove,

Alone, or in the throng,
Do Thee, most Holy! wrong,
Be Thy grace granted for that witless sin!
For Thou art, now I know,
Father of all below,
Of all above, of all the worlds within

Guru of Gurus; more

To reverence and adore
Than all which is adorable and high!
How, in the wide worlds three
Should any equal be?
Should any other share Thy Majesty?

Therefore, with body bent
And reverent intent,
I praise, and serve, and seek Thee, asking grace.
As father to a son,
As friend to friend, as one
Who loveth to his lover, turn Thy face

In gentleness on me!
Good is it I did see
This unknown marvel of Thy Form! But fear
Mingles with joy! Retake,
Dear Lord! for pity's sake
Thine earthly shape, which earthly eyes may bear!

Be merciful, and show
The visage that I know;
Let me regard Thee, as of yore, arrayed
With disc and forehead-gem,
With mace and anadem,
Thou that sustainest all things! Undismayed

Let me once more behold
The form I loved of old,
Thou of the thousand arms and countless eyes!
This frightened heart is fain
To see restored again
My Charioteer, in Krishna's kind disguise.

Krishna.
Yea! thou hast seen, Arjuna! because I loved thee well,
The secret countenance of Me, revealed by mystic spell,
Shining, and wonderful, and vast, majestic, manifold,
Which none save thou in all the years had favour to behold;
For not by Vedas cometh this, nor sacrifice, nor alms,
Nor works well-done, nor penance long, nor prayers, nor chaunted

psalms,
That mortal eyes should bear to view the Immortal Soul unclad,
Prince of the Kurus! This was kept for thee alone! Be glad!
Let no more trouble shake thy heart, because thine eyes have seen
My terror with My glory. As I before have been
So will I be again for thee; with lightened heart behold!
Once more I am thy Krishna, the form thou knew'st of old!

Sanjaya.
These words to Arjuna spake
Vasudev, and straight did take
Back again the semblance dear
Of the well-loved charioteer;
Peace and joy it did restore
When the Prince beheld once more
Mighty BRAHMA's form and face
Clothed in Krishna's gentle grace.

Arjuna.
Now that I see come back, Janardana!
This friendly human frame, my mind can think
Calm thoughts once more; my heart beats still again!

Krishna.
Yea! it was wonderful and terrible
To view me as thou didst, dear Prince! The gods
Dread and desire continually to view!
Yet not by Vedas, nor from sacrifice,
Nor penance, nor gift-giving, nor with prayer
Shall any so behold, as thou hast seen!
Only by fullest service, perfect faith,
And uttermost surrender am I known
And seen, and entered into, Indian Prince!
Who doeth all for Me; who findeth Me
In all; adoreth always; loveth all
Which I have made, and Me, for Love's sole end
That man, Arjuna! unto Me doth wend.

Religion of Faith

Arjuna.
Lord! of the men who serve Thee—true in heart—
As God revealed; and of the men who serve,
Worshipping Thee Unrevealed, Unbodied, Far,
Which take the better way of faith and life?

Krishna.
Whoever serve Me—as I show Myself—
Constantly true, in full devotion fixed,
Those hold I very holy. But who serve—
Worshipping Me The One, The Invisible,
The Unrevealed, Unnamed, Unthinkable,
Uttermost, All-pervading, Highest, Sure—
Who thus adore Me, mastering their sense,
Of one set mind to all, glad in all good,
These blessed souls come unto Me.

Yet, hard
The travail is for such as bend their minds
To reach th' Unmanifest That viewless path
Shall scarce be trod by man bearing the flesh!
But whereso any doeth all his deeds
Renouncing self for Me, full of Me, fixed
To serve only the Highest, night and day
Musing on Me—him will I swiftly lift
Forth from life's ocean of distress and death,
Whose soul clings fast to Me. Cling thou to Me!
Clasp Me with heart and mind! so shalt thou dwell
Surely with Me on high. But if thy thought
Droops from such height; if thou be'st weak to set
Body and soul upon Me constantly,
Despair not! give Me lower service! seek
To reach Me, worshipping with steadfast will;
And, if thou canst not worship steadfastly,
Work for Me, toil in works pleasing to Me!
For he that laboureth right for love of Me
Shall finally attain! But, if in this
Thy faint heart fails, bring Me thy failure! find

Refuge in Me! let fruits of labour go,
Renouncing hope for Me, with lowliest heart,
So shalt thou come; for, though to know is more
Than diligence, yet worship better is
Than knowing, and renouncing better still.
Near to renunciation—very near—
Dwelleth Eternal Peace!

Who hateth nought
Of all which lives, living himself benign,
Compassionate, from arrogance exempt,
Exempt from love of self, unchangeable
By good or ill; patient, contented, firm
In faith, mastering himself, true to his word,
Seeking Me, heart and soul; vowed unto Me,—
That man I love! Who troubleth not his kind,
And is not troubled by them; clear of wrath,
Living too high for gladness, grief, or fear,
That man I love! Who, dwelling quiet-eyed,[25]
Stainless, serene, well-balanced, unperplexed,
Working with Me, yet from all works detached,
That man I love! Who, fixed in faith on Me,
Dotes upon none, scorns none; rejoices not,
And grieves not, letting good or evil hap
Light when it will, and when it will depart,
That man I love! Who, unto friend and foe
Keeping an equal heart, with equal mind
Bears shame and glory; with an equal peace
Takes heat and cold, pleasure and pain; abides
Quit of desires, hears praise or calumny
In passionless restraint, unmoved by each;
Linked by no ties to earth, steadfast in Me,
That man I love! But most of all I love
Those happy ones to whom 'tis life to live
In single fervid faith and love unseeing,
Drinking the blessed Amrit of my Being!

Religion by Separation of Matter and Spirit

Arjuna.
Now would I hear, O gracious Kesava![26]
Of Life which seems, and Soul beyond, which sees,
And what it is we know-or think to know.

Krishna.
Yea! Son of Kunti! for this flesh ye see
Is Kshetra, is the field where Life disports;
And that which views and knows it is the Soul,
Kshetrajna. In all "fields," thou Indian prince!
I am Kshetrajna. I am what surveys!
Only that knowledge knows which knows the known
By the knower![27] What it is, that "field" of life,
What qualities it hath, and whence it is,
And why it changeth, and the faculty
That wotteth it, the mightiness of this,
And how it wotteth-hear these things from Me![28]

The elements, the conscious life, the mind,
The unseen vital force, the nine strange gates
Of the body, and the five domains of sense;
Desire, dislike, pleasure and pain, and thought
Deep-woven, and persistency of being;
These all are wrought on Matter by the Soul!

Humbleness, truthfulness, and harmlessness,
Patience and honour, reverence for the wise.
Purity, constancy, control of self,
Contempt of sense-delights, self-sacrifice,
Perception of the certitude of ill
In birth, death, age, disease, suffering, and sin;
Detachment, lightly holding unto home,
Children, and wife, and all that bindeth men;
An ever-tranquil heart in fortunes good
And fortunes evil, with a will set firm
To worship Me—Me only! ceasing not;
Loving all solitudes, and shunning noise
Of foolish crowds; endeavours resolute

To reach perception of the Utmost Soul,
And grace to understand what gain it were
So to attain,—this is true Wisdom, Prince!
And what is otherwise is ignorance!

Now will I speak of knowledge best to know-
That Truth which giveth man Amrit to drink,
The Truth of HIM, the Para-Brahm, the All,
The Uncreated;; not Asat, not Sat,
Not Form, nor the Unformed; yet both, and more;—
Whose hands are everywhere, and everywhere
Planted His feet, and everywhere His eyes
Beholding, and His ears in every place
Hearing, and all His faces everywhere
Enlightening and encompassing His worlds.
Glorified in the senses He hath given,
Yet beyond sense He is; sustaining all,
Yet dwells He unattached: of forms and modes
Master, yet neither form nor mode hath He;
He is within all beings—and without—
Motionless, yet still moving; not discerned
For subtlety of instant presence; close
To all, to each; yet measurelessly far!
Not manifold, and yet subsisting still
In all which lives; for ever to be known
As the Sustainer, yet, at the End of Times,
He maketh all to end—and re-creates.
The Light of Lights He is, in the heart of the Dark
Shining eternally. Wisdom He is
And Wisdom's way, and Guide of all the wise,
Planted in every heart.

So have I told
Of Life's stuff, and the moulding, and the lore
To comprehend. Whoso, adoring Me,
Perceiveth this, shall surely come to Me!

Know thou that Nature and the Spirit both
Have no beginning! Know that qualities
And changes of them are by Nature wrought;
That Nature puts to work the acting frame,

But Spirit doth inform it, and so cause
Feeling of pain and pleasure. Spirit, linked
To moulded matter, entereth into bond
With qualities by Nature framed, and, thus
Married to matter, breeds the birth again
In good or evil yonis.[29]

Yet is this
Yea! in its bodily prison!—Spirit pure,
Spirit supreme; surveying, governing,
Guarding, possessing; Lord and Master still
PURUSHA, Ultimate, One Soul with Me.

Whoso thus knows himself, and knows his soul
PURUSHA, working through the qualities
With Nature's modes, the light hath come for him!
Whatever flesh he bears, never again
Shall he take on its load. Some few there be
By meditation find the Soul in Self
Self-schooled; and some by long philosophy
And holy life reach thither; some by works:
Some, never so attaining, hear of light
From other lips, and seize, and cleave to it
Worshipping; yea! and those—to teaching true—
Overpass Death!

Wherever, Indian Prince!
Life is—of moving things, or things unmoved,
Plant or still seed—know, what is there hath grown
By bond of Matter and of Spirit: Know
He sees indeed who sees in all alike
The living, lordly Soul; the Soul Supreme,
Imperishable amid the Perishing:
For, whoso thus beholds, in every place,
In every form, the same, one, Living Life,
Doth no more wrongfulness unto himself,
But goes the highest road which brings to bliss.
Seeing, he sees, indeed, who sees that works
Are Nature's wont, for Soul to practise by
Acting, yet not the agent; sees the mass
Of separate living things—each of its kind—

Issue from One, and blend again to One:
Then hath he BRAHMA, he attains!

O Prince!
That Ultimate, High Spirit, Uncreate,
Unqualified, even when it entereth flesh
Taketh no stain of acts, worketh in nought!
Like to th" ethereal air, pervading all,
Which, for sheer subtlety, avoideth taint,
The subtle Soul sits everywhere, unstained:
Like to the light of the all-piercing sun
[Which is not changed by aught it shines upon,]
The Soul's light shineth pure in every place;
And they who, by such eye of wisdom, see
How Matter, and what deals with it, divide;
And how the Spirit and the flesh have strife,
Those wise ones go the way which leads to Life!

Religion by Separation from the Qualities

Krishna.
Yet farther will I open unto thee
This wisdom of all wisdoms, uttermost,
The which possessing, all My saints have passed
To perfectness. On such high verities
Reliant, rising into fellowship
With Me, they are not born again at birth
Of Kalpas, nor at Pralyas suffer change!

This Universe the womb is where I plant
Seed of all lives! Thence, Prince of India, comes
Birth to all beings! Whoso, Kunti's Son!
Mothers each mortal form, Brahma conceives,
And I am He that fathers, sending seed!

Sattwan, Rajas, and Tamas, so are named
The qualities of Nature, "Soothfastness,"
"Passion," and "Ignorance." These three bind down
The changeless Spirit in the changeful flesh.
Whereof sweet "Soothfastness," by purity
Living unsullied and enlightened, binds
The sinless Soul to happiness and truth;
And Passion, being kin to appetite,
And breeding impulse and propensity,
Binds the embodied Soul, O Kunti's Son!
By tie of works. But Ignorance, begot
Of Darkness, blinding mortal men, binds down
Their souls to stupor, sloth, and drowsiness.
Yea, Prince of India! Soothfastness binds souls
In pleasant wise to flesh; and Passion binds
By toilsome strain; but Ignorance, which blots
The beams of wisdom, binds the soul to sloth.
Passion and Ignorance, once overcome,
Leave Soothfastness, O Bharata! Where this
With Ignorance are absent, Passion rules;
And Ignorance in hearts not good nor quick.
When at all gateways of the Body shines
The Lamp of Knowledge, then may one see well

Soothfastness settled in that city reigns;
Where longing is, and ardour, and unrest,
Impulse to strive and gain, and avarice,
Those spring from Passion—Prince!—engrained; and where
Darkness and dulness, sloth and stupor are,
'Tis Ignorance hath caused them, Kuru Chief!

Moreover, when a soul departeth, fixed
In Soothfastness, it goeth to the place—
Perfect and pure—of those that know all Truth.
If it departeth in set habitude
Of Impulse, it shall pass into the world
Of spirits tied to works; and, if it dies
In hardened Ignorance, that blinded soul
Is born anew in some unlighted womb.

The fruit of Soothfastness is true and sweet;
The fruit of lusts is pain and toil; the fruit
Of Ignorance is deeper darkness. Yea!
For Light brings light, and Passion ache to have;
And gloom, bewilderments, and ignorance
Grow forth from Ignorance. Those of the first
Rise ever higher; those of the second mode
Take a mid place; the darkened souls sink back
To lower deeps, loaded with witlessness!

When, watching life, the living man perceives
The only actors are the Qualities,
And knows what rules beyond the Qualities,
Then is he come nigh unto Me!

The Soul,
Thus passing forth from the Three Qualities—
Whereby arise all bodies—overcomes
Birth, Death, Sorrow, and Age; and drinketh deep
The undying wine of Amrit.

Arjuna.
Oh, my Lord!
Which be the signs to know him that hath gone
Past the Three Modes? How liveth he? What way

Leadeth him safe beyond the threefold Modes?

Krishna.
He who with equanimity surveys
Lustre of goodness, strife of passion, sloth
Of ignorance, not angry if they are,
Not wishful when they are not: he who sits
A sojourner and stranger in their midst
Unruffled, standing off, saying—serene—
When troubles break, "These be the Qualities!"
He unto whom—self-centred—grief and joy
Sound as one word; to whose deep-seeing eyes
The clod, the marble, and the gold are one;
Whose equal heart holds the same gentleness
For lovely and unlovely things, firm-set,
Well-pleased in praise and dispraise; satisfied
With honour or dishonour; unto friends
And unto foes alike in tolerance;
Detached from undertakings,—he is named
Surmounter of the Qualities!

And such—
With single, fervent faith adoring Me,
Passing beyond the Qualities, conforms
To Brahma, and attains Me!

For I am
That whereof Brahma is the likeness! Mine
The Amrit is; and Immortality
Is mine; and mine perfect Felicity!

Religion by Attaining the Supreme

Krishna.
Men call the Aswattha,—the Banyan-tree,—
Which hath its boughs beneath, its roots above,—
The ever-holy tree. Yea! for its leaves
Are green and waving hymns which whisper Truth!
Who knows the Aswattha, knows Veds, and all.

Its branches shoot to heaven and sink to earth,[30]
Even as the deeds of men, which take their birth
  From qualities: its silver sprays and blooms,
And all the eager verdure of its girth,
Leap to quick life at kiss of sun and air,
As men's lives quicken to the temptings fair
  Of wooing sense: its hanging rootlets seek
The soil beneath, helping to hold it there,

As actions wrought amid this world of men
Bind them by ever-tightening bonds again.
  If ye knew well the teaching of the Tree,
What its shape saith; and whence it springs; and, then

How it must end, and all the ills of it,
The axe of sharp Detachment ye would whet,
  And cleave the clinging snaky roots, and lay
This Aswattha of sense-life low,—to set

New growths upspringing to that happier sky,—
Which they who reach shall have no day to die,
  Nor fade away, nor fall—to Him, I mean,
FATHER and FIRST, Who made the mystery

Of old Creation; for to Him come they
From passion and from dreams who break away;
  Who part the bonds constraining them to flesh,
And,—Him, the Highest, worshipping alway—

No longer grow at mercy of what breeze
Of summer pleasure stirs the sleeping trees,

What blast of tempest tears them, bough and stem
To the eternal world pass such as these!

Another Sun gleams there! another Moon!
Another Light,—not Dusk, nor Dawn, nor Noon—
  Which they who once behold return no more;
They have attained My rest, life's Utmost boon!

When, in this world of manifested life,
The undying Spirit, setting forth from Me,
Taketh on form, it draweth to itself
From Being's storehouse,—which containeth all,—
Senses and intellect. The Sovereign Soul
Thus entering the flesh, or quitting it,
Gathers these up, as the wind gathers scents,
Blowing above the flower-beds. Ear and Eye,
And Touch and Taste, and Smelling, these it takes,—
Yea, and a sentient mind;—linking itself
To sense-things so.

The unenlightened ones
Mark not that Spirit when he goes or comes,
Nor when he takes his pleasure in the form,
Conjoined with qualities; but those see plain
Who have the eyes to see. Holy souls see
Which strive thereto. Enlightened, they perceive
That Spirit in themselves; but foolish ones,
Even though they strive, discern not, having hearts
Unkindled, ill-informed!

Know, too, from Me
Shineth the gathered glory of the suns
Which lighten all the world: from Me the moons
Draw silvery beams, and fire fierce loveliness.
I penetrate the clay, and lend all shapes
Their living force; I glide into the plant—
Root, leaf, and bloom—to make the woodlands green
With springing sap. Becoming vital warmth,
I glow in glad, respiring frames, and pass,
With outward and with inward breath, to feed
The body by all meats.[31]

For in this world
Being is twofold: the Divided, one;
The Undivided, one. All things that live
Are "the Divided." That which sits apart,
"The Undivided."

Higher still is He,
The Highest, holding all, whose Name is LORD,
The Eternal, Sovereign, First! Who fills all worlds,
Sustaining them. And—dwelling thus beyond
Divided Being and Undivided—I
Am called of men and Vedas, Life Supreme,
The PURUSHOTTAMA.

Who knows Me thus,
With mind unclouded, knoweth all, dear Prince!
And with his whole soul ever worshippeth Me.

Now is the sacred, secret Mystery
Declared to thee! Who comprehendeth this
Hath wisdom! He is quit of works in bliss!

The Separateness of the Divine and Undivine

Krishna.
Fearlessness, singleness of soul, the will
Always to strive for wisdom; opened hand
And governed appetites; and piety,
And love of lonely study; humbleness,
Uprightness, heed to injure nought which lives,
Truthfulness, slowness unto wrath, a mind
That lightly letteth go what others prize;
And equanimity, and charity
Which spieth no man's faults; and tenderness
Towards all that suffer; a contented heart,
Fluttered by no desires; a bearing mild,
Modest, and grave, with manhood nobly mixed,
With patience, fortitude, and purity;
An unrevengeful spirit, never given
To rate itself too high;—such be the signs,
O Indian Prince! of him whose feet are set
On that fair path which leads to heavenly birth!

Deceitfulness, and arrogance, and pride,
Quickness to anger, harsh and evil speech,
And ignorance, to its own darkness blind,—
These be the signs, My Prince! of him whose birth
Is fated for the regions of the vile.[32]

The Heavenly Birth brings to deliverance,
So should'st thou know! The birth with Asuras
Brings into bondage. Be thou joyous, Prince!
Whose lot is set apart for heavenly Birth.

Two stamps there are marked on all living men,
Divine and Undivine; I spake to thee
By what marks thou shouldst know the Heavenly Man,
Hear from me now of the Unheavenly!

They comprehend not, the Unheavenly,

How Souls go forth from Me; nor how they come
Back unto Me: nor is there Truth in these,
Nor purity, nor rule of Life. "This world
Hath not a Law, nor Order, nor a Lord,"
So say they: "nor hath risen up by Cause
Following on Cause, in perfect purposing,
But is none other than a House of Lust."
And, this thing thinking, all those ruined ones—
Of little wit, dark-minded—give themselves
To evil deeds, the curses of their kind.
Surrendered to desires insatiable,
Full of deceitfulness, folly, and pride,
In blindness cleaving to their errors, caught
Into the sinful course, they trust this lie
As it were true—this lie which leads to death—
Finding in Pleasure all the good which is,
And crying "Here it finisheth!"

Ensnared
In nooses of a hundred idle hopes,
Slaves to their passion and their wrath, they buy
Wealth with base deeds, to glut hot appetites;
"Thus much, to-day," they say, "we gained! thereby
Such and such wish of heart shall have its fill;
And this is ours! and th' other shall be ours!
To-day we slew a foe, and we will slay
Our other enemy to-morrow! Look!
Are we not lords? Make we not goodly cheer?
Is not our fortune famous, brave, and great?
Rich are we, proudly born! What other men
Live like to us? Kill, then, for sacrifice!
Cast largesse, and be merry!" So they speak
Darkened by ignorance; and so they fall—
Tossed to and fro with projects, tricked, and bound
In net of black delusion, lost in lusts—
Down to foul Naraka. Conceited, fond,
Stubborn and proud, dead-drunken with the wine
Of wealth, and reckless, all their offerings
Have but a show of reverence, being not made
In piety of ancient faith. Thus vowed
To self-hood, force, insolence, feasting, wrath,

These My blasphemers, in the forms they wear
And in the forms they breed, my foemen are,
Hateful and hating; cruel, evil, vile,
Lowest and least of men, whom I cast down
Again, and yet again, at end of lives,
Into some devilish womb, whence—birth by birth—
The devilish wombs re-spawn them, all beguiled;
And, till they find and worship Me, sweet Prince!
Tread they that Nether Road.

The Doors of Hell
Are threefold, whereby men to ruin pass,—
The door of Lust, the door of Wrath, the door
Of Avarice. Let a man shun those three!
He who shall turn aside from entering
All those three gates of Narak, wendeth straight
To find his peace, and comes to Swarga's gate.[33]

Religion by the Threefold Faith

Arjuna.
If men forsake the holy ordinance,
Heedless of Shastras, yet keep faith at heart
And worship, what shall be the state of those,
Great Krishna! Sattwan, Rajas, Tamas? Say!

Krishna.
Threefold the faith is of mankind and springs
From those three qualities,—becoming "true,"
Or "passion-stained," or "dark," as thou shalt hear!

The faith of each believer, Indian Prince!
Conforms itself to what he truly is.
Where thou shalt see a worshipper, that one
To what he worships lives assimilate,
[Such as the shrine, so is the votary,]
The "soothfast" souls adore true gods; the souls
Obeying Rajas worship Rakshasas[34]
Or Yakshas; and the men of Darkness pray
To Pretas and to Bhutas.[35] Yea, and those
Who practise bitter penance, not enjoined
By rightful rule—penance which hath its root
In self-sufficient, proud hypocrisies—
Those men, passion-beset, violent, wild,
Torturing—the witless ones—My elements
Shut in fair company within their flesh,
(Nay, Me myself, present within the flesh!)
Know them to devils devoted, not to Heaven!
For like as foods are threefold for mankind
In nourishing, so is there threefold way
Of worship, abstinence, and almsgiving!
Hear this of Me! there is a food which brings
Force, substance, strength, and health, and joy to live,
Being well-seasoned, cordial, comforting,
The "Soothfast" meat. And there be foods which bring
Aches and unrests, and burning blood, and grief,
Being too biting, heating, salt, and sharp,
And therefore craved by too strong appetite.

And there is foul food—kept from over-night,[36]
Savourless, filthy, which the foul will eat,
A feast of rottenness, meet for the lips
Of such as love the "Darkness."

Thus with rites;—
A sacrifice not for rewardment made,
Offered in rightful wise, when he who vows
Sayeth, with heart devout, "This I should do!"
Is "Soothfast" rite. But sacrifice for gain,
Offered for good repute, be sure that this,
O Best of Bharatas! is Rajas-rite,
With stamp of "passion." And a sacrifice
Offered against the laws, with no due dole
Of food-giving, with no accompaniment
Of hallowed hymn, nor largesse to the priests,
In faithless celebration, call it vile,
The deed of "Darkness!"—lost!

Worship of gods
Meriting worship; lowly reverence
Of Twice-borns, Teachers, Elders; Purity,
Rectitude, and the Brahmacharya's vow,
And not to injure any helpless thing,—
These make a true religiousness of Act.

Words causing no man woe, words ever true,
Gentle and pleasing words, and those ye say
In murmured reading of a Sacred Writ,—
These make the true religiousness of Speech.

Serenity of soul, benignity,
Sway of the silent Spirit, constant stress
To sanctify the Nature,—these things make
Good rite, and true religiousness of Mind.

Such threefold faith, in highest piety
Kept, with no hope of gain, by hearts devote,
Is perfect work of Sattwan, true belief.

Religion shown in act of proud display

To win good entertainment, worship, fame,
Such—say I—is of Rajas, rash and vain.

Religion followed by a witless will
To torture self, or come at power to hurt
Another,—'tis of Tamas, dark and ill.

The gift lovingly given, when one shall say
"Now must I gladly give!" when he who takes
Can render nothing back; made in due place,
Due time, and to a meet recipient,
Is gift of Sattwan, fair and profitable.

The gift selfishly given, where to receive
Is hoped again, or when some end is sought,
Or where the gift is proffered with a grudge,
This is of Rajas, stained with impulse, ill.

The gift churlishly flung, at evil time,
In wrongful place, to base recipient,
Made in disdain or harsh unkindliness,
Is gift of Tamas, dark; it doth not bless![37]

Religion by Deliverance and Renunciation

Arjuna.
Fain would I better know, Thou Glorious One!
The very truth—Heart's Lord!—of Sannyas,
Abstention; and enunciation, Lord!
Tyaga; and what separates these twain!

Krishna.
The poets rightly teach that Sannyas
Is the foregoing of all acts which spring
Out of desire; and their wisest say
Tyaga is renouncing fruit of acts.

There be among the saints some who have held
All action sinful, and to be renounced;
And some who answer, "Nay! the goodly acts—
As worship, penance, alms—must be performed!"
Hear now My sentence, Best of Bharatas!

'Tis well set forth, O Chaser of thy Foes!
Renunciation is of threefold form,
And Worship, Penance, Alms, not to be stayed;
Nay, to be gladly done; for all those three
Are purifying waters for true souls!

Yet must be practised even those high works
In yielding up attachment, and all fruit
Produced by works. This is My judgment, Prince!
This My insuperable and fixed decree!

Abstaining from a work by right prescribed
Never is meet! So to abstain doth spring
From "Darkness," and Delusion teacheth it.
Abstaining from a work grievous to flesh,
When one saith "'Tisunpleasing!" this is null!
Such an one acts from "passion;" nought of gain
Wins his Renunciation! But, Arjun!
Abstaining from attachment to the work,
Abstaining from rewardment in the work,

While yet one doeth it full faithfully,
Saying, "Tis right to do!" that is "true " act
And abstinence! Who doeth duties so,
Unvexed if his work fail, if it succeed
Unflattered, in his own heart justified,
Quit of debates and doubts, his is "true" act:
For, being in the body, none may stand
Wholly aloof from act; yet, who abstains
From profit of his acts is abstinent.

The fruit of labours, in the lives to come,
Is threefold for all men,—Desirable,
And Undesirable, and mixed of both;
But no fruit is at all where no work was.

Hear from me, Long-armed Lord! the makings five
Which go to every act, in Sankhya taught
As necessary. First the force; and then
The agent; next, the various instruments;
Fourth, the especial effort; fifth, the God.
What work soever any mortal doth
Of body, mind, or speech, evil or good,
By these five doth he that. Which being thus,
Whoso, for lack of knowledge, seeth himself
As the sole actor, knoweth nought at all
And seeth nought. Therefore, I say, if one—
Holding aloof from self—with unstained mind
Should slay all yonder host, being bid to slay,
He doth not slay; he is not bound thereby!

Knowledge, the thing known, and the mind which knows,
These make the threefold starting-ground of act.
The act, the actor, and the instrument,
These make the threefold total of the deed.
But knowledge, agent, act, are differenced
By three dividing qualities. Hear now
Which be the qualities dividing them.

There is "true" Knowledge. Learn thou it is this:
To see one changeless Life in all the Lives,
And in the Separate, One Inseparable.

There is imperfect Knowledge: that which sees
The separate existences apart,
And, being separated, holds them real.
There is false Knowledge: that which blindly clings
To one as if 'twere all, seeking no Cause,
Deprived of light, narrow, and dull, and "dark."

There is "right" Action: that which being enjoined—
Is wrought without attachment, passionlessly,
For duty, not for love, nor hate, nor gain.
There is "vain" Action: that which men pursue
Aching to satisfy desires, impelled
By sense of self, with all-absorbing stress:
This is of Rajas—passionate and vain.
There is "dark" Action: when one doth a thing
Heedless of issues, heedless of the hurt
Or wrong for others, heedless if he harm
His own soul—'tis of Tamas, black and bad!

There is the "rightful"doer. He who acts
Free from self-seeking, humble, resolute,
Steadfast, in good or evil hap the same,
Content to do aright-he "truly" acts.
There is th' "impassioned" doer. He that works
From impulse, seeking profit, rude and bold
To overcome, unchastened; slave by turns
Of sorrow and of joy: of Rajas he!
And there be evil doers; loose of heart,
Low-minded, stubborn, fraudulent, remiss,
Dull, slow, despondent—children of the "dark."

Hear, too, of Intellect and Steadfastness
The threefold separation, Conqueror-Prince!
How these are set apart by Qualities.

Good is the Intellect which comprehends
The coming forth and going back of life,
What must be done, and what must not be done,
What should be feared, and what should not be feared,
What binds and what emancipates the soul:
That is of Sattwan, Prince! of "soothfastness."

Marred is the Intellect which, knowing right
And knowing wrong, and what is well to do
And what must not be done, yet understands
Nought with firm mind, nor as the calm truth is:
This is of Rajas, Prince! and "passionate!"
Evil is Intellect which, wrapped in gloom,
Looks upon wrong as right, and sees all things
Contrariwise of Truth. O Pritha's Son!
That is of Tamas, "dark" and desperate!

Good is the steadfastness whereby a man
Masters his beats of heart, his very breath
Of life, the action of his senses; fixed
In never-shaken faith and piety:
That is of Sattwan, Prince! "soothfast" and fair!
Stained is the steadfastness whereby a man
Holds to his duty, purpose, effort, end,
For life's sake, and the love of goods to gain,
Arjuna! 'tis of Rajas, passion-stamped!
Sad is the steadfastness wherewith the fool
Cleaves to his sloth, his sorrow, and his fears,
His folly and despair. This—Pritha's Son!—
Is born of Tamas, "dark" and miserable!

Hear further, Chief of Bharatas! from Me
The threefold kinds of Pleasure which there be.

Good Pleasure is the pleasure that endures,
Banishing pain for aye; bitter at first
As poison to the soul, but afterward
Sweet as the taste of Amrit. Drink of that!
It springeth in the Spirit's deep content.
And painful Pleasure springeth from the bond
Between the senses and the sense-world. Sweet
As Amrit is its first taste, but its last
Bitter as poison. 'Tis of Rajas, Prince!
And foul and "dark" the Pleasure is which springs
From sloth and sin and foolishness; at first
And at the last, and all the way of life
The soul bewildering. 'Tis of Tamas, Prince!

For nothing lives on earth, nor 'midst the gods
In utmost heaven, but hath its being bound
With these three Qualities, by Nature framed.

The work of Brahmans, Kshatriyas, Vaisyas,
And Sudras, O thou Slayer of thy Foes!
Is fixed by reason of the Qualities
Planted in each:

A Brahman's virtues, Prince!
Born of his nature, are serenity,
Self-mastery, religion, purity,
Patience, uprightness, learning, and to know
The truth of things which be. A Kshatriya's pride,
Born of his nature, lives in valour, fire,
Constancy, skilfulness, spirit in fight,
And open-handedness and noble mien,
As of a lord of men. A Vaisya's task,
Born with his nature, is to till the ground,
Tend cattle, venture trade. A Sudra's state,
Suiting his nature, is to minister.

Whoso performeth—diligent, content—
The work allotted him, whate'er it be,
Lays hold of perfectness! Hear how a man
Findeth perfection, being so content:
He findeth it through worship—wrought by work—
Of Him that is the Source of all which lives,
Of HIM by Whom the universe was stretched.

Better thine own work is, though done with fault,
Than doing others' work, ev'n excellently.
He shall not fall in sin who fronts the task
Set him by Nature's hand! Let no man leave
His natural duty, Prince! though it bear blame!
For every work hath blame, as every flame
Is wrapped in smoke! Only that man attains
Perfect surcease of work whose work was wrought
With mind unfettered, soul wholly subdued,
Desires for ever dead, results renounced.

Learn from me, Son of Kunti! also this,
How one, attaining perfect peace, attains
BRAHM, the supreme, the highest height of all!

Devoted—with a heart grown pure, restrained
In lordly self-control, forgoing wiles
Of song and senses, freed from love and hate,
Dwelling 'mid solitudes, in diet spare,
With body, speech, and will tamed to obey,
Ever to holy meditation vowed,
From passions liberate, quit of the Self,
Of arrogance, impatience, anger, pride;
Freed from surroundings, quiet, lacking nought—
Such an one grows to oneness with the BRAHM;
Such an one, growing one with BRAHM, serene,
Sorrows no more, desires no more; his soul,
Equally loving all that lives, loves well
Me, Who have made them, and attains to Me.
By this same love and worship doth he know
Me as I am, how high and wonderful,
And knowing, straightway enters into Me.
And whatsoever deeds he doeth—fixed
In Me, as in his refuge—he hath won
For ever and for ever by My grace
Th' Eternal Rest! So win thou! In thy thoughts
Do all thou dost for Me! Renounce for Me!
Sacrifice heart and mind and will to Me!
Live in the faith of Me! In faith of Me
All dangers thou shalt vanquish, by My grace;
But, trusting to thyself and heeding not,
Thou can'st but perish! If this day thou say'st,
Relying on thyself, "I will not fight!"
Vain will the purpose prove! thy qualities
Would spur thee to the war. What thou dost shun,
Misled by fair illusions, thou wouldst seek
Against thy will, when the task comes to thee
Waking the promptings in thy nature set.
There lives a Master in the hearts of men
Maketh their deeds, by subtle pulling—strings,
Dance to what tune HE will. With all thy soul
Trust Him, and take Him for thy succour, Prince!

So—only so, Arjuna!—shalt thou gain—
By grace of Him—the uttermost repose,
The Eternal Place!

Thus hath been opened thee
This Truth of Truths, the Mystery more hid
Than any secret mystery. Meditate!
And—as thou wilt—then act!

Nay! but once more
Take My last word, My utmost meaning have!
Precious thou art to Me; right well-beloved!
Listen! I tell thee for thy comfort this.
Give Me thy heart! adore Me! serve Me! cling
In faith and love and reverence to Me!
So shalt thou come to Me! I promise true,
For thou art sweet to Me!

And let go those—
Rites and writ duties! Fly to Me alone!
Make Me thy single refuge! I will free
Thy soul from all its sins! Be of good cheer!

[Hide, the holy Krishna saith,
This from him that hath no faith,
Him that worships not, nor seeks
Wisdom's teaching when she speaks:
Hide it from all men who mock;
But, wherever, 'mid the flock
Of My lovers, one shall teach
This divinest, wisest, speech—
Teaching in the faith to bring
Truth to them, and offering
Of all honour unto Me—
Unto Brahma cometh he!
Nay, and nowhere shall ye find
Any man of all mankind
Doing dearer deed for Me;
Nor shall any dearer be
In My earth. Yea, furthermore,
Whoso reads this converse o'er,

Held by Us upon the plain,
Pondering piously and fain,
He hath paid Me sacrifice!
(Krishna speaketh in this wise!)
Yea, and whoso, full of faith,
Heareth wisely what it saith,
Heareth meekly,—when he dies,
Surely shall his spirit rise
To those regions where the Blest,
Free of flesh, in joyance rest.]

Hath this been heard by thee, O Indian Prince!
With mind intent? hath all the ignorance—
Which bred thy trouble—vanished, My Arjun?

Arjuna.
Trouble and ignorance are gone! the Light
Hath come unto me, by Thy favour, Lord!
Now am I fixed! my doubt is fled away!
According to Thy word, so will I do!

Sanjaya.
Thus gathered I the gracious speech of Krishna, O my King!
Thus have I told, with heart a-thrill, this wise and wondrous thing
By great Vyasa's learning writ, how Krishna's self made known
The Yoga, being Yoga's Lord. So is the high truth shown!
And aye, when I remember, O Lord my King, again
Arjuna and the God in talk, and all this holy strain,
Great is my gladness: when I muse that splendour, passing speech,
Of Hari, visible and plain, there is no tongue to reach
My marvel and my love and bliss. O Archer-Prince! all hail!
O Krishna, Lord of Yoga! surely there shall not fail
Blessing, and victory, and power, for Thy most mighty sake,
Where this song comes of Arjun, and how with God he spake.

Footnotes

[1] Some repetitionary lines are here omitted.

[2] Technical phrases of Vedic religion.

[3] The whole of this passage is highly involved and difficult to render.

[4] I feel convinced sankhyanan and yoginan must be transposed here in sense.

[5] I am doubtful of accuracy here.

[6] A name of the sun.

[7] Without desire of fruit.

[8] That is,"joy and sorrow, success and failure, heat and cold,"&c.

[9] i.e., the body.

[10] The Sanskrit has this play on the double meaning of Atman.

[11] So in original.

[12] Beings of low and devilish nature.

[13] Krishna.

[14] I read here janma, "birth;" not jara,"age"

[15] I have discarded ten lines of Sanskrit text here as an undoubted interpolation by some Vedantist

[16] The Sanskrit poem here rises to an elevation of style and manner which I have endeavoured to mark by change of metre.

[17] Ahinsa.

[18] The nectar of immortality.

[19] Called "The Jap."

[20] The compound form of Sanskrit words.

[21] "Kamalapatraksha"

[22] These are all divine or deified orders of the Hindoo Pantheon.

[23] "Hail to Thee, God of Gods! Be favourable!"

[24] The wind.

[25] "Not peering about,"anapeksha.

[26] The Calcutta edition of the Mahabharata has these three opening lines.

[27] This is the nearest possible version of Kshetrakshetrajnayojnanan yat tajnan matan mama.

[28] I omit two lines of the Sanskrit here, evidently interpolated by some Vedantist.

[29] Wombs.

[30] I do not consider the Sanskrit verses here-which are somewhat freely rendered—"an attack on the authority of the Vedas," with Mr Davies, but a beautiful lyrical episode, a new "Parable of the fig-tree."

[31] I omit a verse here, evidently interpolated.

[32] "Of the Asuras,"lit.

[33] I omit the ten concluding shlokas, with Mr Davis.

[34] Rakshasas and Yakshas are unembodied but capricious beings of great power, gifts, and beauty, same times also of benignity.

[35] These are spirits of evil wandering ghosts.

[36] Yatayaman, food which has remained after the watches of the night. In India this would probably "go bad."

[37] I omit the concluding shlokas, as of very doubtful authenticity.

Bhagavad Gita

translated by Swami Swarupananda

Table of Contents

The Grief of Arjuna

Dhritarashtra said:

1) Tell me, O Sanjaya! Assembled on Kurukshetra, the center of religious activity, desirous to fight, what indeed did my people and the Pandavas do?

Sanjaya said:

2) But then King Duryodhana, having seen the Pandava forces in battle array, approached his teacher Drona and spoke these words:

3) "Behold, O Teacher! this mighty army of the sons of Pandu, arrayed by the son of Drupada, your gifted pupil.

4-6) "Here [are] heroes, mighty archers, the equals in battle of Bhima and Arjuna-the great warriors Yuyudhana, Virata, Drupada; the valiant Dhrishtaketu, Chekitana, and the king of Kashi; the best of men, Purujit, Kuntibhoja, and Shaibya; the powerful Yudhamanyu, and the brave Uttamaujas, the son of Subhadra and the sons of Draupadi-all of whom are lords of great chariots.

7) "Hear also, O best of the twice-born! the names of those who [are] distinguished amongst ourselves, the leaders of my army. These I relate [to you] for your information.

8) "Yourself and Bhishma and Karna and Kripa, the victorious in war. Ashvatthama and Vikarna and Jayadratha, the son of Somadatta.

9) "And many other heroes also, well-skilled in fight, and armed with many kinds of weapons, are here, determined to lay down their lives for my sake.

10) "This our army defended by Bhishma [is] impossible to be counted, but that army of theirs, defended by Bhima [is] easy to number.

11) "[Now] do, being stationed in your proper places in the divisions of the army, support Bhishma alone."

12) That powerful, oldest of the Kurus, Bhishma the grandsire, in order to cheer Duryodhana, now sounded aloud a lion-roar and blew his conch.

13) Then following Bhishma, conchs and kettle-drums, tabors, trumpets, and cowhorns blared forth suddenly from the Kaurava side, and the noise was tremendous.

14) Then, also, Madhava and Pandava, stations in their magnificent Chariot yoked with white horses, blew their divine conchs with a furious noise.

15) Hrishikesha blew the Panchajanya, Dhananjaya, the Devadatta,and Vrikodara, the doer of terrific deeds, his large conch Paundra.

16) King Yudhishthira, son of Kunti, blew the conch named Anantavijaya, and Nakula and Sahadeva, their Sughosha and Manipushpaka.

17) The expert bowman, king of Kashi, and the great warrior Shikhandi, Dhristadyumna, and Virata, and the unconquered Satyaki;

18) O Lord of Earth! Drupada and the sons of Draupadi, and the mighty-armed son of Subhadra, all, also blew each his own conch.

19) And the terrific noise resounding throughout heaven and earth rent the hearts of Dhritarashtra's party.

20) Then, O Lord of Earth, seeing Dhritarashtra's party standing marshalled and the shooting about to begin, the Pandava, whose ensign was the monkey, raising his bow, said the following words to Krishna:

Arjuna said:

21-22) Place my chariot, O Achyuta! between the two armies that I may see those who stand here prepared for war. On this eve of battle [let me know] with whom I have to fight.

23) For I desire to observe those who are assembled here for fight, wishing to please the evil-minded Duryodhana by taking his side on this battle-field.

Sanjaya said:

24-25) O Bharata, commanded thus by Gudakesha, Hrishikesha drove that grandest of chariots to a place between the two hosts, facing Bhishma, Drona, and all the rulers of the earth, and then spoke thus, "Behold, O Partha, all the Kurus gathered together!"

26) Then saw Partha stationed there in both the armies, grandfathers, fathersin- law, and uncles, brothers and cousins, his own and their sons and grandsons, and comrades, teachers, and other friends as well.

27) Then, he, the son of Kunti, seeing all those kinsmen stationed in their ranks, spoke thus sorrowfully, filled with deep compassion.

Arjuna said:

28-29) Seeing, O Krishna, these my kinsmen gathered here eager for fight, my limbs fail me, and my mouth is parched up. I shiver all over, and my hair stands on end. The bow Gandiva slips from my hand, and my skin burns.

30) Neither, O Keshava, can I stand upright. My mind is in a whirl. And I see adverse omens.

31) Neither, O Krishna, do I see any good in killing these my own people in battle. I desire neither victory nor empire, nor yet pleasure.

32-34) Of what avail is dominion to us, of what avail are pleasures and even life, if these, O Govinda! for whose sake it is desired that empire, enjoyment, 3 and pleasure should be ours, themselves stand here in battle, having renounced life and wealth–teachers, uncles, sons, and also grandfathers, maternal uncles, fathers-in-law, grandsons, brothers-in-law, besides other kinsmen.

35) Even tough these were to kill me, O slayer of Madhu, I could not wish to kill them–not even for the sake of dominion over the three worlds, how much less for the sake of the earth!

36) What pleasure indeed could be ours, O Janardana, from killing these sons of Dhritarashtra? Sin only could take hold of us by the slaying of these felons.

37) Therefore we ought not to kill our kindred, the sons of Dhritarashtra. For how could we, O Madhava, gain happiness by the slaying of our own kinsmen?

38-39) Though these, with understanding overpowered by greed, see no evil due to decay of families, and no sin in hostility to friends, why should we O Janaradana, who see clearly the evil due to the decay of families, not turn away from this sin?

40) On the decay of a family the immemorial religious rites of that family die out. On the destruction of spirituality, impiety further overwhelms the whole of the family.

41) On the prevalence of impiety, O Krishna, the women of the family become corrupt; and women being corrupted, there arises, O Varshneya, intermingling of castes.

42) Admixture of castes, indeed is for the hell of the family and the destroyers of the family; their ancestors fall, deprived of the offerings of rice-ball and water.

43) By these misdeeds of the destroyers of the family, bringing about confusion of castes, are the immemorial religious rites of the caste and the family destroyed.

44) We have heard, O Janardana, that dwelling in hell is inevitable for those men in whose families religious practices have been destroyed.

45) Alas, we are involved in a great sin, in that we are prepared to slay our kinsmen, out of greed for the pleasures of a kingdom!

46) Verily, if the sons of Dhritarashtra, weapons in hand, were to slay me, unresisting and unarmed, in the battle, that would be better for me.

Sanjaya said:
47) Speaking thus in the midst of the battle-field, Arjuna, casting away his bow and arrows, sank down on the seat of his chariot, with his mind distressed with sorrow.

The Way of Knowledge

Sanjaya said:

1) To him who was thus overwhelmed with pity and sorrowing, and whose eyes were dimmed with tears, Madhusudana spoke these words.

The Blessed Lord said:

2) In such a crisis, whence comes upon you, O Arjuna, this dejection, un-Arya-like, disgraceful, and contrary to the attainment of heaven?

3) Yield not to unmanliness, O son of Pritha! Ill does it become you. Cast off this mean faintheartedness and arise, O scorcher of your enemies!

Arjuna said:

4) But how can I, in battle, O slayer of Madhu, fight with arrows against Bhishma and Drona, who are rather worthy to be worshipped, O destroyer of foes!

5) Surely it would be better even to eat the bread of beggary in this life than to slay these great-souled masters. But if I kill them, even in this world, all my enjoyment of wealth and desires will be stained with blood.

6) And indeed I can scarcely tell which will be better, that we should conquer them, or that they should conquer us. The very sons of Dhritarashtra–after slaying whom we should not care to live–stand facing us.

7) With my nature overpowered by weak commiseration, with a mind in confusion about duty, I supplicate You. Say decided what is good for me. I am Your disciple. Instruct me who have taken refuge in You.

8) I do not see anything to remove this sorrow which blasts my senses, even were I to obtain unrivalled and flourishing dominion over the earth, and mastery over the gods.

Sanjaya said:

9) Having spoken thus to the Lord of the senses, Gudakesha, the scorcher of foes, said to Govinda, "I shall not fight," and became silent.

10) To him who was sorrowing in the midst of the two armies, Hrishikesha, as if smiling, O descendant of Bharata, spoke these words.

The Blessed Lord said:

11) You have been mourning for them who should not be mourned for. Yet you speak words of wisdom. The [truly] wise grieve neither for the living nor for the dead.

12) It is not that I have never existed, nor you, nor these kings. Nor is it that we shall cease to exist in the future.

13) As are childhood, youth, and old age, in this body, to the embodied soul, so also is the attaining of another body. Calm souls are not deluded thereat.

14) Notions of heat and cold, of pain and pleasure, are born, O son of Kunti, only of the contact of the senses with their objects. They have a beginning and an end. They are impermanent in their nature. Bear them patiently, O descendant of Bharata.

15) That calm man who is the same in pain and pleasure, whom these cannot disturb, alone is able, O great amongst men, to attain to immortality.

16) The unreal never is. The real never is not. Men possessed of the knowledge of the Truth fully know both these.

17) That by which all this is pervaded–That know for certain to be indestructible. None has the power to destroy this Immutable.

18) Of this indwelling self–the ever-changeless, the indestructible, the illimitable–these bodies are said to have an end. Fight, therefore, O descendant of Bharata.

19) He who takes the self to be the slayer, and he who takes it to be the slain, neither of these knows. It does not slay, nor is it slain.

20) This is never born, nor does it die. It is not that, not having been, it again comes into being. [Or according to another view: It is not that having been, it again ceases to be.] This is unborn, eternal, changeless, ever-itself. It is not killed when the body is killed.

21) He that knows this to be indestructible, changeless, without birth, and immutable, how is he, O son of Pritha, to slay or cause another to slay?

22) Even as a man casts off worn-out clothes, and puts on others which are new, so the embodied casts off worn-out bodies, and enters into others which are new.

23) This [self], weapons cut not; this, fire burns not; this, water wets not; and this, wind dries not.

24) This self cannot be cut, nor burnt, nor wetted, nor dried. Changeless, all-pervading, unmoving, immovable, the self is eternal.

25) This [self] is said to be unmanifested, unthinkable, and unchangeable. Therefore, knowing this to be such, you ought not to mourn.

26) But if you should take this to have constant birth and death, even in that case, O mighty-armed, you ought not to mourn for this.

27) Of that which is born, death is certain; of that which is dead, birth is certain. Over the unavoidable, therefore, you ought not to grieve.

28) All beings are unmanifested in their beginning, O Bharata, manifested in their middle state, and unmanifested again in their end. What is there then to grieve about?

29) Some look upon the self as marvelous. Others speak of it as wonderful. Others again hear of it as a wonder. And still others, though hearing, do not understand it at all.

30) This, the indweller in the bodies of all, is ever indestructible, O descendant of Bharata. Therefore you ought not to mourn for any creature.

31) Looking at your own dharma, also, you ought not to waver, for there is nothing higher for a kshatriya than a righteous war.

32) Fortunate certainly are the kshatriyas, O son of Pritha, who are called to fight in such a battle that comes unsought as an open gate to heaven.

33) But if you refuse to engage in this righteous warfare, then forfeiting your own dharma and honor, you shall incur sin.

34) The world also will ever hold you in reprobation. To the honored, disrepute is surely worse than death.

35) The great chariot-warriors will believe that you have withdrawn from the battle through fear. And you will be lightly esteemed by them who have thought much of you.

36) your enemies also, cavilling at your great prowess, will say of you things that are not to be uttered. What could be more intolerable than this?

37) Dying you gain heaven; conquering you enjoy the earth. Therefore, O son of Kunti, arise, resolved to fight

38) Having made pain and pleasure, gain and loss, conquest and defeat, the same, engage then in battle. So shall you incur no sin.

39) The wisdom of self-realization has been declared unto you. Hearken now to the wisdom of yoga, endued with which, O son of Pritha, you shall break through the bonds of karma.

40) In this, there is no waste of the unfinished attempt, nor is there production of contrary results. Even very little of this dharma protects from the great terror.

41) In this, O scion of Kuru, there is but a single one-pointed determination. The purposes of the undecided are innumerable and many-branching.

42-44) O Partha, no set determination is formed in the minds of those that are deeply attached to pleasure and power, and whose discrimination is stolen away by the flowery words of the unwise, who are full of desires and look upon heaven as their highest goal and who, taking pleasure in the panegyric words of the Vedas, declare that there is nothing else. Their flowery words are exuberant with various specific rites as the means to pleasure and power and are the causes of [new] births as the result of their works [performed with desire].

45) The Vedas deal with the three gunas. Be free, O Arjuna, from the triad of the gunas, free from the pairs of opposites, ever-balanced, free from [the thought of] getting and keeping, and established in the self.

46) To the Brahmin who has known the self, all the Vedas are of so much use as a reservoir is, when there is a flood everywhere.

47) Your right is to work only; but never to the fruits thereof. Be not the producer of the fruits of [your] actions; neither let your attachment be towards inaction.

48) Being steadfast in yoga, O Dhananjaya, perform actions, abandoning attachment, remaining unconcerned as regards success and failure. This evenness of mind [in regard to success and failure] is known as yoga.

49) Word [with desire] is verily far inferior to that performed with the mind undisturbed by thoughts of results. O Dhananjaya, seek refuge in this evenness of mind. Wretched are they who act for results.

50) Endued with this evenness of mind, one frees oneself in this life, alike from vice and virtue. Devote yourself, therefore, to this yoga. Yoga is the very dexterity of work.

51) The wise, possessed of this evenness of mind, abandoning the fruits of their actions, freed for ever from the fetters of birth, go to that state which is beyond all evil.

52) When your intellect crosses beyond the taint of illusion, then shall you attain to indifference, regarding things heard and things yet to be heard.

53) When your intellect, tossed about by the conflict of opinions, has become immovable and firmly established in the self, then you shall attain self-realization.

Arjuna said:

54) What, O Keshava, is the description of the man of steady wisdom, merged in samadhi? How [on the other hand] does the man of steady wisdom speak, how sit, how walk?

The Blessed Lord said:

55) When a man completely casts away, O Partha, all the desires of the mind, satisfied in the self alone by the self, then is he said to be one of steady wisdom.

56) He whose mind is not shaken by adversity, who does not hanker after happiness, who has become free from affection, fear, and wrath, is indeed the muni of steady wisdom.

57) He who is everywhere unattached, not pleased at receiving good, nor vexed at evil, his wisdom is fixed.

58) When also, like the tortoise withdrawing its limbs, he can completely withdraw the senses from their objects, then his wisdom becomes steady.

59) Objects fall away from the abstinent man, leaving the longing behind. But his longing also ceases, who see the Supreme.

60) The turbulent senses, O son of Kunti, do violently snatch away the mind of even a wise man, striving after perfection.

61) The steadfast, having controlled them all, sits focussed on Me as the Supreme. His wisdom is steady, whose senses are under control.

62) Thinking of objects, attachment to them is formed in a man. From attachment longing, and from longing anger grows.

63) From anger comes delusion, and from delusion loss of memory. From loss of memory comes the ruin of discrimination, and from the ruin of discrimination he perishes.

64) But the self-controlled man, moving among objects with senses under restraint, and free from attraction and aversion, attains to tranquillity.

65) In tranquillity, all sorrow is destroyed. For the intellect of him, who is tranquil-minded, is soon established in firmness.

66) No knowledge [of the self] has the unsteady. Nor has he meditation. To the unmeditative there is no peace. And how can one without peace have happiness?

67) For, the mind, which follows in the wake of the wandering senses, carries away his discrimination, as a wind [carries away from its course] a boat on the waters.

68) Therefore, O mighty-armed, his knowledge is steady, whose senses are completely restrained from their objects.

69) That which is night to all beings, in that the self-controlled man wakes. This in which all being wake, is night to the self-seeing muni.

70) As into the ocean–brimful, and still–flow the waters, even so the muni into whom enter all desires, he, and not the desirer of desires, attains to peace.

71) That man who lives devoid of longing, abandoning all desires, without the sense of "I" and "mine," he attains to peace.

72) This is to have one's being in Brahma, O son of Pritha. None, attaining to this, becomes deluded. Being established therein, even at the end of life, a man attains to oneness with Brahman.

The Way of Action

Arjuna said:

1) If, O Janardana, according to You, knowledge is superior to action, why then, O Keshava, do You engage me in this terrible action?

2) With these seemingly conflicting words You are, as it were, bewildering my understanding. Tell me that one thing for certain by which I can attain to the highest.

The Blessed Lord said:

3) In the beginning [of creation], O sinless one, the twofold path of devotion was given by Me to this world: the path of knowledge for the meditating, the path of work for the active.

4) By non-performance of work none reaches worklessness; by merely giving up action no one attains to perfection.

5) Verily none can ever rest for even an instant without performing action; for all are made to act, helplessly indeed, by the gunas, born of Prakriti.

6) He who, restraining the organs of action, sit revolving in the mind thought regarding objects of sense, he, of deluded understanding, is called a hypocrite.

7) But, O Arjuna, he who, controlling by the senses by the mind, unattached, directs his organs of action to the path of work, excels.

8) Do you perform obligatory action; for action is superior to inaction; and even the bare maintenance of your body would not be possible if you are inactive.

9) The world is bound by actions other than those performed for the sake of yajna; do you, therefore, O son of Kunti, perform action for yajna alone, devoid of attachment.

10) The Prajapati, having in the beginning created mankind together with yajna, said, "By this shall you multiply: this shall be the milk cow of your desire."

11) "Cherish the devas with this, and may those devas cherish you: thus cherishing one another, you shall gain the highest good.

12) "The devas, cherished by yajna, will give you desired-for-objects." So, he who enjoys objects given by the devas without offering [in return] to them, is verily a thief.

13) The good, eating the remnants of yajna, are freed from all sins: but those who cook food [only] for themselves, those sinful ones eat sin.

14) From food come forth beings: from rain food is produced: from yajna 10 arises rain; and yajna is born of karma.

15) Know karma to have risen from the Veda, and the Veda from the Imperishable. Therefore the all-pervading Veda is ever centered in yajna.

16) He who here follows not the wheel thus set revolving, living in sin, and satisfied in the senses, O son of Pritha–he lives in vain.

17) But the man who is devoted to the self, and is satisfied with the self, and content in the self alone, has no obligatory duty.

18) He has no object in this world [to gain] by doing [an action], nor [does he incur any loss] by non-performance of action–nor has he [need of] depending on any being for any object.

19) Therefore, do you always perform actions which are obligatory, without attachment; by performing action without attachment, one attains to the highest.

20) Verily by action alone, Janaka and others attained perfection; also, simply with the view for the guidance of men, you should perform action.

21) Whatsoever the superior person does, that is followed by others. What he demonstrates by action, that people follow.

22) I have, O son of Pritha, no duty, nothing that I have not gained; and nothing that I have to gain in the three worlds; yet, I continue in action.

23) If ever I did not continue in work without relaxation, O son of Pritha, men would, in every way, follow in My wake.

24) If I did not do work, these worlds would perish. I should be the cause of the admixture [of races], and I should ruin these beings.

25) As do the unwise, attached to work, act, so should the wise act, O descendant of Bharata, [but] without attachment, desirous of the guidance of the world.

26) One should not unsettle the understanding of the ignorant, attached to action; the wise one, [himself] steadily acting, should engage [the ignorant] in all work.

27) The gunas of Prakriti perform all action. With the understanding deluded by egoism, man thinks, "I am the doer."

28) But one, with true insight into the domains of guna and karma, knowing that gunas as senses merely rest on gunas as objects, does not become attached.

29) Men of perfect knowledge should not unsettle [the understanding of] people of dull wit and imperfect knowledge, who deluded by the gunas of Prakriti attach [themselves] to the functions of the gunas.

30) Renouncing all actions to Me, with mind centered on the self, getting rid of hope and selfishness, fight-free from [mental] fever.

31) Those men who constantly practice this teaching of Mine, full of shraddha and without cavilling, they too are freed from work.

32) But those who decrying this teaching of Mine do not practice [it], deluded 11 in all knowledge, and devoid of discrimination, know them to be ruined.

33) Even a wise man acts in accordance with his own nature; beings follow nature: what can restraint to?

34) Attachment and aversion of the senses for their respective objects are natural: let none come under their sway: they are his foes.

35) Better is one's own dharma, [though] imperfect, than the dharma of another well-performed. Better is death in one's own dharma: the dharma of another is fraught with fear.

Arjuna said:
36) But impelled by what does man commit sin, though against his wishes, O Varshneya, constrained as it were by force?

The Blessed Lord said:
37) it is desire–it is anger, born of the Rajo-guna: of great craving, and of great sin; know this as the foe here [in this world].

38) As fire is enveloped by smoke, as a mirror by dust, as an embryo by the secundine, so is it covered by that.

39) Knowledge is covered by this, the constant foe of the wise, O son of Kunti, the unappeasable fire of desire.

40) The senses, the mind, and the intellect are said to be its abode: through these, it deludes the embodied by veiling his wisdom.

41) Therefore, O Bull of the Bharata race, controlling the senses at the outset, kill it–the sinful,the destroyer of knowledge and realization.

42) The senses are said to be superior [to the body]; the mind is superior to the senses; the intellect is superior to the mind; and that which is superior to the intellect is he [the atman].

43) Thus, knowing Him who is superior to the intellect, and restraining the self by the self, destroy, O mighty-armed, that enemy, the unseizable foe, desire.

The Way of Renunciation of Action in Knowledge

The Blessed Lord said:

1) I told this imperishable yoga to Vivasvat; Vivasvat told it to Manu; [and] Manu told it to Ikshvaku:

2) Thus handed down in regular succession, the royal sages knew it. This yoga, by long lapse of time, declined in this world, O scorcher of foes.

3) I have this day told you that same ancient yoga, [for] you are My devotee, and My friend, and this secret is profound indeed.

Arjuna said:

4) Later was Your birth, and that if Vivasvat prior; how then should I understand that You told this in the beginning?

The Blessed Lord said:

5) Many are the births that have been passed by Me and you, O Arjuna. I know them all, while you know not, O scorcher of foes.

6) Though I am unborn, of changeless nature and Lord of beings, yet subjugating My Prakriti, I come into being by My own Maya.

7) Whenever, O descendant of Bharata, there is decline of dharma, and rise of Adharma, then I body Myself forth.

8) For the protection of the good, for the destruction of the wicked, and for the establishment of dharma, I come into being.

9) He who thus knows, in true light, My divine birth and action, leaving the body, is not born again: he attains to Me, O Arjuna.

10) Freed from attachment, fear, and anger, absorbed in Me, taking refuge in Me, purified by the fire of knowledge, many have attained My Being.

11) In whatever way men worship Me, in the same way do I fulfil their desires; [it is] My path, O son of Pritha, [that] men tread, in all ways.

12) Longing for success in action, in this world, [men] worship the gods. Because success, resulting from action, is quickly attained in the human world.

13) The fourfold caste was created by Me, by the differentiation of guna and karma. Though I am the author thereof, know Me to be the non-doer, and changeless.

14) Actions do not taint Me, nor have I any thirst for the result of action. He who knows Me thus is not fettered by action.

15) Knowing thus, the ancient seekers after freedom also performed action. Do you, therefore, perform action, as did the ancients in olden times.

16) Even sages are bewildered as to what is action and what is inaction. I shall, therefore, tell you what action is, by knowing which you will be freed from evil.

17) For verily, [the true nature] even of action [enjoined by the shastras] should be known, as also [that] of forbidden action, and of inaction: the nature of karma is impenetrable.

18) He who sees inaction in action, and action in inaction is intelligent among men, he is a yogi and a doer of all action.

19) Whose undertakings are all devoid of plan and desire for results, and whose actions are burnt by the fire of knowledge, him the sages call wise.

20) Forsaking the clinging to fruits of action, ever satisfied, depending on nothing, though engaged in action, he does not do anything.

21) Without hope, the body and mind controlled, and all possessions relinquished, he does not suffer any evil consequences, by doing mere bodily action.

22) Content with what comes to him without effort, unaffected by the pairs of opposites, free from envy, even-minded in success and failure, though acting, he is not bound.

23) Devoid of attachment, liberated, with mind centered in knowledge, performing work for yajna alone, his whole karma dissolves away.

24) The process is Brahman, the clarified butter is Brahman, offered by Brahman in the fire of Brahman; by seeing Brahman in action, he reaches Brahman alone.

25) Some yogis perform sacrifices to devas alone, while others offer the self as sacrifice by the self in the fire of Brahman alone.

26) Some again offer hearing and other senses as sacrifice in the fire of control, while others offer sound and other sense-objects as sacrifice in the fire of the senses.

27) Some again offer all the actions of senses and the functions of the vital energy, as sacrifice in the fire of control in self, kindled by knowledge.

28) Others again offer wealth, austerity, and yoga, as sacrifice, while others, of self-restraint and rigid vows, offer study of the scriptures and knowledge, as sacrifice.

29) Yet some offer as sacrifice, the outgoing into the incoming breath, and the incoming into the outgoing, stopping the courses of the incoming and outgoing breaths, constantly practicing the regulation of the vital energy; while others yet of regulated food, offer in the pranas the functions thereof.

30-31) All of these are knowers of yajna, having their sins consumed by yajna, and eating of the nectar—the remnant of yajna—they go to the Eternal Brahman. [Even] this world is not for the non-performer of yajna, how then another, O best of the Kurus?

32) Various yajnas, like the above, are strewn in the storehouse of the Veda. Know them all to be born of action; and thus knowing, you shall be free.

33) Knowledge-sacrifice, O scorcher of foes, is superior to sacrifice [performed] with [material] objects. All action in its entirety, O Partha, attains its consummation in knowledge.

34) Know that, by prostrating yourself, by questions, and by service; the wise, those who have realized the Truth, will instruct you in that knowledge.

35) Knowing which, you shall not, O Pandava, again get deluded like this, and by which you shall see the whole of creation in [your] self and in Me.

36) Even if you are the most sinful among all the sinful, yet by the raft of knowledge alone you shall go across all sin.

37) As blazing fire reduces wood into ashes, so, O Arjuna, does the fire of knowledge reduce all karma to ashes.

38) Verily there exists nothing in this world purifying like knowledge. In good time, having reached perfection in yoga, one realizes that oneself in one's own heart.

39) The man with shraddha, the devoted, the master of one's senses, attains [this] knowledge. Having attained knowledge one goes at once to the Supreme Peace.

40) The ignorant, the man without shraddha, the doubting self, goes to destruction. The doubting self has neither this world, nor the next, nor happiness.

41) With work renounced by yoga and doubts rent asunder by knowledge, O Dhananjaya, actions do not bind him who is poised in the self.

42) Therefore, cutting with the sword of knowledge, this doubt about the self, born of ignorance, residing in your heart, take refuge in yoga. Arise, O Bharata!

The Way of Renunciation

Arjuna said:

1) Renunciation of action, O Krishna, you commend, and again, its performance. Which is the better one of these? Do You tell me decisively.

The Blessed Lord said:

2) Both renunciation and performance of action lead to freedom: of these, performance of action is superior to the renunciation of action.

3) He should be known a constant sannyasi, who neither likes nor dislikes: for, free from the pairs of opposites, O mighty-armed, he is easily set free from bondage.

4) Children, not the wise, speak of knowledge and performance of action as distinct. He who truly lives in one, gains the fruits of both.

5) The plane which is reached by the jnanis is also reached by the karma yogis. He who sees knowledge and performance of action as one alone sees.

6) Renunciation of action, O mighty-armed, is hard to attain to without performance of action; the man of meditation, purified by devotion to action, quickly goes to Brahman.

7) With the mind purified by devotion to performance of action, and the body conquered, and senses subdues, one who realizes one's self as the self in all beings, though acting, is not tainted.

8-9) The knower of Truth, [being] centered [in the self] should think, "I do nothing at all"–though seeing, hearing, touching, smelling, eating, going, sleeping, breathing, speaking, letting go, holding, opening, and closing the eyes–convinced that it is the senses that move among sense objects.

10) He who does actions forsaking attachment, resigning them to Brahman, is not soiled by evil, like unto a lotus leaf by water.

11) Devotees in the path of work perform action, only with body, mind, senses, and intellect, forsaking attachment, for the purification of the heart.

12) The well-poised, forsaking the fruit of action, attains peace, born of steadfastness; the unbalanced one, led by desire, is bound by being attached to the fruit (of action).

13) The subduer (of the senses), having renounced all actions by discrimination, rests happily in the city of the nine gates, neither acting, nor causing (others) to act.

14) Neither agency, nor actions does the Lord create for the world, nor (does he bring about) the union with the fruit of action. It is universal ignorance that does (it all).

15) The Omnipresent takes note of the merit or demerit of none. Knowledge is enveloped in ignorance, hence do beings get deluded.

16) But whose ignorance is destroyed by the knowledge of self–that knowledge of theirs, like the sun, reveals the Supreme (Brahman).

17) Those who have their intellect absorbed in That, whose self is That, whose steadfastness is in That, whose consummation is That, their impurities cleansed by knowledge, they attain to non-return (Moksha).

18) The knowers of the self look with an equal eye on a Brahmana endowed with learning and humility, a cow, an elephant, a dog, and a pariah.

19) (Relative) existence has been conquered by them, even in this world, whose mind rests in evenness, since Brahman is even and is without imperfection: therefore they indeed rest in Brahman.

20) Resting in Brahman, with intellect steady, and without delusion, the knower of Brahman neither rejoiceth on receiving what is pleasant, nor grieveth on receiving what is unpleasant.

21) With the heart unattached to external objects, he realizes the joy that is in the self. With the heart devoted to the meditation of Brahman, he attains undecaying happiness.

22) Since enjoyments that are contact-born are parents of misery alone, and with beginning and end, O son of Kunti, a wise man does not seek pleasure in them.

23) He who can withstand in this world, before the liberation from the body, the impulse arising from lust and anger, he is steadfast (in yoga), he is a happy man.

24) Whose happiness is within, whose relaxation is within, whose light is within, that Yogi alone, becoming Brahman, gains absolute freedom.

25) With imperfections exhausted, doubts dispelled, senses controlled, engaged in the good of all beings, the Rishis obtain absolute freedom.

26) Released from lust and anger, the heart controlled, the self realized, absolute freedom is for such Sannyasins, both here and hereafter.

27-28) Shutting out external objects; steadying the eyes between the eyebrows; restricting the even currents of prana and apana inside the nostrils; the senses, mind, and intellect controlled; with Moksha as the supreme goal; freed from desire, fear, and anger: such a man of moderation is verily free for ever.

29) Knowing Me as the dispenser of yajnas and asceticisms, as the Great Lord of all worlds, as the friend of all beings, he attains Peace.

The Way of Meditation

The Blessed Lord said:

1) He who performs his bounden duty without leaning to the fruit of action–he is a renouncer of action as well as of steadfast mind: not he who is without fire, nor he who is without action.

2) Know that to be devotion to action, which is called renunciation, O Pandava, for none becomes a devotee to action without forsaking Sankalpa.

3) For the man of meditation wishing to attain purification of heart leading to concentration, work is said to be the way: For him, when he has attained such (concentration), inaction is said to be the way.

4) Verily, when there is no attachment, either to sense-objects, or to actions, having renounced all Sankalpas, then is one said to have attained concentration.

5) A man should uplift himself by his own self, so let him not weaken this self. For this self is the friend of oneself, and this self is the enemy of oneself.

6) The self (the active part of our nature) is the friend of the self, for him who has conquered himself by this self. But to the unconquered self, this self is inimical, (and behaves) like (an external) foe.

7) To the self-controlled and serene, the Supreme Self is the object of constant realization, in cold and heat, pleasure and pain, as well as in honour and dishonour.

8) Whose heart is filled with satisfaction by wisdom and realization, and is changeless, whose senses are conquered, and to whom a lump of earth, stone, and gold are the same: that Yogi is called steadfast.

9) He attains excellence who looks with equal regard upon well-wishers, friends, foes, neutrals, arbiters, the hateful, the relatives, and upon the righteous and the unrighteous alike.

10) The yogi should constantly practise concentration of the heart, retiring into solitude, alone, with the mind and body subdued, and free from hope and possession.

11) Having established in a cleanly spot his seat, firm, neither too high nor too low, made of a cloth, a skin, and Kusha-grass, arranged in consecution.

12) There, seated on that seat, making the mind one-pointed and subduing the action of the imaging faculty and the senses, let him practise yoga for the purification of the heart.

13) Let him firmly hold his body, head, and neck erect and still, (with the eye-balls fixed, as if) gazing at the tip of his nose, and not looking around.

14) With the heart serene and fearless, firm in the vow of a Brahmachari, with the mind controlled, and ever thinking of Me, let his sit (in yoga) having Me as his supreme goal.

15) Thus always keeping the mind steadfast, the Yogi of subdued mind attains the peace residing in Me-the peace which culminates in Nirvana (Moksha).

16) (Success in) yoga is not for him who eats too much or too little-nor, O Arjuna, for him who sleeps too much or too little.

17) To him who is temperate in eating and recreation, in his effort for work, and in sleep and wakefulness, yoga becomes the destroyer of misery.

18) When the completely controlled mind rests serenely in the self alone, free from longing after all desires, then is one called steadfast (in the self).

19) "As a lamp in a spot sheltered from the wind does not flicker"-even such has been the simile used for a Yogi of subdued mind, practising concentration in the self.

20-23) When the mind, absolutely restrained by the practice of concentration, attains quietude, and when seeing the self by the self, one is satisfied in his own self; when he feels that infinite bliss-which is perceived by the (purified) intellect and which transcends the senses, and established wherein he never departs from his real state; and having obtained which, regards no other acquisition superior to that, and where established, he is not moved even by heavy sorrow; let that be known as the state, called by the name of yoga-a state of severance from the contact of pain. This yoga should be practised with perseverance, undisturbed by depression of heart.

24) Abandoning without reserve all desires born of Sankalpa, and completely restraining, by the mind alone, the whole group of senses from their objects in all directions;

25) With the intellect set in patience, with the mind fastened on the self, let him attain quietude by degrees: let him not think of anything.

26) Through wahtever reason the restless, unsteady mind wanders away, let him, curbing it from that, bring it under the subjugation of the self alone.

27) Verily, the supreme bliss comes to that Yogi, of perfectly tranquil mind, with passions quieted, Brahman-become, and freed from taint.

28) The Yogi, freed from tain (of good and evil), constantly engaging the mind thus, with ease attains the infinite bliss of contact with Brahman.

29) With the heart concentrated by yoga, with the eye of evenness for all things, he beholds the self in all beings and all beings in the self.

30) He who sees Me in all things, and sees all things in Me, he never becomes separated from Me, nor do I become separated from him.

31) Hw who being established in unity, worships Me, who am dwelling in all beings, whatever his mode of life, that yogi abides in Me.

32) He who judges of pleasure or pain everywhere, by the same standard as he applies to himself, that Yogi, O Arjuna, is regarded as the highest.

Arjuna said:

33) This yoga which has been taught by You, O slayer of Madhu, as characterized by evenness, I do not see (the possibility of) its lasting endurance, owing to restlessness (of the mind.)

34) Verily, the mind, O Krishna, is restless, turbulent, strong, and unyielding; I regard it quite as hard to achieve its control, as that of the wind.

The Blessed Lord said:

35) Without doubt, O mighty-armed, the mind is restless, and difficult to control; but through practice and renunciation, O son of Kunti, it may be governed.

36) Yoga is hard to be attained by one of uncontrolled self: such is My conviction; but the self-controlled, striving by right means can obtain it.

Arjuna said:

37) Though possess of shraddha but unable to control himself, with the mind wandering away from yoga, what end does one, failing to gain perfection in yoga, meet, O Krishna?

38) Does he not, fallen from both, perish, without support, like a rent cloud, O mighty-armed, deluded in the path of Brahman?

39) This doubt of mine, O Krishna, you should completely dispel; for it is not possible for any but you to dispel this doubt.

The Blessed Lord said:

40) Verily, O son of Pritha, there is destruction for him, neither here nor hereafter for, the doer of good, O my son, never comes to grief.

41) Having attained to the worlds of the righteous, and dwelling there for everlasting years, one falled from yoga reincarnates in the home of the pure and the prosperous.

42) Or else he is born into a family of wise yogis only; verily, a birth such as that is very rare to obtain in this world.

43) There he is united with the intelligence acquired in his former body, and strives more than before, for perfection, O son of the Kurus.

44) By that previous practice alone, he is borne on in spite of himself. Even the enquirer after yoga rises superior to the performer of Vedic actions

45) The Yogi, striving assiduously, purified of taint, gradually gaining perfection through many births, then reaches the highest goal.

46) The Yogi is regarded as superior to those who practice asceticism, also to those who have obtained wisdom (through the shastras). He is also superior to the performers of action (enjoined in the Vedas). Therefore, be a Yogi, O Arjuna!

47) And of all Yogis, he who with the inner self merged in Me, with shraddha devotes himself to Me, is considered by Me the most steadfast.

The Way of Knowledge With Realization

The Blessed Lord said:

1) With the mind intent on me, O son of Pritha, taking refuge in Me, and practicing yoga, how you shall without doubt know Me fully, that do you hear.

2) I shall tell you in full, of knowledge, speculative and practical, knowing which, nothing more here remains to be know.

3) One, perchance, in thousands of men, strives for perfection; and one perchance, among the blessed ones, striving thus, knows Me in reality.

4) Bhumi (earth, Ap (water), Anala (fire), Vayu (air), Kha (ether), intellect, and egoism: thus is My Prakriti divided eightfold.

5) This is the lower (Prakriti). But different from it, know, O mighty-armed, My higher Prakriti-the principle of self-consciousness, by which this universe is sustained.

6) Know that these (two Prakritis) are the womb of all beings, I am the origin and dissolution of the whole universe.

7) Beyond Me, O Dhananjaya, there is naught. All this is strung in Me, as a row of jewels on a thread.

8) I am the sapidity in water, O son of Kunti; I, the radiance in the moon and the sun; I am the Om in all the Vedas, sound in Akasha, and manhood in men.

9) I am the sweet fragrance in earth, and the brilliance in fire am I; the life in all beings, and the austerity am I in ascetics.

10) Know me, O son of Pritha, as the eternal seed of all beings. I am the intellect of the intelligent, and the heroism of the heroic.

11) Of the strong, I am the strength devoid of desire and attachment. I am, O bull among the Bharatas, desire in beings, unopposed to dharma.

12) And whatever states pertaining to sattwa, and those pertaining to rajas, and to tamas, know them to proceed from Me alone; still I am not in them, but they are in Me.

13) Deluded by these states, the modifications of the three gunas (of Prakriti), all this world does not know Me who is beyond them, and immutable.

14) Verily, this divine illusion of Mine, constituted of the gunas, is difficult to cross over; those who devote themselves to Me alone, cross over this illusion.

15) They do not devote themselves to Me-the evil-doers, the deluded, the lowest of men, deprived of discrimination by Maya, and following the way of the Asuras.

16) Four kinds of virtuous men worship Me, O Arjuna-the distressed, the seeker of knowledge, the seeker of enjoyment, and the wise, O bull among the Bharatas.

17) Of them, the wise man, ever-steadfast, (and fired) with devotion to the One, excels; for supremely dear am I to the wise, and he is dear to Me.

18) Noble indeed are they all, but the wise man I regard as My very self; for with the mind steadfast, he is established in Me alone, as the supreme goal.

19) At the end of many births, the man of wisdom takes refuge in Me, realizing that all this is Vasudeva (the innermost self). Very rare is that great soul.

20) Others, again, deprived of discrimination by this or that desire, following this or that rite, devote themselves to other gods, led by their own natures.

21) Whatsoever form any devotee seeks to worship with shraddha-the shraddha of his do I make unwavering.

22) Endued with that shraddha, he engages in the worship of that, and from it, gains his desires-these being verily dispensed by Me alone.

23) But the fruit (accruing) to these men of little understanding is limited. The worshippers of the devas go to the devas; My devotees too come to me.

24) The foolish regard Me, the unmanifested, as come into manifestation, not knowing My supreme state-immutable and transcendental.

25) Veiled by the illusion born of the congress of the gunas, I am not manifest to all. This deluded world knows Me not-the Unborn, the Immutable.

26) I know, O Arjuna, the beings of the whole past, and the present, and the future, but Me none knoweth.

27) By the delusion of the pairs of opposites, arising from desire and aversion, O descendant of Bharata, all beings fall into delusion at birth, O scorcher of foes.

28) Those men of virtuous deeds, whose sin has come to an end-they, freed from the delusion of the pairs of opposites, worship Me with firm resolve.

29) Those who strive for freedom from old age and death, taking refuge in Me-they know Brahman, the whole of Adhyatma, and karma in its entirety.

30) Those who know Me with the Adhibhuta, the Adhidaiva, and the Adhiyajna, (continue to) know Me even at the time of death, steadfast in mind.

The Way to the Imperishable Brahman

Arjuna said:

1) What is the Brahman, what is Adhyatma, what is karma, O best of Purushas? What is called Adhibhuta, and what Adhidaiva?

2) Who, and in what way, is Adhiyajna here in this body, O destroyer of Madhu? And how are You known at the time of death, by the self-controlled?

The Blessed Lord said:

3) The Imperishable is the Supreme Brahman. Its dwelling in each individual body is called Adhyatma; the offering in sacrifice which causes the genesis and support of beings, is called karma.

4) The perishable adjunct is the Adhibhuta, and the Indweller is the Adhidaivata; I alone am the Adhiyajna here in this body, O best of the embodied.

5) And he who at the time of death, meditating on Me alone, goes forth, leaving the body, attains My Being: there is no doubt about this.

6) Remembering whatever object, at the end, he leaves the body, that alone is reached by him, O son of Kunti, (because) of his constant thought of that object.

7) Therefore, at all times, constantly remember Me, and fight. With mind and intellect absorbed in Me, you shall doubtless come to Me.

8) With the mind not moving towards anything else, made steadfast by the method of habitual meditation, and dwelling on the Supreme, Resplendent Purusha, O son of Pritha, one goes to Him. 9-

10) The Omniscient, the Ancient, the Overruler, minuter than an atom, the Sustainer of all, of form inconceivable, self-luminous like the sun, and beyond the darkness of Maya–he who meditates on Him thus, at the time of death, full of devotion, with the mind unmoving, and also by the power of yoga, fixing the whole prana betwixt the eyebrows, he goes to that Supreme, Resplendent Purusha.

11) What the knowers of the Veda speak of as Imperishable, what the selfcontrolled (Sannyasis), freed from attachment enter, and to gain which goal they live the life of a Brahmachari, that I shall declare unto thee in brief.

12-13) Controlling all the senses, confining the mind in the heart, drawing the prana into the head, occupied in the practice of concentration, uttering the one-syllabled "Om"–the Brahman, and meditating on Me–he who so departs, leaving the body, attains the Supreme Goal.

14) I am easily attainable by that ever-steadfast Yogi who remembers Me constantly and daily, with a single mind, O son of Pritha.

15) Reaching the highest perfection and having attained Me, the great-souled ones are no more subject to rebirth–which is the home of pain, and ephemeral.

16) All the worlds, O Arjuna, including the realm of Brahma, are subject to return, but after attaining Me, O son of Kunti, there is no rebirth.

17) They who know (the true measure of) day and night, know the day of Brahma, which ends in a thousand Yugas, and the night which (also) ends in a thousand Yugas.

18) At the approach of (Brahma's) day, all manifestations proceed from the unmanifested state; at the approach of night, they merge verily into that alone, which is called the unmanifested.

19) The very same multitude of beings (that existed in the preceding day of Brahma), being born again and again, merge, in spite of themselves, O son of Pritha, (into the unmanifested), at the approach of night, and re-manifest at the approach of day.

20) But beyond this unmanifested, there is that other Unmanifested, Eternal Existence–That which is not destroyed at the destruction of all beings.

21) What has been called Unmanifested and Imperishable, has been described as the Goal Supreme. That is My highest state, having attained which, there is no return.

22) And that Supreme Purusha is attainable, O son of Pritha, by whole-souled devotion to Him alone, in Whom all beings dwell, and by Whom all this is pervaded.

23) Now I shall tell thee, O bull of the Bharatas, of the time (path) travelling in which, the Yogis return, (and again of that, taking which) they do not return.

24) Fire flame, daytime, the bright fortnight, the six months of the Northern passage of the sun–taking this path, the knowers of Brahman go to Brahman.

25) Smoke, night-time, the dark fortnight, the six months of the Southern passage of the sun–taking this path the Yogi, attaining the lunar light, returns.

26) Truly are these bright and dark paths of the world considered eternal: one leads to non-return; by the other, one returns.

27) No Yogi, O son of Pritha, is deluded after knowing these paths. Therefore, O Arjuna, be steadfast in yoga, at all times.

28) Whatever meritorious effect is declared (in the Scriptures) to accrue from (the study of) the Vedas, (the performance of) yajnas, (the practice of) austerities and gifts–above all this rises the Yogi, having known this, and attains to the primeval, supreme Abode.

The Way of the Kingly Knowledge and the Kingly Secret

The Blessed Lord said:

1) To thee, who dost not carp, verily shall I now declare this, the most profound knowledge, united with realization, having known which, you shall be free from evil (Samsara).

2) Of sciences, the highest; of profundities, the deepest; of purifiers, the supreme, is this; realizable by direct perception, endowed with (immense) merit, very easy to perform, and of an imperishable nature.

3) Persons without shraddha for this dharma, return, O scorcher of foes, without attaining Me, to the path of rebirth fraught with death.

4) All this world is pervaded by Me in My unmanifested form: all beings exist in Me, but I do not dwell in them.

5) Nor do beings exists in Me, (in reality), behold My divine yoga! Bringing forth and supporting the beings, My Self does not dwell in them.

6) As the mighty wind, moving always everywhere, rests ever in the Akasha, know that even so do all beings rest in Me.

7) At the end of a Kalpa, O son of Kunti, all beings go back to My Prakriti: at the beginning of (another) Kalpa, I send them forth again.

8) Animating My Prakriti, I project again and again this whole multitude of beings, helpless under the sway of Prakriti.

9) These acts do not bind Me, sitting as one neutral, unattached to them, O Dhananjaya.

10) By reason of My proximity, Prakriti produces all this, the moving and the unmoving; the world wheels round and round, O son of Kunti, because of this.

11) Unaware of My higher state, as the great Lord of being, fools disregard Me, dwelling in the human form.

12) Of vain hopes, of vain works, of vain knowledge, and senseless, they verily are possessed of the delusive nature of Rakshasas and Asuras.

13) But the great-souled ones, O son of Pritha, possessed of the Divine Prakriti, knowing Me to be the origin of beings and immutable, worship Me with a single mind.

14) Glorifying Me always and striving with firm resolve, bowing down to Me in devotion, always steadfast, they worship Me.

15) Others, too, sacrificing by the yajna of knowledge (I.e., seeing the self in all), worship Me the All-Formed, as one, as distinct, as manifold.

16) I am the Kratu, I the Yajna, I the Svadha, I the Aushadha, I the Mantra, I the Ajya, I the fire, and I the oblation.

17) I am the Father of this world–the Mother, the Sustainer, the Grandfather, the Purifier, the (one) thing to be known, (the syllable) Om, and also the Rik, Saman, and Yajus.

18) The Goal, the Supporter, the Lord, the Witness, the Abode, the Refuge, the Friend, the Origin, the Dissolution, the Substratum, the Storehouse, the Seed immutable.

19) (As the sun) I give heat; I withhold and send forth rain; I am immortality and also death; being and non-being am I, O Arjuna!

20) The knowers of the three Vedas, worshipping Me by yajna, drinking the Soma, and (thus) being purified from sin, pray for passage to heaven; reaching the holy world of the Lord of the devas, they enjoy in heaven the divine pleasures of the devas.

21) Having enjoyed the vast Svarga-world, they enter the mortal world, on the exhaustion of their merit: Thus, abiding by the injunctions of the three (Vedas), desiring desires, they (constantly) come and go.

22) Persons who, meditating on Me as non-separate, worship Me in all beings, to them thus ever zealously engaged, I carry what they lack and preserve what they already have.

23) Even those devotees, who endued with shraddha, worship other gods, they too worship Me alone, O son of Kunti, (but) by the wrong method

24) For I alone am the Enjoyer, and Lord of all yajnas; but because they do not know Me in reality, they return, (to the mortal world).

25) Votaries of the devas go to the devas' to the Pitris, go their votaries; to the Bhutas, go the Bhuta worshippers; My votaries too come unto Me.

26) Whoever with devotion offers Me a leaf, a flower, a fruit, or water, that I accept–the devout gift of the pure-minded.

27) Whatever you do, whatever you eat, whatever you off in sacrifice, whatever you give away, whatever austerity ou practice, O son of Kunti, do that as an offering unto Me.

28) Thus shall you be freed from the bondages of actions, bearing good and evil results: with the heart steadfast in the yoga of renunciation, and liberated you shall come unto Me.

29) I am the same to all beings: to Me there is none hateful or dear. But those who worship Me with devotion, are in Me, and I too am in them.

30) If even a very wicked person worships Me, with devotion to none else, he should be regarded as good, for he has rightly resolved.

31) Soon does he become righteous, and attain eternal Peace, O son of Kunti; boldly can you proclaim, that My devotee is never destroyed.

32) For, taking refuge in Me, they also, O son of Pritha, who might be of inferior birth-women, Vaishyas, as well as Shudras-even they attain to the Supreme Goal.

33) What need to mention holy Brahmanas, and devoted Rajarshis! Having obtained this transient, joyless world, worship Me.

34) Fill your mind with Me, be My devotee, sacrifice unto Me, bow down to Me; thus having made your heart steadfast in Me, taking Me as the Supreme Goal, you shall come to Me.

Glimpses of the Divine Glory

The Blessed Lord said:

1) Again, O mighty-armed, listen to My supreme word, which I wishing your welfare, will tell thee who art delighted (to hear Me).

2) Neither the hosts of devas, nor the great Rishis, know My origin, for in every way I am the source of all the devas and the great Rishis.

3) He who knows Me, birthless and beginningless, the great Lord of worlds–he, among mortals, is undeluded, he is freed from all sins.

4-5) Intellect, knowledge, non-delusion, forbearance, truth, restraint of the external senses, calmness of heart, happiness, misery, birth, death, fear, as well as fearlessness, non-injury, evenness, contentment, austerity, benevolence, good name, (as well as) ill-fame–(these) different kinds of qualities of beings arise from Me alone.

6) The seven great Rishis as well as the four ancient manus, possessed of powers like Me (due to their thoughts being fixed on Me), were born of (My) mind; from them are these creatures in the world.

7) He who in reality knows these manifold manifestations of My being and (this) yoga power of Mine, becomes established in the unshakable yoga; there is no doubt about it.

8) I am the origin of all, from Me everything evolves–thus thinking, the wise worship Me with loving consciousness.

9) With their minds wholly in Me, with their senses absorbed in Me, enlightening one another, and always speaking of Me, they are satisfied and delighted.

10) To them, ever steadfast and serving Me with affection, I give that buddhiyoga by which they come unto Me.

11) Out of mere compassion for them, I, abiding in their hearts, destroy the darkness (in them) born of ignorance, by the luminous lamp of knowledge.

Arjuna said:

12-13) The Supreme Brahman, the Supreme Abode, the Supreme Purifier, are You. All the Rishis, the deva-Rishi Narada as well as Asita, Devala, and Vyasa have declared You as the Eternal, the self-luminous Purusha, the first Deva, Birthless, and All-pervading. So also you yourself say to me.

14) I regard all this that you say to me as true, O Keshava. Verily, O Bhagavan, neither the devas nor the Danavas know Your manifestation.

15) Verily, you yourself know yourself by yourself, O Supreme Purusha, O Source of being, O Lord of beings, O Deva of Devas, O Ruler of the World.

16) You should indeed speak, without reserve of Your divine attributes by which, filling all these worlds, you existest.

17) How shall I, O Yogi, meditate ever to know You? In what things, O Bhagavan, are you to be thought of by me?

18) Speak to me again in detail, O Janardana, of your yoga-powers and attributes; for I am never satiated in hearing the ambrosia (of Your speech).

The Blessed Lord said:

19) I shall speak to thee now, O best of the Kurus, of my divine attributes, according to their prominence; there is no end to the particulars of My manifestation.

20) I am the Self, O Gudakesha, existent in the heart of all beings; I am the beginning, the middle, and also the end of all beings.

21) Of the Adityas, I am Vishnu; of luminaries, the radiant Sun; of the winds, I am Marichi; of the asterisms, the Moon.

22) I am the Sama-Veda of the Vedas, and Vasava (Indra) of the gods; of the senses I am the mind and intelligence in living beings am I.

23) And of the Rudras I am Shankara; of the Yakshas and Rakshasas, the Lord of wealth (Kubera); of the Vasus I am Pavaka; and of mountains, Meru am I.

24) And of priests, O son of Pritha, know Me the chief, Brihaspati; of generals, I am Skanda; of bodies of water, I am the ocean.

25) Of the great Rishis I am Bhrigu; of words I am the one syllable "Om;" of yajnas I am the yajna of japa (silent repetition); of immovable things the Himalaya.

26) Of all trees (I am) the Ashvattha, and Narada of deva-Rishis; Chitraratha of Gandharvas am I, and the Muni Kapila of the perfected ones.

27) Know me among horses as Uchchaisshravas, Amrita-born; of lordly elephants Airavata, and of men the king.

28) Of weapons I am the thunderbolt, of cows I am Kamadhuk; I am the Kandarpa, the cause of offspring; of serpents I am Vasuki.

29) And Ananta of snakes I am, I am Varuna of water-beings; and Aryaman of Pitris I am, I am Yama of controllers.

30) And Prahlada am I of Diti's progeny, of measurers I am Time; and of beasts I am the lord of beasts [lion], and Garuda of birds.

31) Of purifiers I am the wind, Rama of warriors am I; of fishes I am the shark, of streams I am Jahnavi (the Ganga).

32) Of manifestations I am the beginning, the middle and also the end; of all knowledges I am the knowledge of the self, and Vada of disputants.

33) Of letters the letter A am I, and Dvandva of all compounds; I alone am the inexhaustible Time, I the Sustainer (by dispensing fruits of actions) All-formed.

34) An I am the all-seizing Death, and the prosperity of those who are to be prosperous; of the feminine qualities (I am) Fame, Prosperity (or beauty, Inspiration, Memory, Intelligence, Constancy and Forbearance.

35) Of Samas also I am the Brihat-Sama, of metres Gayatri am I; of months I am Margashirsha, of seasons the flowery season.

36) I am the gambling of the fraudulent, I am the power of the powerful; I am victory, I am effort, I am sattwa of the sattwic.

37) Of the Vrishnis I am Vasudeva; of the Pandavas, Dhananjaya; and also of the Munis I am Vyasa; of the sages, Ushanas the sage.

38) Of punishers I am the sceptre; of those who seek to conquer, I am statesmanship; and also of things secret I am silence, and the knowledge of knowers am I.

39) And whatsoever is the seed of all beings, that also am I, O Arjuna. There is no being, whether moving or unmoving, that can exist without Me.

40) There is no end of My divine attributes, O scorcher of foes; but this is a brief statement by Me of the particulars of My divine attributes.

41) Whatever being there is great, prosperous, or powerful, that know to be a product of a part of My splendour.

42) Or what avails thee to know all this diversity, O Arjuna? (Know this that) I exist, supporting this whole world by a portion of Myself.

The Vision of the Universal Form

Arjuna said:

1) By the supremely profound words, on the discrimination of self, that have been spoken by You out of compassion towards me, this my delusion is gone.

2) Of You, O lotus-eyed, I have heard at length, of the origin and dissolution of beings, as also Your inexhaustible greatness.

3) So it is, O Supreme Lord,! as You have declared Yourself. (Still) I desire to see Your Ishvara-Form, O Supreme Purusha.

4) If, O Lord, You think me capable of seeing it, the, O Lord of Yogis, show me Your immutable Self.

The Blessed Lord said:

5) Behold, O son of Pritha, by hundreds and thousands, My different forms celestial, of various colours and shapes.

6) Behold the Adityas, the Vasus, the Rudras, the twin Ashvins, and the Maruts; behold, O descendant of Bharata, many wonders never seen before.

7) See now, O Gudakesha, in this My body, the whole universe centred in one–including the moving and the unmoving–and all else that you desirest to see.

8) But you cannot see me with these eyes of yours; I give thee supersensuous sight; behold My supreme yoga power. Sanjaya said:

9) Having thus spoken, O King, Hari, the Great Lord of Yoga, showed unto the son of Pritha, His Supreme Ishvara-Form:

10) With numerous mouths and eyes, with numerous wondrous sights, with numerous celestial ornaments, with numerous celestial weapons uplifted;

11) Wearing celestial garlands and apparel, anointed with celestial-scented unguents, the All-wonderful Resplendent, Boundless, and All-formed.

12) If the splendour of a thousand suns were to rise up simultaneously in the sky, that would be like the splendour of that Mighty Being.

13) There in the body of the God of gods, the son of Pandu then saw the whole universe resting in one, with its manifold divisions.

14) Then Dhananjaya, filled with wonder, with his hairs standing on end, bending down his head to the Deva in adoration, spoke with joined palms.

Arjuna said:

15) I see all the devas, O Deva, in Your body, and hosts of all grades of beings; Brahma, the Lord, seated on the lotus, and all the Rishis and celestial serpents.

16) I see You of boundless form on every side with manifold arms, stomachs, mouths, and eyes; neither the end nor the middle, nor also the beginning of You do I see, O Lord of the universe, O Universal Form.

17) I see You with diadem, club, and discus; a mass of radiance shining everywhere, very hard to look at, all around blazing like burning fire and sun, and immeasurable.

18) You are the Imperishable, the Supreme Being, the one thing to be known. You are the great Refuge of this universe; You are the undying Guardian of the Eternal dharma, You are the Ancient Purusha, I ween.

19) I see You without beginning, middle, or end, infinite in power, of manifold arms; the sun and the moon Your eyes, the burning fire Your mouth; heating the whole universe with Your radiance.

20) This space betwixt heaven and earth and all the quarters are filled by You alone; having seen this, Your marvelous and awful form, the three worlds are trembling with fear, O Great-souled One.

21) Verily, into You enter these hosts of devas; some extol You in fear with joined palms; "May it be well!" thus saying, bands of great Rishis and Siddhas praise You with splendid hymns.

22) The Rudras, Adityas, Vasus, Sadhyas, Vishva-devas, the two Ashvins, Maruts, Ushmapas, and hosts of Gandharvas, Yakshas, Asuras, and Siddhas–all these are looking at You, all quite astounded.

23) Having seen Your immeasurable Form–with many mouths and eyes, O mighty-armed, with many arms, thighs, and feet, with many stomachs, and fearful with many tusks–the worlds are terrified, and so am I.

24) On seeing You touching the sky, shining in many a colour, with mouths wide open, with large fiery eyes, I am terrified at heart, and find no courage nor peace, O Vishnu.

25) Having seen Your mouths, fearful with tusks, (blazing) like Pralaya-fires, I know not the four quarters, nor do I find peace; have mercy, O Lord of the devas, O Abode of the universe.

26-27) All those sons of Dhritarashtra, with hosts of monarchs, Bhishma, Drona, and Sutaputra, with the warrior chiefs of ours, enter precipitately into Your mouth, terrible with tusks and fearful to behold. Some are found sticking in the interstices of Your teeth, with their heads crushed to powder.

28) Verily, as the many torrents of rivers flow towards the ocean, so do those heroes in the world of men enter Your fiercely flaming mouths.

29) As moths precipitately rush into a blazing fire only to perish, even so do these creatures also precipitately rush into Your mouths only to perish.

30) Swallowing all the worlds on every side with Your flaming mouths, You are licking Your lips. Your fierce rays, filling the whole world with radiance, are burning, O Vishnu!

31) Tell me who You are, fierce in form. Salutation to You, O Supreme Deva! have mercy. I desire to know You, O Primeval One. I know not indeed Your purpose.

The Blessed Lord said:

32) I am the mighty world-destroying Time, here made manifest for the purpose of infolding the world. Even without thee, none of the warriors arrayed in the hostile armies shall live.

33) Therefore arise and acquire fame. Conquer the enemies, and enjoy the unrivalled dominion. Verily by Myself have they been already slain; be merely an apparent cause, O Savyasachin (Arjuna).

34) Drona, Bhishma, Jayadratha, Karna as well as other brave warriors–these already killed by Me, do you kill. Be not distressed with fear; fight, and you shall conquer your enemies in battle. **Sanjaya said:**

35) Having heard this speech of Keshava, the diademed one (Arjuna), with joined palms, trembling, prostrated himself, and again addresssed Krishna in a choked voice, bowing down, overwhelmed with fear.

Arjuna said:

36) It is meet, O Hrishikesha, that the world is delighted and rejoices in Your praise, that rakshasas fly in fear to all quarters and all the hosts of Siddhas bow down to You in adoration.

37) And why should they not, O Great-souled One, bow to You, greater than, and the Primal Cause of even Brahma, O Infinite Being, O Lord of the devas, O Abode of the universe? You are the Imperishable, the Being and the non-Being, (as well as) That which is Beyond (them).

38) You are the Primal Deva, the Ancient Purusha; You are the Supreme Refuge of this universe, You are the Knower, and the One Thing to be known; You are the Supreme goal. By You is the universe pervaded, O boundless Form.

39) You are Vayu, Yama, Agni, Varuna, the Moon, Prajapati, and the Greatgrandfather. Salutation, salutation to You, a thousand times, and again and again salutation, salutation to You!

40) Salutation to You before and behind, salutation to You on every side, O All! You, infinite in power and infinite in prowess, pervadest all; wherefore You are All.

41-42) Whatever I have presumptuously said from carelessness or love, addressing You as "O Krishna, O Yadava, O friend," regarding You merely as a friend, unconscious of this Your greatness–in whatever way I may have been disrespectful to You in fun, while walking, reposing, sitting, or at meals, when alone (with You), O Achyuta, or in company–I implore You, Immeasurable One, to forgive all this.

43) You are the Father of the world, moving and unmoving; the object of its worship; greater than the great. None there exists who is equal to You in the three worlds; who then can excel You, O You of power incomparable?

44) So prostrating my body in adoration, I crave Your forgiveness, Lord adorable! As a father forgiveth his son, friend a dear friend, a eloed one his love, even so should You forgive me, O Deva.

45) Overjoyed am I to have seen what I saw never before; yet my mind is distracted with terror. Show me, O Deva, only that form of Yours. Have mercy, O Lord of Devas, O Abode of the universe.

46) Diademed, bearing a mace and a discus, You I desire to see as before. Assume that same four-armed Form, O You of thousand arms, of universal Form.

The Blessed Lord said:

47) Graciously have I shown to thee, O Arjuna, this Form supreme, by My own yoga power, this resplendent, primeval, infinite, universal Form of Mine, which hathnot been seen before by anyone else.

48) Neither by the study of the Veda and yajna, nor by gifts, nor by rituals, nor by severe austerities, am I in such Form seen, in the world of men, by any other than thee, O great hero of the Kurus.

49) Be not afraid nor bewildered, having beheld this Form of Mine, so terrific. With your fears dispelled and with gladdened heart, now see again this former Form of Mine. **Sanjaya said:**

50) So Vasudeva, having thus spoken to Arjuna, showed again His own Form; and the Great-souled One, assuming His gently Form, pacified him who was terrified.

Arjuna said:

51) Having seen this Your gentle human Form, O Janardana, my thoughts are now composed, and I am restored to my nature.

The Blessed Lord said:

52) Very hard indeed it is to see this Form of Mine which you have hast seen. Even the devas ever long to behold this Form.

53) Neither by the Vedas, nor by austerity, nor by gifts, nor by sacrifice can I be seen as you have seen Me.

54) But by single-minded devotion I may in this form, be known, O Arjuna, and seen in reality, and also entered into O scorcher of foes.

55) He who does work for Me alone and has Me for his goal, is devoted to Me, is freed from attachment, and bears enmity towards no creature-he entereth into Me, O Pandava.

The Way of Devotion

Arjuna said:
1) Those devotees who, ever-steadfast, thus worship You, and those also who worship the Imperishable, the Unmanifested–which of them are better versed in yoga?

The Blessed Lord said:
2) Those who, fixing their mind on Me, worship Me, ever-steadfast, and endowed with supreme shraddha, they in My opinion are the best versed in yoga.

3-4) But those also, who worship the Imperishable, the Indefinable, the Unmanifested, the Omnipresent, the Unthinkable, the Unchangeable, the Immovable, the Eternal–having subdued all the senses, even-minded everywhere, engaged in the welfare of all beings–verily they read only Myself.

5) Greater is their trouble whose minds are set on the Unmanifested; for the goal of the Unmanifested is very hard for the embodied to reach.

6-7) But those who worship Me, resigning all actions in Me, regarding me as the Supreme Goal, meditating on Me with single-minded yoga–to those whose mind is set on Me, verily, I become ere long, O son of Pritha, the Saviour out of the ocean of the mortal Samsara.

8) Fix your mind on Me only, place your intellect in Me: (then) you shall no doubt live in Me hereafter.

9) If you are unable to fix your mind steadily on Me, then by abhyasa-yoga do you seek to reach Me, O Dhananjaya.

10) If also you are unable to practice Abhyasa, be intent on doing actions for my sake. Even by doing actions for My sake, you shall attain perfection.

11) If you are unable to do even this, then taking refuge in Me, abandon the fruit of all action, being self-controlled.

12) Better indeed is knowledge than (blind) Abhyasa; meditation (with knowledge) is more esteemed than (mere) knowledge; than meditation the renunciation of the fruit of action; peace immediately follows renunciation.

13-14) He who hates no creature, and is friendly and compassionate towards all, who is free from the feelings of "I" and "mine," even-minded in pain and pleasure, forbearing, ever content, steady in meditation, self-controlled, and possessed of firm conviction, with mind and intellect fixed on Me–he who is thus devoted to Me, is dear to Me.

15) He by whom the world is not agitated and who cannot be agitated by the world, who is freed from joy, envy, fear, and anxiety–he is dear to Me.

16) He who is free from dependence, who is pure, prompt, unconcerned, untroubled, renouncing every undertaking–he who is thus devoted to Me, is dear to Me.

17) He who neither rejoices, nor hates, nor grieves, nor desires, renouncing good and evil, full of devotion, he is dear to Me.

18-19) He who is the same to friend and foe, and also in honor and dishonor; who is the same in heat and cold, and in pleasure and pain; who is free from attachment; to whom censure and praise are equal; who is silent, contend with anything, homeless, steady-minded, full of devotion–that man is dear to Me.

20) And they who follow this Immortal Dharma, as described above, endued with shraddha, regarding Me as the Supreme Goal, and devoted–they are exceedingly dear to Me.

The Discrimination of the Kshetra and the Kshetrajna

Arjuna said: Prakriti and Purusha, also the kshetra and the knower of the kshetra, knowledge, and that which ought to be known—these, O Keshava, I desire to learn.

The Blessed Lord said:

1) This body, O son of Kunti, is called kshetra, and he who knows it is called kshetrajna by those who know of them (kshetra and kshetrajna).

2) Me do you also know, O descendant of Bharata, to be kshetrajna in all kshetras. The knowledge of kshetra and kshetrajna is considered by Me to be the knowledge.

3) What the kshetra is, what is properties are, what its modifications are, what effects arise from what causes, and also who He is and what His powers are, that hear from Me in brief.

4) (This truth) has been sung by Rishis in many ways, in various distinctive chants, in passages indicative of Brahman, full of reasoning, and convincing.

5-6) The great Elements, Egoism, Intellect, as also the Unmanifested (Mula Prakriti), the ten senses and the one (mind), and the five objects of the senses; desire, hatred, pleasure, pain, the aggregate, intelligence, fortitude—the kshetra has been thus briefly described with its modifications.

7) Humility, unpretentiousness, non-injury, forbearance, uprightness, service to the teacher, purity, steadiness, self-control;

8) The renunciation of sense-objects, and also absence of egoism; reflection on the evils of birth, death, old age, sickness, and pain;

9) Non-attachment, non-identification of self with son, wife, home, and the rest, and constant even-mindedness in the occurrence of the desirable and the undesirable;

10) Unswerving devotion to Me by the yoga of non-separation, resort to sequestered places, distaste for the society of men;

11) Constant application to spiritual knowledge, understanding of the end of true knowledge; this is declared to be knowledge, and what is opposed to it is ignorance.

12) I shall describe that which has to be known, knowing which one attains to immortality, the beginningless Supreme Brahman. It is called neither being nor non-being.

13) With hands and feet everywhere, with eyes, heads, and mouths everywhere, with ears everywhere in the universe–That exists pervading all.

14) Shining by the functions of all the senses, yet without the senses; Absolute, yet sustaining all; devoid of gunas, yet their experiencer.

15) Without and within (all) beings; the unmoving and also the moving; because of Its subtlety incomprehensible; It is far and near.

16) Impartible, yet It exists as if divided in beings: It is to be known as sustaining beings; and devouring, as well as generating (them).

17) The Light even of lights, It is said to be beyond darkness; Knowledge, and the One Thing to be known, the Goal of knowledge, dwelling in the hearts of all.

18) Thus kshetra, knowledge, and that which has to be known, have been briefly stated. Knowing this, My devotee is fitted for My state.

19) Know that Prakriti and Purusha are both beginningless; and know also that all modifications and gunas are born of Prakriti.

20) In the production of the body and the senses, Prakriti is said to be the cause; in the experience of pleasure and pain, Purusha is said to be the cause.

21) Purusha seated in Prakriti, experiences the gunas born of Prakriti; the reason of his birth in good and evil wombs is his attachment to the gunas.

22) And the Supreme Purusha in this body is also called the Looker-on, the Permitter, the Supporter, the Experiencer, the Great Lord, and the Highest Self.

23) He who thus knows the Purusha and Prakriti together with the gunas, whatever his life, is not born again.

24) Some by meditation behold the self in their own intelligence by the purified heart, others by the path of knowledge, others again by karma-yoga.

25) Others again not knowing thus, worship as they have heard from others. Even these go beyond death, regarding what they have heard as the Supreme Refuge.

26) Whatever being is born, the moving or the unmoving, O bull of the Bharatas, know it to be from the union of kshetra and kshetrajna.

27) He sees, who sees the Supreme Lord, existing equally in all beings, deathless in the dying.

28) Since seeing the Lord equally existent everywhere, he injures not self by self, and so goes to the highest Goal.

29) He sees, who sees that all actions are done by Prakriti alone and that the self is actionless.

30) When he sees the separate existence of all being inherent in the One, and their expansion from That (One) alone, he then becomes Brahman.

31) Being without beginning and devoid of gunas, this Supreme Self, immutable, O son of Kunti, though existing in the body neither acts nor is affected.

32) As the all-pervading Akasha, because of its subtlety, is not tainted, so the self existent everywhere in the body is not tainted.

33) As the one sun illumines all this world, so does He who abides in the kshetra, O descendant of Bharata, illumine the whole kshetra.

34) They who thus with the eye of knowledge perceive the distinction between the kshetra and the kshetrajna, and also the emancipation from the Prakriti of beings, they go to the Supreme.

The Discrimination of the Three Gunas

The Blessed Lord said:

1) Again I shall tell you that supreme knowledge which is above all knowledge, having known which all the Munis have attained to high perfection after this life.

2) They who, having devoted themselves to this knowledge, have attained to My Being, are neither born at the time of creation, nor are they troubled at the time of dissolution.

3) My womb is the great Prakriti; in that I place the germ; from thence, O descendant of Bharata, is the birth of all beings.

4) Whatever forms are produced, O son of Kunti, in all the wombs, the great Prakriti is their womb, and I the seed-giving Father.

5) Sattwa, rajas, and tamas-these gunas, O mighty-armed, born of Prakriti, bind fast in the body the indestructible embodied one.

6) Of these sattwa, because of its stainlessness, luminous and free from evil, binds, O sinless one, by attachment to happiness, and by attachment to knowledge.

7) Know rajas to be of the nature of passion, giving rise to thirst and attachment; it binds fast, O son of Kunti, the embodied one, by attachment to action.

8) And know tamas to be born of ignorance, stupefying all embodied beings; it binds fast, O descendant of Bharata, by miscomprehension, indolence, and sleep.

9) Sattwa attaches to happiness, and rajas to action, O descendant of Bharata; while tamas, verily, shrouding discrimination, attaches to miscomprehension.

10) Sattwa arises, O descendant of Bharata, predominating over rajas and tamas; likewise rajas over sattwa and tamas; so, tamas over sattwa and rajas.

11) When through every sense in this body, the light of intelligence shines, then it should be known that sattwa is predominant.

12) Greed, activity, the undertaking of actions, unrest, longing-these arise when rajas is predominant, O bull of the Bharatas.

13) Darkness, inertness, miscomprehension, and delusion-these arise when tamas is predominant, O descendant of Kuru.

14) If the embodied one meets death when sattwa is predominant, then he attains to the spotless regions of the worshippers of the Highest.

15) Meeting death in rajas he is born among those attached to action; so dying in tamas, he is born in the wombs of the irrational.

16) The fruit of good action, they say, is Sattvika and pure; verily, the fruit of rajas is pain, and ignorance is the fruit of tamas.

17) From sattwa arises wisdom, and from rajas greed; miscomprehension, delusion and ignorance arise from tamas.

18) The sattwa-abiding go upwards; the rajasic dwell in the middle; and the tamasic, abiding in the function of the lowest guna, go downwards.

19) When the seer beholds no agent other than the gunas and knows That which is higher than the gunas, he attains to My being.

20) The embodied one having gone beyond these three gunas, out of which the body is evilved, is freed from birth, death, decay, and pain, and attains to immortality.

Arjuna said:
21) By what marks, O Lord, is he (known) who has gone beyond these three gunas? What is his conduct, and how does he pass beyond these three gunas?

The Blessed Lord said:
22) He who hates not the appearance of light (the effect of sattwa), activity (the effect of rajas), and delusion (the effect of tamas), (in his own mind), O Pandava, nor longs for them when absent;

23) He who, sitting like one unconcerned, is moved not by the gunas, who knowing that the gunas operate, is self-centered and swerves not;

24) Alike in pleasure and apin, self-abiding, regarding a clod of earth, a stone and gold alike; the same to agreeable and disagreeable, firm, the same in censure and praise;

25) The same in honor and disgrace, the same to friend and foe, relinquishing all undertakings-he is said to have gone beyond the gunas.

26) And he who serves Me with unswerving devotion, he, going beyond the gunas, is fitted for becoming Brahman.

27) For I am the abode of Brahman, the Immortal and Immutable, of everlasting dharma and of Absolute Bliss.

The Way to the Supreme Spirit

The Blessed Lord said:

1) They speak of an eternal Ashvattha rooted above and branching below whose leaves are the Vedas; he who knows it, is a Veda-knower.

2) Below and above spread its branches, nourished by the gunas; sense-objects are its buds; and below in the world of man stretch forth the roots, originating action.

3-4) Its form is not here perceived as such, neither its end, nor its origin, nor its existence. Having cut asunder this firm-rooted Ashvattha with the strong axe of non-attachment–then that Goal is to be sought for, going whither they (the wise) do not return again. I seek refuge in that Primeval Purusha whence streamed forth the Eternal Activity.

5) Free from pride and delusion, with the evil of attachment conquered, ever dwelling in the self, with desires completely receded, liberated from the pairs of opposites known as pleasure and pain, the undeluded reach that Goal Eternal.

6) That the sun illumines not, nor the moon, nor fire; that is My Supreme Abode, going whither they return not.

7) An eternal portion of Myself having become a living soul in the world of life, draws (to itself) the (five) senses with mind for the sixth, abiding in Prakriti.

8) When the Lord obtains a body and when He leaves it, He takes these and goes, as the wind takes the scents from their seats (the flowers).

9) Presiding over the ear, the eye, the touch, the taste, and the smell, as also the mind, He experiences objects.

10) While transmigrating (from one body to another), or residing (in the same) or experiencing, or when united with the gunas–the deluded do not see Him; but those who have the eye of wisdom behold Him.

11) The Yogis striving (for perfection) behold Him dwelling in themselves; but the unrefined and unintelligent, even though striving, see Him not.

12) The light which residing in the sun illumines the whole world, that which is in the moon and in the fire–know that light to be Mine.

13) Entering the earth with My energy, I support all beings, and I nourish all the herbs, becoming the watery moon.

14) Abiding in the body of living beings as (the fire) Vaishvanara, I, associated with prana and apana, digest the fourfold food.

15) I am centered in the hearts of all; memory and perception as well as their loss come from Me. I am verily that which has to be known by all the Vedas, I indeed am the Author of the Vedanta, and the Knower of the Veda am I.

16) There are two Purushas in the world–the Perishable and the Imperishable. All beings are the Perishable, and the Kutastha is called Imperishable.

17) But (there is) another, the Supreme Purusha, called the Highest Self, the immutable Lord, who pervading the three worlds, sustains them.

18) As I transcend the Perishable and am above even the Imperishable, therefore am I in the world and in the Veda celebrated as Purushottama (the Highest Purusha).

19) He who, free from delusion, thus knows Me, the Highest Spirit, he knowing all, worships Me with all his heart, O descendant of Bharata.

20) Thus, O sinless one, has this most profound teaching been imparted by Me. Knowing this one attains the highest intelligence and will have accomplished all one's duties, O descendant of Bharata.

The Classification of the Divine and the Nondivine Attributes

The Blessed Lord said:

1) Fearlessness, purity of heart, steadfastness in knowledge and yoga; almsgiving, control of the senses, yajna, reading of the shastras, austerity, uprightness;

2) Non-injury, truth, absence of anger, renunciation, tranquillity, absence of calumny, compassion to beings, uncovetousness, gentleness, modesty, absence of fickleness;

3) Boldness, forgiveness, fortitude, purity, absence of hatred, absence of pride; these belong to one born for a divine state, O descendant of Bharata.

4) Ostentation, arrogance, and self-conceit, anger as also harshness and ignorance, belong to one who is born, O Partha, for an asuric state.

5) The divine state is deemed to make for liberation, the asuric for bondage; grieve not, O Pandava, you are born for a divine state.

6) There are two types of beings in this world, the divine and the asuric. The divine have been described at length; hear from Me, O Partha, of the asuric.

7) The persons of asuric nature know not what to do and what to refrain from; neither is purity found in them nor good conduct, nor truth.

8) They say, "The universe is without truth, without a (moral) basis, without a God, brought about by mutual union, with lust for its cause; what else?"

9) Holding this view, these ruined souls of small intellect and fierce deeds, rise as the enemies of the world for its destruction.

10) Filled with insatiable desires, full of hypocrisy, pride, and arrogance, holding evil ideas through delusion, they work with impure resolve.

11) Beset with immense cares ending only with death, regarding gratification of lust as the highest, and feeling sure that that is all;

12) Bound by a hundred ties of hope, given over to lust and wrath, they strive to secure by unjust means hoards of wealth for sensual enjoyment.

13) "This today has been gained by me; this desire I shall obtain; this is mind, and this wealth also shall be mine in the future.

14) "That enemy has been slain by me, and others also shall I slay. I am the Lord, I enjoy, I am successful, powerful, and happy.

15) "I am rich and well-born. Who else is equal to me? I will sacrifice, I will give, I will rejoice." Thus deluded by ignorance,

16) Bewildered by many a fancy, covered by the meshes of delusion, addicted to the gratification of lust, they fall down into a foul hell.

17) Self-conceited, haughty, filled with the pride and intoxication of wealth, they perform sacrifices in name, out of ostentation, disregarding ordinance.

18) Possessed of egoism, power, insolence, lust, and wrath, these malignant people hate Me (the self within) in their own bodies and those of others.

19) These malicious and cruel evil-doers, most degraded of men, I hurl perpetually into the wombs of Asuras only, in these worlds.

20) Obtaining the asuric wombs, and deluded birth after birth, not attaining to Me, they thus fall, O son of Kunti, into a still lower condition.

21) Triple is this gate of hell, destructive of the self—lust, anger and greed; therefore one should forsake these three.

22) The man who has got beyond these three gates of darkness, O son of Kunti, practices what is good for himself, and thus goes to the Goal Supreme.

23) He who, setting aside the ordinance of the shastra, acts under the impulse of desire, attains not to perfection, nor happiness, nor the Goal Supreme.

24) So let the shastra be your authority in ascertaining what ought to be done and what ought not to be done. Having known what is said in the ordinance of the shastra, ou should act here.

The Enquiry into the Threefold Shraddha

Arjuna said:

1) Those who, setting aside the ordinance of the shastra, perform sacrifice with shraddha, what is their condition, O Krishna? (Is it) sattwa, rajas, or tamas?

The Blessed Lord said:

2) Threefold is the shraddha of the embodied, which is inherent in their nature-the satwic, rajasic, and the tamasic. Do you hear of it.

3) The shraddha of each is according to his natural disposition, O descendant of Bharata. The man consists of his shraddha; he verily is what his shraddha is.

4) Sattwic men worship the devas; rajasika, the yakshas and the rakshasa; the others-the tamasic men-the pretas and the hosts of bhutas.

5-6) Those men who practice severe austerities not enjoined by the shastras, given to ostentation and egoism, endowed with the power of lust and attachment, torture senseless as they are, all the organs in the body, and Me dwelling in the body within; know them to be of asuric resolve.

7) The food also which is liked by each of them is threefold, as also yajna, austerity, and almsgiving. Do you hear this, their distinction.

8) The foods which augment vitality, energy, strength, health, cheerfulness, and appetite, which are savory and oleaginous, substantial and agreeable, ae liked by the sattwic.

9) The foods that are bitter, sour, saline, excessively hot, pungent, dry, and burning, are liked by the rajasic, and are productive of pain, grief, and disease.

10) That which is stale, tasteless, stinking, cooked overnight, refuse, and impure, is the food liked by the tamasic.

11) That yajna is sattwic which is performed by men desiring no fruit, as enjoined by ordinance, with their mind fixed on the yajna only, for its own sake.

12) That which is performed, O best of the Bharatas, seeking for fruit and for ostentation, know it to be a rajasic yajna.

13) The yajna performed without heed to ordinance, in which no food is distributed, which is devoid of mantras, gifts, and shraddha, is said to be tamasic.

14) Worship of the devas, the twice-born, the gurus, and the wise; purity, straightforwardness, continence, and non-injury are called the austerity of the body.

15) Speech which causes no vexation, and is true, as also agreeable and beneficial, and regular study of the Vedas-these are said to form the austerity of speech.

16) Serenity of mind, kindliness, silence, self-control, honesty of motive-this is called the mental austerity.

17) This threefold austerity practiced by steadfast men, with great Shraddha, desiring no fruit, is said to be sattwic.

18) That austerity which is practiced with the object of gaining welcome, honor, and worship, and with ostentation, is here said to be rajasic, unstable, and transitory.

19) That austerity which is practiced out of a foolish notion, with self-torture, or for the purpose of ruining another, is declared to be tamasic.

20) "To give is right"-gift given with this idea, to one who does no service in return, in a fit place and to a worthy person, that gift is held to be sattwic.

21) And what is given with a view to receiving in return, or looking for the fruit, or again reluctantly, that gift is held to be rajasic.

22) The gift that is given at the wrong place or time, to unworthy persons, without regard or with disdain, that is declared to be tamasic.

23) "Om, Tat, Sat": this has been declared to be the triple designation of Brahman. By that were made of old the Brahmanas, the Vedas, and the yajnas.

24) Therefore, uttering "Om" are the acts of sacrifice, gift, and austerity as enjoined in the ordinances, always begun by the followers of the Vedas.

25) Uttering "Tat," without aiming at fruits, are the various acts of yajna, austerity, and gift performed by the seekers of Moksha.

26) The word "Sat" is used in the sense of reality and of goodness; and so also, O Partha, the word "Sat" is used in the sense of an auspicious act.

27) Steadiness in yajna, austerity, and gift is also called "Sat": as also action in connection with these (or, action for the sake of the Lord) is called "Sat."

28) Whatever is sacrificed, given, or performed and whatever austerity is practiced without shraddha, it is called Asat, O Partha; it is naught here or hereafter.

The Way of Liberation in Renunciation

Arjuna said:

1) I desire to know severally, O mighty-armed, the truth of sannyasa, O Hrishikesha, as also of tyaga, O slayer of Keshi.

The Blessed Lord said:

2) The renunciation of kamya actions the sages understand as sannyasa: the wise declare the abandonment of the fruit of all works as tyaga.

3) Some philosophers declare that all actions should be relinquished as an evil, whilst others (say) that the work of yajna, gift, and austerity should not be relinquished.

4) Hear from Me the final truth about relinquishment, O best of the Bharatas. For relinquishment has been declared to be of three kinds, O tiger among men.

5) The work of yajna, gift, and austerity should not be relinquished, but it should indeed be performed; (for) yajna, gift, and austerity are purifying to the wise.

6) But even these works, O Partha, should be performed, leaving attachment and the fruits; such is My best and certain conviction.

7) But the renunciation of obligatory action is not proper. Abandonment of the same from delusion is declared to be tamasic.

8) He who from fear of bodily trouble relinquishes action, because it is painful, thus performing a rajasic relinquishment, he obtains not the fruit thereof.

9) When obligatory work is performed, O Arjuna, only because it ought to be done, leaving attachment and fruit, such relinquishment is regarded as sattwic.

10) The relinquisher endued with sattwa and a steady understanding and with his doubts dispelled, hates not a disagreeable work nor is attached to an agreeable one.

11) Actions cannot be entirely relinquished by an embodied being, but he who relinquishes the fruits of actions is called a relinquisher.

12) The threefold fruit of action–disagreeable, agreeable, and mixed–accrues to non-relinquishers after death, but never to relinquishers.

13) Learn from Me, O mighty-armed, these five causes for the accomplishment of all works as declared in the wisdom which is the end of all action;

14) The body, the agent, the various senses, the different functions of a manifold kind, and the presiding divinity, the fifth or these;

15) Whatever action a man performs by his body, speech, and mind–whether right or the reverse–these five are its causes.

16) Such being the case, he who through a non-purified understanding looks upon his self, the Absolute, as the agent–he of perverted mind sees not.

17) He who is free from the notion of egoism, whose intelligence is not affected (by good or evil), though he kills these people, he kills not, nor is bound (by the action).

18) Knowledge, the known and the knower form the threefold cause of action. The instrument, the object, and the agent are the threefold basis of action.

19) Knowledge, action and agent are declared in the Sankhya philosophy to be of three kinds only, from the distinction of gunas: hear them also duly.

20) That by which the one indestructible Substance is seen in all being, inseparate in the separated, know that knowledge to be sattwic.

21) But that knowledge which sees in all beings various entities of distinct kinds as different from one another, know that knowledge as rajasic

22) Whilst that which is confined to one single effect as if it were the whole, without reason, without foundation in truth, and trivial–that is declared to be tamasic.

23) An ordained action done without love or hatred by one not desirous of the fruit and free from attachment, is declared to be sattwic.

24) But the action which is performed desiring desires, or with self-conceit and with much effort, is declared to be rajasic.

25) That action is declared to be tamasic which is undertaken through delusion, without heed to the consequence, loss (of power and wealth), injury (to others), and (one's own) ability.

26) An agent who is free from attachment, non-egotistic, endued with fortitude and enthusiasm, and unaffected in success or failure, is called sattwic.

27) He who is passionate, desirous of the fruits of action, greedy, malignant, impure, easily elated or dejected, such an agent is called rajasic.

28) Unsteady, vulgar, arrogant, dishonest, malicious, indolent, desponding, and procrastinating, such an agent is called tamasic.

29) Hear the triple distinction of intellect and fortitude, according to the gunas, as I declare them exhaustively and severally, O Dhananjaya.

30) That which knows the paths of work and renunciation, right and wrong action, fear and fearlessness, bondage and liberation, that intellect, O Partha, is sattwic.

31) That which has a distorted apprehension of dharma and its opposite and also of right action and its opposite, that intellect, O Partha, is rajasic.

32) That which, enveloped in darkness, regards adharma as dharma and views all things in a perverted light, that intellect, O Partha, is tamasic.

33) The fortitude by which the functions of the mind, the prana, and the senses, O Partha, are regulated, that fortitude, unswerving through yoga, is sattwic.

34) But the fortitude by which one regulates (one's mind) to dharma, desire, and wealth, desirous of the fruit of each from attachment, that fortitude, O Partha, is rajasic.

35) That by which a stupid man does not give up sleep, fear, grief, despondency, and also overweening conceit, that fortitude, O Partha, is tamasic.

36) And now hear from Me, O bull of the Bharatas, of the threefold happiness that one learns to enjoy by habit, and by which one comes to the end of pain.

37) That which is like poison at first, but like nectar at the end; that happiness is declared to be sattwic, born of the translucence of intellect due to self-realization.

38) That which arises from the contact of object with sense, at first like nectar, but at the end like poison, that happiness is declared to be rajasic.

39) That happiness which begins and results in self-delusion arising from sleep, indolence, and miscomprehension, that is declared to be tamasic.

40) There is no entity on earth, or again in heaven among the devas, that is devoid of these three gunas, born of Prakriti.

41) Of Brahmanas and kshatriyas and vaishyas, as also of shudras, O scorcher of foes, the duties are distributed according to the Gunas born of their own nature.

42) The control of the mind and the senses, austerity, purity, forbearance, and also uprightness, knowledge, realization, belief in a hereafter-these are the duties of the brahmanas, born of (their own) nature.

43) Prowess, boldness, fortitude, dexterity, and also not flying from battle, generosity and sovereignty are the duties of the kshatriyas, born of (their own) nature.

44) Agriculture, cattle-rearing, and trade are the duties of the Vaishyas, born of (their own) nature; and action consisting of service is the duty of the shudras, born of (their own) nature.

45) Devoted each to his own duty, man attains the highest perfection. How engaged in his own duty, he attains perfection, that hear.

46) From whom is the evolution of all beings, by whom all this is pervaded, worshipping Him with his own duty, a man attains perfection.

47) Better is one's own dharma, (though) imperfect than the dharma of another well-performed. He who does the duty ordained by his own nature incurs no evil.

48) One should not relinquish, O son of Kunti, the duty to which one is born, though it is attended with evil; for, all undertakings are enveloped by evil, as fire by smoke.

49) He who intellect is unattached everywhere, who has subdued his heart, whose desires have fled, he attains by renunciation to the supreme perfection, consisting of freedom from action.

50) Learn from Me in brief, O son of Kunti, how reaching such perfection, he attains to Brahman, that supreme consummation of knowledge.

51) Endued with a pure intellect; subduing the body and the senses with fortitude; relinquishing sound and such other sense-objects; abandoning attraction and hatred;

52) Resorting to a sequestered spot; eating but little; body, speech, and mind controlled; ever engaged in meditation and concentration; possessed of dispassion;

53) Forsaking egoism, power, pride, lust, wrath, and property; freed from the notion of "mine;" and tranquil–he is fit for becoming Brahman.

54) Brahman-become, tranquil-minded, he neither grieves nor desires; the same to all beings, he attains to supreme devotion unto Me.

55) By devotion he knows me in reality, what and who I am; then having known Me in reality, he forthwith enters into Me.

56) Even doing all actions always, taking refuge in Me–by My grace he attains to the eternal, immutable State.

57) Resigning mentally all deeds to Me, having Me as the highest goal, resorting to buddhi-yoga do you ever fix your mind on Me.

58) Fixing your mind on Me, you shall, by My grace, overcome all obstacles; but if from self-conceit you will not hear Me, you shall perish.

59) If, filled with self-conceit, you think, "I will not fight," vain is this your resolve; your prakriti will constrain you.

60) Fettered, O son of Kunti, by your own karma, born of your own nature, what you, from delusion, desire not to do, you shall have to do in spite of yourself.

61) The Lord, O Arjuna, dwells in the hearts of all beings, causing all beings, by His Maya, to revolve, (as if) mounted on a machine.

62) Take refuge in Him with all your heart, O Bharata; by His grace you shall attain supreme peace (and) the eternal abode.

63) Thus has wisdom, more profound than all profundities, been declared to you by Me; reflecting over it fully, act as you like.

64) Hear again My supreme word, the profoundest of all; because you are dearly beloved of Me, therefore, will I speak what is good to you.

65) Occupy your mind with Me, be devoted to Me, sacrifice to Me, bow down to Me. You shall reach Myself; truly do I promise unto you, (for) you are dear to Me.

66) Relinquishing all dharmas take refuge in Me alone; I will liberate you from all sins; grieve not.

67) This is never to be spoken by you to one who is devoid of austerities or devotion, nor to one who does not render service, nor to one who cavils at Me.

68) He who with supreme devotion to Me will teach this deeply profound philosophy to My devotees, shall doubtless come to Me alone.

69) Nor among men is there any who does dearer service to Me, nor shall there be another on earth dearer to Me, than he.

70) And he who will study this sacred dialogue of ours, by him shall I have been worshipped by the yajna of knowledge; such is My conviction.

71) And even that man who hears this, full of shraddha and free from malice, he too, liberated shall attain to the happy worlds of those of righteous deeds.

72) Has this been heard by you, O Partha, with an attentive mind? Has the delusion of your ignorance been destroyed, O Dhananjaya?

Arjuna said:

73) Destroyed is my delusion, and I have gained my memory through Your grace, O Achyuta. I am firm; my doubts are gone. I will do Your word.

Sanjaya said:

74) Thus have I heard this wonderful dialogue between Vasudeva and the high-souled Partha, causing my hair to stand on end.

75) Through the grace of Vyasa have I heard this supreme and most profound Yoga, direct from Krishna, the Lord of Yoga, Himself declaring it.

76) O King, as I remember and remember this wonderful and holy dialogue between Keshava and Arjuna, I rejoice again and again.

77) And as I remember and remember that most wonderful form of Hari, great is my wonder, O King; and I rejoice again and again. 78) Wherever is Krishna, the Lord of Yoga, wherever is Partha, the wielder of the bow, there are prosperity, victory, expansion, and sound policy: such is my conviction.

The Greatness of the Gita

Arjuna said:

1) I desire to know severally, O mighty-armed, the truth of Sannyâsa, O Hrishikesha, as also of Tyâga, O slayer of Keshi.

The Blessed Lord said:

2) The renunciation of Kâmya actions, the sages understand as. Sannyâsa: the wise declare the abandonment of the fruits of all works as Tyâga.

3) Some philosophers declare that all action should be relinquished as an evil, whilst others (say) that the work of Yajna, gift and austerity should not be relinquished.

4) Hear from Me the final truth about relinquishment, O best of the Bhâratas. For relinquishment has been declared to be of three kinds, O tiger among men.

5) The work of Yajna, gift and austerity should not be relinquished, but it should indeed be performed; (for) Yajna, gift and austerity are purifying to the wise.

6) But even these works, O Pârtha, should be performed, leaving attachment and the fruits;—such is My best and certain conviction.

7) But the renunciation of obligatory action is not proper. Abandonment of the same from delusion is declared to be Tâmasika.

8) He who from fear of bodily trouble relinquishes action, because it is painful, thus performing a Râjasika relinquishment, he obtains not the fruit thereof.

9) When obligatory work is performed, O Arjuna, only because it ought to be done, leaving attachment and fruit, such relinquishment is regarded as Sâttvika.

10) The relinquisher endued with Sattva and a steady understanding and with his doubts dispelled, hates not a disagreeable work nor is attached to an agreeable one.

11) Actions cannot be entirely relinquished by an embodied being, but he who relinquishes the fruits of action is called a relinquisher.

12) The threefold fruit of action—disagreeable, agreeable and mixed,—accrues to non-relinquishers after death, but never to relinquishers.

13) Learn from Me, O mighty-armed, these five causes for the accomplishment of all works as declared in the wisdom which is the end of all action:

14) The body, the agent, the various senses, the different functions of a manifold kind, and the presiding divinity, the fifth of these;

15) Whatever action a man performs by his body, speech and mind—whether right or the reverse—these five are its causes.

16) Such being the case, he who through a non-purified understanding looks upon his Self, the Absolute, as the agent, he of perverted mind sees not.

17) He who is free from the notion of egoism, whose intelligence is not affected (by good or evil), though he kills these people, he kills not, nor is bound (by the action);

18) Knowledge, the known and the knower form the threefold cause of action. The instrument, the object and the agent are the threefold basis of action.

19) Knowledge, action and agent are declared in the Sânkhya philosophy to be of three kinds only, from the distinction of Gunas: hear them also duly.

20) That by which the one indestructible Substance is seen in all beings, inseparate in the separated, know that knowledge to be Sâttvika.

21) But that knowledge which sees in all beings various entities of distinct kinds as different from one another, know thou that knowledge as Râjasika.

22) Whilst that which is confined to one single effect as if it were the whole, without reason, without foundation in truth, and trivial,—that is declared to be Tâmasika.

23) An ordained action done without love or hatred by one not desirous of the fruit and free from attachment, is declared to be Sâttvika.

24) But the action which is performed desiring desires, or with self-conceit and with much effort, is declared to be Râjasika.

25) That action is declared to be Tâmasika which is undertaken through delusion, without heed to the consequence, loss (of power and wealth), injury (to others) and (one's own) ability.

26) An agent who is free from attachment, non-egotistic, endued with fortitude and enthusiasm and unaffected in success or failure, is called Sâttvika.

27) He who is passionate, desirous of the fruits of action, greedy, malignant, impure, easily elated or dejected, such an agent is called Râjasika.

28) Unsteady, vulgar, arrogant, dishonest, malicious, indolent, desponding and procrastinating, such an agent is called Tâmasika.

29) Hear thou the triple distinction of intellect and fortitude, according to the Gunas, as I declare them exhaustively and severally, O Dhananjaya.

30) That which knows the paths of work and renunciation, right and wrong action, fear and fearlessness, bondage and liberation, that intellect, O Pârtha, is Sâttvika.

31) That which has a distorted apprehension of Dharma and its opposite and also of right action and its opposite, that intellect, O Pârtha, is Râjasika.

32) That which enveloped in darkness regards Adharma as Dharma and views all things in a perverted light, that intellect, O Pârtha, is Tâmasika.

33) The fortitude by which the functions of the mind, the Prâna and the senses, O Pârtha, are regulated, that fortitude, unswerving through Yoga, is Sâttvika.

34) But the fortitude by which one regulates (one's mind) to Dharma, desire and wealth, desirous of the fruit of each from attachment, that fortitude, O Pârtha, is Râjasika.

35) That by which a stupid man does not give up sleep, fear, grief, despondency and also overweening conceit, that fortitude, O Pârtha, is Tâmasika.

36) And now hear from Me, O bull of the Bhâratas, of the threefold happiness. That happiness which one learns to enjoy by habit, and by which one comes to the end of pain;

37) That which is like poison at first, but like nectar at the end; that happiness is declared to be Sâttvika, born of the translucence of intellect due to Self-realisation.

38) That which arises from the contact of object with sense, at first like nectar, but at the end like poison, that happiness is declared to be Râjasika.

39) That happiness which begins and results in self-delusion arising from sleep, indolence and miscomprehension, that is declared to be Tâmasika.

40) There is no entity on earth, or again in heaven among the Devas, that is devoid of these three Gunas, born of Prakriti.

41) Of Brâhmanas and Kshatriyas and Vaishyas, as also of Sudras, O scorcher of foes, the duties are distributed according to the Gunas born of their own nature.

42) The control of the mind and the senses, austerity, purity, forbearance, and also uprightness, knowledge, realisation, belief in a hereafter,—these are the duties of the Brâhmanas, born of (their own) nature.

43) Prowess, boldness, fortitude, dexterity, and also not flying from battle, generosity and sovereignty are the duties of the Kshatriyas, born of (their own) nature.

44) Agriculture, cattle-rearing and trade are the duties of the Vaishyas, born of (their own) nature; and action consisting of service is the duty of the Sudras, born of (their own) nature.

45) Devoted each to his own duty, man attains the highest perfection. How engaged in his own duty, he attains perfection, that hear.

46) From whom is the evolution of all beings, by whom all this is pervaded, worshipping Him with his own duty, a man attains perfection.

47) Better is one's own Dharma, (though) imperfect, than the Dharma of another well-performed. He who does the duty ordained by his own nature incurs no evil.

48) One should not relinquish, O son of Kunti, the duty to which one is born, though it is attended with evil; for, all undertakings are enveloped by evil, as fire by smoke.

49) He whose intellect is unattached everywhere, who has subdued his heart, whose desires have fled, he attains by renunciation to the supreme perfection, consisting of freedom from action.

50) Learn from Me in brief, O son of Kunti, how reaching such perfection, he attains to Brahman, that supreme consummation of knowledge.

51) Endued with a pure intellect, subduing the body and the senses with fortitude, relinquishing sound and such other sense-objects, abandoning attraction and hatred;

52) Resorting to a sequestered spot, eating but little, body, speech and mind controlled, ever engaged in meditation and concentration, possessed of dispassion;

53) Forsaking egoism, power, pride, lust, wrath and property, freed from the notion of "mine," and tranquil, he is fit for becoming Brahman.

54) Brahman-become, tranquil-minded, he neither grieves nor desires; the same to all beings, he attains to supreme devotion unto Me.

55) By devotion he knows Me in reality, what and who I am; then having known Me in reality, he forthwith enters into Me.

56) Even doing all actions always, taking refuge in Me,—by My grace he attains to the eternal, immutable State.

57) Resigning mentally all deeds to Me, having Me as the highest goal, resorting to Buddhi-Yoga do thou ever fix thy mind on Me.

58) Fixing thy mind on Me, thou shalt, by My grace, overcome all obstacles; but if from self-conceit thou wilt not hear Me, thou shalt perish.

59) If filled with self-conceit thou thinkest, "I will not fight," vain is this thy resolve; thy Prakriti will constrain thee.

60) Fettered, O son of Kunti, by thy own Karma, born of thy own nature, what thou, from delusion, desirest not to do, thou shalt have to do in spite of thyself.

61) The Lord, O Arjuna, dwells in the hearts of all beings, causing all beings, by His Mâyâ, to revolve, (as if) mounted on a machine.

62) Take refuge in Him with all thy heart, O Bhârata; by His grace shalt thou attain supreme peace (and) the eternal abode.

63) Thus has wisdom more profound than all profundities, been declared to. thee by Me; reflecting over it fully, act as thou likest.

64) Hear thou again My supreme word, the profoundest of all; because thou art dearly beloved of Me, therefore will I speak what is good to thee.

65) Occupy thy mind with Me, be devoted to Me, sacrifice to Me, bow down to Me. Thou shalt reach Myself; truly do I promise unto thee, (for) thou art dear to Me.

66) Relinquishing all Dharmas take refuge in Me alone; I will liberate thee from all sins; grieve not. 66

67) This is never to be spoken by thee to one who is devoid of austerities or devotion, nor to one who does not render service, nor to one who cavils at Me.

68) He who with supreme devotion to Me will teach this deeply profound philosophy to My devotees, shall doubtless come to Me alone.

69) Nor among men is there any who does dearer service to Me, nor shall there be another on earth dearer to Me, than he.

70) And he who will study this sacred dialogue of ours, by him shall I have been worshipped by the Yajna of knowledge; such is My conviction.

71) And even that man who hears this, full of Shraddhâ and free from malice, he too, liberated, shall attain to the happy worlds of those of righteous deeds.

72) Has this been heard by thee, Pârtha, with an attentive mind? Has the delusion of thy ignorance been destroyed, O Dhananjaya?

Arjuna said:
73) Destroyed is my delusion, and I have gained my memory through Thy grace, O Achyuta. I am firm; my doubts are gone. I will do Thy word.

Sanjaya said:

74) Thus have I heard this wonderful dialogue between Vâsudeva and the high-souled Pârtha, causing my hair to stand on end.

75) Through the grace of Vyâsa have I heard this supreme and most profound Yoga, direct from Krishna, the Lord of Yoga, Himself declaring it.

76) O King, as I remember and remember this wonderful and holy dialogue between Keshava and Arjuna, I rejoice again and again.

77) And as I remember and remember that most wonderful Form of Hari, great is my wonder, O King; and I rejoice again and again.

78) Wherever is Krishna, the Lord of Yoga, wherever is Pârtha, the wielder of the bow, there are prosperity, victory, expansion, and sound policy: such is my conviction.

www.ingramcontent.com/pod-product-compliance
Lightning Source LLC
LaVergne TN
LVHW011325080426
835513LV00006B/194